Improving Teacher Education
Practices Through Self-study

D0221561

Self-study in teacher education is a growing field and a natural progression from the concept of reflective practice in shaping the nature of teaching and learning in teacher education. This book is designed to introduce teacher educators to the theory and practice of self-study, in order to explore, understand and improve their teaching about teaching.

With studies from an international range of contributors, this book illustrates a variety of approaches to self-study. It describes the issues that teacher educators have chosen to study, how they carried out their research and what the learning outcomes were. Throughout, the emphasis is on placing teacher educators' knowledge and practice at the center of their academic work. The book is divided into four sections:

- understanding teaching in teacher education
- studying teacher educators' roles and responsibilities
- fostering social justice in teaching about teaching
- exploring myths in teacher education.

This book will be of interest to all teacher educators wishing to improve their knowledge and practice.

John Loughran is a teacher educator at Monash University, Australia.
Tom Russell is Professor in the Faculty of Education at Queen's University, Canada. The authors have previously collaborated on *Teaching about Teaching* (RoutledgeFalmer, 1999).

Improving Teacher Education Practices Through Self-study

Edited by John Loughran
and Tom Russell

London and New York

First published 2002
by RoutledgeFalmer
11 New Fetter Lane, London EC4P 4EE

Simultaneously published in the USA and Canada
by RoutledgeFalmer
29 West 35th Street, New York, NY 10001

RoutledgeFalmer is an imprint of the Taylor & Francis Group

Typeset in Goudy by Taylor & Francis Books Ltd
Printed and bound in Great Britain by The Cromwell Press,
Trowbridge, Wiltshire

British Library Cataloguing in Publication Data
A catalogue record for this book is available from the British Library

Library of Congress Cataloging in Publication Data
Improving teacher education practices through self-study / edited by John
Loughran and Tom Russell
    p.cm.
Includes bibliographical references and index
1. Teachers–Training of. 2. Teacher educators. 3. Education–Study and
teaching (Higher) I. Loughran, J. John. II. Russell, Tom.

LB1707 .I52 2002
370'.71'–dc21   2001048823

ISBN 0–415–27670–5 (hbk)
ISBN 0–415–27671–3 (pbk)

Contents

Contributors

Jerry Allender, though retired, still works with teachers to discover more about the teaching and learning process. His humanistic educational views found support in the College of Education at Temple University over much of his career, although they offered quite a challenge to colleagues during the nine years that he chaired the Department of Psychoeducational Processes. He lives in Philadelphia with his wife, Donna, and divides his time among writing, family, travel, and playing classical and jazz trumpet.

Vicky Anderson-Patton is an Adjunct Professor in Elementary Education at West Chester University, Pennsylvania. She teaches a variety of graduate and undergraduate courses, although her current passion and research interest is teaching teachers how to identify and encourage creative thinking, problem solving, and creative expression in the classroom utilizing reflective processes and teaching portfolios. As a mother of three sons of elementary-school age, she spends lots of time in her truck running them between sports, activities, and play-dates.

Lis Bass is an Associate Professor and currently chair of the Reading/Writing Department of Camden County College in New Jersey. She is active as a speaker and organizer for the New Jersey Project on Inclusive Scholarship, Research, and Pedagogy. Lis is also affiliated with Rutgers University where she teaches a practicum on the teaching of writing and mentors graduate students who work for her department.

Amanda Berry taught general science and biology for ten years in high schools before joining Monash University as a science teacher educator. She is responsible for science teacher education in both pre-service and in-service programs. Mandi has had a strong and continuing involvement in teacher research groups (for example, PEEL and PAVOT) at both school and university levels. She has a keen interest in developing approaches to science teaching and learning that focus on conceptual change, as well as collaborative classroom inquiry.

Enora R. Brown is an Associate Professor in the Social and Cultural Foundations Program in the School of Education at DePaul University. Her primary areas of inquiry include discourse analyses of children's social conflict and the identity formation processes of youth and adults in educational settings. Her publications include articles on culture and mental health; the significance of power, positionality, and "reason" in verbal conflicts; racial identity of European-American pre-service teachers; and the conceptual and practical limits and possibilities for two-generation family/school-based interventions. Her current work examines the disciplines of developmental psychology and mental health as cultural constructions. She addresses the philosophical and theoretical underpinnings that frame traditional psychological inquiry, and their implications for educational policies and practice, and constructions of racial and social-class identities in school contexts.

Mary C. Dalmau is an Australian with many years' experience in teaching, administration, professional development, school improvement, and educational change. She is currently preparing to return to Australia after nine years of study and work at the University of Oregon in the western United States. Her current interests include knowledge creation in education, international education, and forms of educational research that question stereotypic perceptions and judgments and invite participants to share in a critically reflective dialogue.

Deborah Deemer is an Associate Professor of Educational Psychology and Foundations and is head of the team who teach developmental psychology courses in the Teacher Education Program. Her scholarly work contributes to feminist pedagogy and qualitative inquiry. Her expertise in alternative forms of assessment is being tapped as the University of Northern Iowa moves toward performance-based teacher education in response to new state licensure standards.

Denise Drevdahl is an Assistant Professor in the Nursing Program at the University of Washington, Tacoma, where she has taught courses in community health, community change and organization, and race, racism and health since 1996. Her research interests center on women's health issues, particularly the effects of welfare reform on women's health, as well as the role of race in science and health care. She has authored or co-authored a number of research and theoretical papers, including articles on teaching; community theory and practice; theory, research, and practice in nursing; and social justice.

Joan E. Farstad is an adjunct instructor in educational psychology. She teaches human development courses (Development of the Young Child, Child Development, Adolescent Psychology) for pre-service teachers. Joan is a second-year doctoral student in Counseling Psychology at Walden University. In addition to self-study of teacher education practice, her current research and writing focuses on the search for meaning and the addicted self.

Linda May Fitzgerald is Associate Professor of Curriculum and Instruction at the University of Northern Iowa and Research Fellow in the Regents' Center for Early Developmental Education. She tries to prepare pre-service teachers to accept into their early childhood classroom communities a wide variety of children. In addition to self-study of teacher education practice, her current research and writing focuses on the inclusion of individuals with disabilities into everyday settings.

Morwenna Griffiths is Professor of Educational Research at Nottingham Trent University. Her current research interests focus on social justice, gender, and educational research. She tries to combine her interests in philosophy, feminism, action research, and self-study with her commitments to teaching, learning, and finding ways of dealing with injustices. She thinks that seeking for wisdom is enhanced if it is done with joy and justice. Her current research focus is on partnerships and collaborations as a way of working, and she has recently (with Graham Impey) co-edited *Working Partnerships: Better Research and Learning*, which includes a number or self-studies. She is the author of *Educational Research for Social Justice: Getting Off the Fence*, *Feminisms and the Self: The Web of Identity*, and *Self-identity, Self-esteem, and Social Justice*, and co-author (with Carol Davies) of *In Fairness to Children: Working for Social Justice in the Primary School*.

Hafdís Guðjónsdóttir is Assistant Professor of Education and Director of the Division of Developmental Education at the Iceland University of Education (IUE). She worked for twenty-five years as a general classroom teacher and special educator in elementary and high schools. Teaching is her primary profession, and she emphasizes partnership with teachers through teacher education, university–school projects, consultancy, and research. Her overall approach to research is qualitative, and research priorities include action, teacher, and self-study research. Current research and writing projects include mathematics for all learners, effective planning and teaching for elementary students, and self-study of framing professional discourse with teachers.

Mary Lynn Hamilton is an Associate Professor in the Teaching and Leadership Department in the School of Education at the University of Kansas. Her research interests include self-study of teacher education practices, teacher beliefs, multicultural issues, and the professional development of teachers. Some of her recent publications include "Confronting the self: Passion and practice in the act of teaching or My Oz-dacious journey to Kansas!" in *Teacher Education Quarterly* and the edited text *Reconceptualizing teaching practice: Self-study in teacher education* published by Falmer.

Jeffrey J. Kuzmic is an Associate Professor of Secondary Education in the School of Education at DePaul University. His research and scholarship have examined the relationship between schooling, society, and the curriculum as a way of understanding educational practice, teacher education, and social and educational change. In particular, his work has focused on the relation-ship between societal values such as democracy, individual freedom, community, and the purpose of schooling within a democratic society. Jeffrey has collaborated with seven beginning teachers in a qualitative study that seeks to explore the lives and work of beginning teachers and their collabo-rative efforts to conduct research in their classrooms. He is currently working on a book, tentatively titled *Democracy, Community, and Difference: Curriculum and Critical Educational Practice*.

John Loughran works in the Faculty of Education at Monash University. He has been actively involved in teacher education for the past decade. His research interests include teacher-as-researcher, reflective practice, science education, and teaching and learning. Recent publications include *Developing Reflective Practice* and *Opening the Classroom Door* (Loughran and Northfield), *Teaching about Teaching* (Loughran and Russell), and *Researching Teaching* (all published by Falmer).

Belinda Y. Louie is an Associate Professor of Education at the University of Washington, Tacoma. She has taught courses in curriculum inquiry, class-room assessment, and children's literature. Her research interests include students' responses to literature, multicultural literature, and self-study in teaching. Currently, she is working on a research project funded by the Spencer Foundation on enhancing diversity education through multicultural literature.

Charles B. Myers is Professor of Social Studies Education and Assistant to the Dean for Teacher Education at Peabody College, Vanderbilt University. He teaches the Beginning Teacher Education course for undergraduates, and two doctoral-level seminars on teacher education. He has written extensively about and conducted research on teaching, teacher education, and school reform. He is co-author (with Lynn K. Myers) of a text, *The Professional Educator: A new introduction to teaching and schools* (Wadsworth, 1995), and (with Douglas J. Simpson) a monograph, *Re-creating Schools: Places Where Everyone Learns and Likes It* (Corwin, 1998).

Jill M. Purdy is an Associate Professor of Business Administration and Graduate Coordinator of the MBA program at the University of Washington, Tacoma. She earned her doctorate from Pennsylvania State University, where her studies focused on organization theory. Currently, Jill's scholarly interests include negotiation, governmental dispute resolution, wisdom in organizations, and teaching in higher education. She has served as a trainer and consultant to a variety of governmental and private organizations.

Tom Russell is a Professor in the Faculty of Education at Queen's University in Kingston, Ontario. He teaches pre-service courses in physics methods and in professional practice, as well as an M.Ed. course in action research. His research focuses on the process of learning to teach, and he is also interested in innovative pedagogy, action research, and self-study of teacher education practices. Recent publications include *Teachers who Teach Teachers* (Munby and Russell), *Teaching about Teaching* (Loughran and Russell), *Finding a Voice While Learning to Teach* (Featherstone, Munby and Russell) (all published by Falmer).

Sandy Schuck is a Senior Lecturer in the Faculty of Education at the University of Technology, Sydney. Her Ph.D. is in mathematics education and concerns the beliefs of student teachers regarding the nature of mathematics and mathematics teaching and learning. She is one of the founding members of the Change in Education Research Group, which is designated as a faculty research strength by the university. Her current research interests include challenging beliefs about mathematics, mentoring and induction experiences, and the use of computer technology in education. Together with Gilda Segal, she is the convenor of a professional development project in the faculty, entitled the e-Change Project, which considers the pedagogy of teaching with technology.

Gilda Segal is a Senior Lecturer in the Faculty of Education at the University of Technology, Sydney. In her Ph.D. in science education, Gilda studied the learning of both student teachers and early childhood children in gender-inclusive learning environments. She has recently been working with Sandy Schuck on a number of research projects that include mentoring and induction of beginning teachers, self-study, and integration of computer-mediated learning in schools. As co-convenor of the e-Change Faculty Development Project, Gilda has expanded her interest in computer-mediated learning. She will carry this interest into her imminent retirement.

Joseph C. Senese has taught junior high and high school English for over twenty-five years. For the last ten years, he has been Assistant Principal for Curriculum, Instruction, Assessment, and Staff Development at Highland Park High School in Highland Park, Illinois. Since initiating the Action Research Laboratory in 1995, he has shared this program of teacher research at local, national, and international conferences (http://www.d113.lake.k12.il.us/hphs/action/page1.htm). Recipient of the award for Best Research in Staff Development for 1999 from the National Council of Staff Development in December 1999, Senese has published several articles about the experience of working with and conducting his own action research.

Richard W. Stackman is an Assistant Professor of Business Administration at the University of Washington, Tacoma. Richard earned his doctorate in Business Administration from the University of British Columbia in 1995. His studies focused on organizational behavior. He holds an undergraduate degree in Business Administration from the University of California, Berkeley, where he graduated with honors and was inducted into Phi Beta Kappa. His scholarly interests include the self-study of teaching, personal work networks, personal values, career and job-search strategies, and organizational stages. He is currently the Secretary for the Western Academy of Management and the Chair of UWT's Faculty Assembly.

Deborah Tidwell is an Associate Professor of Literacy Education in the Department of Curriculum and Instruction at the University of Northern Iowa, where she teaches undergraduate and graduate courses in literacy education and in bilingual education. Her research includes self-study of her own teacher education practices, research on reflective practices in assessment and instruction, and research on classroom instructional practices for diverse linguistic populations. In addition to her university work, Deborah farms organically with her husband, Jeff Klinge, on a fifth-generation family farm in north-east Iowa.

Acknowledgments

To Airlie and LaVerne for their ongoing support in helping us find the time and energy to complete this book.

We are grateful to:

Carrie Paechter for permission to use her poem 'Peripherality'.
Rebekka Jonsdóttir for her Professional Working Theory paper.

Introduction

1 Can self-study improve teacher education?

Tom Russell

Only a few teacher educators, often those most prominent at conferences, are situated in research-intensive universities where they are able to focus most of their attention on research. The vast majority of us work regularly with pre-service teachers in program or course structures that have many minor variations but probably share many common themes and assumptions. In the teacher education classroom, most teacher educators are aware that their students can read every teaching move we make for an implicit message about how to teach. Those of us who are acutely aware of the potential for contradiction between the content and the process of our teaching and who wish to minimize such contradictions seem to be drawn to the self-study of teacher education practices.

Schools for Thought: a science of learning in the classroom is just one of many publications offering advice such as:

> If we want to improve Americans' schools, we will have to apply in the classroom what we know about humans as intelligent, learning, thinking creatures.
>
> (Bruer, 1994, p. 1)

Similarly, many publications tell us that teacher education itself needs to change (Darling-Hammond, 1997). When the Self-Study of Teacher Education Practices (S-STEP) special interest group was formed in 1993, there was considerable interest in the fact that teacher educators, individually and collectively, would be studying their own teaching, going beyond the standard image of telling others how teaching should be done without necessarily following their own advice. S-STEP has held three international conferences (in 1996, 1998 and 2000) at Herstmonceux Castle, located in the south of England and the site of the International Study Centre of Queen's University (Canada). The papers in this collection have their roots in presentations made at the Third International Conference in 2000.

The title of this collection is an ambitious one: *Improving teacher education practices through self-study*. Often it is challenging enough to look critically at one's own teaching practices. While the obvious purpose of self-study is improvement, it is even more challenging to make changes and seek evidence that the changes did indeed represent improvement. Along the way, one often finds that the overall structure in which one's teaching occurs makes change more complex. Much the same can be said for the overall research enterprise associated with teacher education, because the theory/practice gap between teaching and research is just as great in teacher education as it is in education generally.

Four parts provide the broad structure for this collection of sixteen chapters. We open in Part I with four chapters that speak directly to teacher education, and continue in Part II with studies that examine the roles and responsibilities of teacher educators. Part III provides three studies related to a longstanding and elusive theme in teacher education – fostering social justice – while Part IV offers three chapters that explore teacher education myths that often stand in the way of change.

Part I: Understanding teaching in teacher education

Amanda Berry and John Loughran of Monash University (Australia) open this section by reporting their collaborative self-study, "Developing an understanding of learning to teach in teacher education". Together they taught *Developing Pedagogy* to pre-service teachers with goals of creating a learning environment rich in experiences and supportive of risk-taking. By documenting and interpreting their experiences together, they provide a rich array of insights into what is possible in the teacher education classroom. Their conclusions illustrate how in teacher education accepting responsibility for, and genuine caring about, the interpersonal relations that are so embedded in teaching really matters. They highlight that it is crucial to recognize that learning about teaching is just as important for teacher educators as it is for student teachers.

Deborah Tidwell of the University of Northern Iowa (USA) continues the pursuit of understanding teaching in teacher education in a chapter titled "A balancing act: self-study in valuing the individual student". This very personal study of her relationships with three individuals in three different university programs illustrates in rich detail how self-study of teacher education practices can provide insights into assumptions about teaching. Tidwell begins with a sense of tension and conflict between valuing the individual student and the university's expectations for rigor. By documenting for herself her interactions with three students and then sharing these accounts with a colleague, Tidwell gained new understandings of herself and her teaching that drive her to reduce the potential for contradictions between her values and her actions.

Joe Senese of Highland Park (Illinois) High School (USA) focuses his self-study on his return to the English classroom after ten years as an administrator charged with in-service teacher education duties. "Opposites attract: what I learned about being a classroom teacher by being a teacher educator" explores the intriguing question: *What have I learned about myself as a staff developer (teacher educator) that has changed me as a high school English teacher?* Senese extracts three axioms from his practice as a teacher educator and applies them to two instances of teaching British Literature on his return to the role of classroom teacher. This chapter highlights the similarities between learning by students and learning by teachers, and provides compelling insights on issues such as the fostering of self-direction for both students and teachers.

Part I concludes with a collective review of many experiences of self-study by Lis Bass and Vicky Anderson-Patton of West Chester University (USA) and Jerry Allender of Temple University (USA). In "Self-study as a way of teaching and learning: a research collaborative re-analysis of self-study teaching portfolios", these three teacher educators describe their personal approaches to self-study and their experiences as critical friends for each other in the self-study process. Perhaps more than any other chapter in this collection, this one offers detailed accounts of what self-study is and how self-study can lead to changes in teaching practice. Their conclusions are:

> that self study is an emergent and creative process, that change in practice necessarily integrates change in self, that self-study requires a collective, and that self-study's version of professional growth challenges the developmental model that implies that teachers improve simply with experience.

Part II: Studying teacher educators' roles and responsibilities

Part II opens with a chapter by Tom Russell of Queen's University (Canada). "Guiding new teachers' learning from classroom experience: self-study of the faculty liaison role" explores the complexities inherent in learning a new role created by structural changes in a pre-service course. At the center of the new role is the familiar task of supervising teacher candidates. When the practicum placement extends to ten weeks in one school and the responsibilities include supporting each candidate's action research project while also fostering school–university partnership, the apparently familiar becomes unfamiliar and the apparently simple becomes complex. Gathering several types of data over several years generates new insights and understandings about teacher education as well as changes in personal teaching practices.

Sandy Schuck and Gilda Segal of University of Technology, Sydney (Australia), extend the role of teacher educator by identifying the potential importance of contact with new teachers after they leave the university setting. In "Learning about our teaching from our graduates, learning about our learning with critical friends", Schuck and Segal challenge the implicit assumption that neither new teacher nor teacher educator has anything to say to the other as the new teacher begins to teach. While their chapter offers a range of perspectives, perhaps the reflexive look at their own work is most relevant to the theme of this collection. Of their own teaching they conclude:

> We became aware that far more discussion of the school context was needed in our subjects, that more integration with school-based experiences would

be helpful, and that we needed to deal more effectively with issues of resource management, negotiation with other staff members and behavior management in the context of our own disciplines.

"Framing professional discourse with teachers: Professional Working Theory", by Mary C. Dalmau of the University of Oregon (USA) and Hafdís Guðjónsdóttir of Iceland University of Education, explains how the authors developed the notion of Professional Working Theory. They productively challenge the assumption that teachers are practitioners who resist theoretical analysis and are only interested in hearing about practical ideas by identifying with teachers six different but integrated roles that articulate the scope of their professional identities and practice. Their perspective is apparent in the manner in which they dispel views such as teaching practice is non-theoretical in offering thoughtful and responsive details about their work with teachers.

In the closing chapter of Part II, Charles B. Myers of Vanderbilt University (USA) explores the challenges he has faced over several decades of work facilitating change at his own university and in a national context. "Can self-study challenge the belief that telling, showing, and guided practice constitute adequate teacher education?" reveals a teacher educator exploring why self-study is not used to bring about change in teacher education. Myers poses and responds to eleven questions that break down and examine the central question in his title. His conclusions, after examining his personal work within his university's larger setting, will be uncomfortable for teacher educators:

> As a whole, teacher educators are more a part of the problem than part of the solution. ... Few teacher educators, including those who readily critique and criticize classroom teachers and other educators, make serious attempts to improve their personal practice or the programs in which they teach.

Part III: Fostering social justice in teaching about teaching

"The (in)visibility of race in narrative constructions of the self", by Enora R. Brown of DePaul University (USA), is the provocative opening chapter of Part III. This chapter highlights the central role of the personal in a self-study, yet it provides both data and conclusions that every teacher educator must bear in mind, regardless of the degree of racial diversity that happens to exist in a university's community. Brown's own words offer a clear introduction to her self-study:

> Through this inquiry, I challenge the notion that curricular materials and pedagogical practices are unfettered by societal relations of racial and class inequity, and are unrelated to identity formation processes. In essence, I challenge the "myth of racelessness".

Morwenna Griffiths of Nottingham Trent University (UK) contributes a chapter with the title "'Nothing grand': small tales and working for social justice". She provides an account of a small group of educators who came together in the *Fairness Project* to explore the meaning and the pursuit of social justice in terms of their individual actions. One result is a number of interesting insights into and comments about self-study, including:

> self-study is not just about the study of individual human beings nor even about the study of those individuals in context. It is about each of us in relation to others.

In "Change, social justice, and re-liability: reflections of a secret (change) agent", Mary Lynn Hamilton of the University of Kansas (USA) provides a personal account of a teacher education unit that failed to change. She draws us directly into teacher education issues by exploring the complex territory of how beliefs and practices do and do not interact, for both those learning to teach and those who teach them. She and her colleagues set out to create a program that would center on fostering social justice, but in the final analysis they were unwilling to explicitly adopt social justice as a program goal. Hamilton's analysis draws the uncomfortable conclusion that racism may have been implicit in this organizational behavior that failed to produce change.

Part IV: Exploring myths in teacher education

Belinda Y. Louie, Richard W. Stackman, Denise Drevdahl and Jill M. Purdy work in three different disciplines – education, nursing and business adminis-tration – at the University of Washington, Tacoma (USA). Theirs is a collaborative study of "Myths about teaching and the university professor: the power of unexamined beliefs". As in other chapters, the complex relationship between beliefs and practices is placed under scrutiny. Again, the power of collaborative self-study is revealed, this time across several professional disci-plines:

> Despite the highly personal nature of our myths, our collective analysis revealed that the myths could be grouped into three categories: myths about the *control of learning*, myths about *preparation for teaching*, and myths about *how to approach teaching*.

Louie and Stackman provide personal case studies that illustrate the group's generalizations. Their conclusion reminds us that changes in practice often begin with a willingness to examine beliefs:

> Encouraging university faculty to identify myths that they use to make sense of teaching is an important first step in beginning the process of change.

Linda May Fitzgerald, Joan E. Farstad and Deborah Deemer of the University of Northern Iowa (USA) reveal the considerable potential of collaboration in self-study in their chapter on "What gets 'mythed' in the student evaluations of their teacher education professors?" This chapter takes us into the heart of the teacher education classroom, as three teacher educators study their practices in relation to the official evaluation forms on which their students must judge them when they have finished their teaching. They pay particular attention to the embedded assumptions that all teaching is telling and that each teacher stands alone in the assessment of teaching. It is impossible to miss the commitment to improving teacher education practices through self-study, and readers will be inspired by the details provided that may enable them to conduct self-study of their own practices.

In "Research as a way of knowing and seeing: advocacy for the other", Jeff Kuzmic of DePaul University (USA) explores very personally the myth that knowledge about teaching is generated by academic researchers and then used by teachers to improve their practices. Haunted by two statements made by a teacher in one of his courses and by the experience of a committee meeting that prompted one of those statements, Kuzmic names and picks apart a broad range of issues associated with the issue of whether research done by teachers themselves is acceptable as research. Ultimately this issue goes to the heart of self-study by teacher educators, for they too are teachers studying their own teaching. Is self-study research by teacher educators acceptable as research in the larger academic community? Clearly Kuzmic and the contributors to this collection believe that it is, but Kuzmic's efforts to carefully unpack general tensions and his own personal experiences help us better understand the territory in which self-studies are conducted.

This collection of self-studies of teacher education practices focused on the goal of improvement closes with John Loughran's chapter, which looks back over the fourteen studies. As co-editors, John and I were first faced with the complex task of selecting from the conference proceedings that we had already co-edited a set of papers that would come together in this collection. The S-STEP group is strong, cohesive, and committed to supporting its members; the selection process was also, inevitably, one of exclusion and this was painful. Now that we are concluding the editing process, we can better see the whole as well as the individual pieces and trust that the painful decisions made to develop a book that offered a variety of approaches to, and learning from, self-study will offer powerful examples of the breadth of work in this field. We acknowledge our debt to all who have contributed to the first three International Conferences on the Self-Study of Teacher Education Practices. Their commitment to improving the nature of teacher education and to articulating the knowledge that shapes their practice has been crucial in developing the field of self-study.

We are pleased to provide this range of self-studies on the common theme of teacher education. Some of these studies are very close to the daily events of pre-service teacher education, while others stand back some distance to take broader perspectives. Teacher educators working alone, in pairs, and in small groups illustrate ways in which self-study leads to new personal understandings and to changes in teaching practice. While self-study has not transformed teacher education in its first ten years, self-study of teacher education practices has rapidly generated a new landscape for professional dialogue among teacher educators and between teacher educators and both new and experienced teachers. On that new landscape, the self is the focal point for studying the intersection of theory and practice. Teacher education has long been criticized for its inability to practice what it preaches. Self-study appears to be a powerful way to respond to such criticisms. We welcome your critical reading of these self-studies.

References

Bruer, J.T. (1994) *Schools for Thought: a science of learning in the classroom*, Cambridge, MA: MIT Press.

Darling-Hammond, L. (1997). *Doing What Matters Most: investing in quality teaching*, Kutztown, PA: National Commission on Teaching & America's Future, http://www.nctaf.org/publications/DoingWhatMattersMost.pdf.

Part I

Understanding teaching in teacher education

2 Developing an understanding of learning to teach in teacher education

Amanda Berry and John Loughran

Introduction

The self-study described in this chapter draws on the relationship between teaching about teaching and learning about teaching realized through the planning and teaching of a double degree pre-service teacher preparation subject titled *Developing Pedagogy*.

Our purpose in both the construction and the teaching of the subject was to create a learning environment rich in experiences that would be responsive to participants' emerging needs and concerns in learning about teaching. We envisaged that this might be realized through encouraging appropriate risk-taking by ourselves and our students in a joint venture of learning and teaching about teaching. Such learning about practice requires a consistent focus on recognizing alternative perspectives and approaches to learning situations ("reframing" – Schön, 1983). By considering the development of practice in this way, we believed that dilemmas, issues and concerns of practice could be viewed as problematic, and thus we might create a situation through which a diversity of responses might be expected. This could highlight the value and importance of problem recognition as a response to curious and puzzling situations (Dewey, 1933; Loughran and Northfield, 1996) and of reframing as a mediating factor in influencing responses and actions.

This chapter explores the teaching and learning about practice that we have come to understand and articulate by researching three distinctive phases in the development of the *Developing Pedagogy* subject: curriculum planning and purpose, team-teaching, and introducing another teacher educator to the philosophy and pedagogy of the subject. The chapter examines these three phases chronologically in an attempt to maintain – as much as is possible through text – the sense of building on previous learning and experience. We believe that this approach to representation reveals how shifts in the roles and responsibilities of participants leads to learning about pedagogy that is intertwined and recursive rather than simple and linear.

Context

In the Faculty of Education at Monash University there are two teacher preparation programs. One is a one-year Post Graduate Diploma in Education (Dip. Ed.) and the other is a combined Double Degree four-year program (for example, B.Sc./B.Ed., BA/B.Ed.). Whereas the Dip. Ed. has a long-established tradition, the Double Degree program is a relatively recent addition. Both authors have been extensively involved in Dip. Ed. and have developed first-hand understanding of student teachers' learning to teach through this program. With the introduction of the Double Degree, an opportunity emerged to develop and teach a third-year subject designed to help student teachers begin to learn about their own teaching through the use of intensive micro-teaching experiences.

This new subject was organized in ways that were not logistically or organizationally possible in the existing and familiar Dip. Ed. We also arranged the class so that we could co-teach, which meant teaching a larger number of students together, rather than smaller groups individually.

The subject

We organized *Developing Pedagogy* with a curricular focus based on explicitly modeling particular aspects of teaching so that we could "unpack" these aspects of teaching through professional critiques of practice. In conceptualizing the curriculum in this manner, we anticipated tensions and dilemmas in helping student teachers to critique teaching actions rather than criticizing individual(s) conducting the teaching. Therefore we purposely designed teaching and learning situations in which opportunities to "unpack" the teaching, as professional critique, could be modeled.

In order to model this approach, we decided that the first two sessions should focus on one of us teaching specific content to the class followed by a debriefing by the other. These sessions were then followed by a one-to-one teaching experience whereby pairs of student teachers each taught a pair of Year 7 students from a local high school. Both student teachers planned the teaching (as was the case with our teaching in the previous sessions) and one student teacher would do the teaching while the other observed and then interviewed the Year 7 students about the experience. Both student teachers then collaborated in writing a Reflective Assignment on the experience.

We organized the next part of the program around videotaped micro-teaching in which groups of student teachers would teach the rest of their class. The focus was on the teaching rather than the content to be taught, so that a diverse range of teaching procedures might be encouraged. Student teachers were organized into groups of three to prepare the teaching (one-hour sessions) and again one member was responsible for debriefing the experience with the class. The three student teachers then collaborated to "review and write-up" their session, which included analysis of the videotape and written feedback from everyone.

Next the class moved into schools for a five-day school practicum experience during which they would teach lessons and attempt to push the boundaries of their learning about teaching using the approaches for learning about their teaching that they had gained through the subject (ideally having a peer from the subject visit the school and critique their practice). The subject concluded with a debriefing of the school experience/subject and development of the learning about teaching that occurred throughout the semester.

What mattered in putting the subject together

> I'd never worked with double degree students, but I was confident that when it came to learning about teaching, one thing was crystal clear to me: experience precedes understanding. I knew that it would impact not only on what we could do (well) but also on what the students would be ready to see in the experiences we might try to create for them.
>
> (John, e-mail to Mandi)

We were concerned that much of these students' experience of teacher educa-tion had focused on their being told how to teach, and so in developing this subject we were ever conscious of the need to find ways of providing *experiences* of teaching. We wanted to move beyond the vicarious teaching experiences so far created for them in their degree, so that we could provide a basis for them to genuinely raise questions and concerns about *their* teaching and learning and so that we could publicly analyze these experiences. This meant we needed to be ready to recognize and respond to four types of issues.

1 Seeing into experience through professional critique

We believed that modeling particular aspects of teaching for the student teachers was crucial. Our previous experiences with Dip. Ed. students had led us to see that how we taught had much greater impact on student teachers' thinking about practice than what we taught (Russell, 1997). It was therefore inevitable that we *unpack* teaching (ours and theirs) through professional critiques of the experiences. We believed that student teachers needed to *experi-ence* unpacking in order to begin to understand it. They needed to see that teaching and learning is a complex amalgam of decisions that all teachers face. Less clear is how teachers respond and why.

By helping student teachers to see into the decisions of others and consider the effects of particular teaching decisions on different learners in the group, we hoped that they might come to view teaching as a thoughtful, professional, planned activity rather than as a spontaneous performance or the enactment of a prescribed script. Unpacking teaching meant that we needed to help student teachers learn to *critique the teaching rather than the person*, so it was important for us to do it ourselves before we asked them to take similar risks.

2 Recognizing different types of teaching decisions

We also wanted student teachers to recognize that decision-making in teaching happens on different levels: *before teaching* (what do I want students to learn? why?), *during teaching* (how might I respond? what are my choices? what are their consequences?), and *after teaching* (what did my students learn? how do I know? what responses did I apprehend and why?). To help student teachers be informed about their own pedagogical reasoning, we had to highlight differences between the kinds of teaching decisions they made and the impact of their thinking on their subsequent actions.

3 Recognizing differences between action and intent

Similarly, we were concerned that many student teachers (and experienced teachers) struggle to recognize differences between what they intend to teach and their teaching behaviors. We felt that micro-teaching would help them explore and understand the relationship between what they taught, how they taught and what was learnt.

4 Exploring the value of co-teaching

As much as possible, we organized experiences that revolved around collaboration and the sharing of ideas and perspectives on practice. This was a deliberate decision to encourage student teachers to articulate their thinking as they planned, taught and debriefed with others. Through our own teaching we hoped to model the same process, as we taught and publicly debriefed each other about how our plans were enacted and then interpreted by the class.

Experiences of teaching the course

Each week we met to discuss our own, and our students', experiences of the session. These shared teaching and learning experiences and the subsequent discussions were important opportunities to question and reconsider particular situations. New understandings of learning and teaching about teaching emerged in ways that were less likely on an individual level. In addition to our weekly conversations, Mandi maintained a journal and we shared e-mail conversations as the experiences impacted in different ways at different times. This was particularly so in the final weeks of the subject, as the overall experiences of learning were discussed and analyzed.

The following extract from one of our electronic conversations highlights the importance of feeling confident to respond to teachable moments in learning about teaching as opposed to sticking to our initial plan. The extract also illustrates how a teaching partnership based on mutual trust supports the learning of the teacher educators as well as the student teachers. We were teaching each other about teaching as we were helping our student teachers to learn about teaching.

MANDI: This process of working through what was in my head at the time is quite cathartic … I think in some instances I had a funny role, not feeling quite in control of what was going on but in a different place to the students. You didn't ever say it, but I think you were both teaching me and teaching with me. Was that what you intended? I'm thinking about the things you can't plan for in a class and how they are (or have to be?) dealt with when they happen. I wanted to plan for each class because it makes me feel comfortable. I wanted to know how I could feel in control of this experience so that I could walk in knowing the beginning, middle and end of what was going to happen. I know this is an unrealistic expectation. The classes don't work out that way. They are less about planned learning than using the experiences that come out of the plans that the students have for their teaching. I have to trust that I will see and know how to capitalize on these opportunities for learning. That is unsettling. But it's also okay because we do trust each other. I know there is permission to work in different ways and that means being able to take a risk.

JOHN: I couldn't agree more. It's developing a confidence to look into and examine what's happening as it happens through being honest and exposing your own vulnerability so that the "normal" rules of being courteous do not get in the way of genuinely exploring (and feeling) what it means to make sense of a situation and develop new ways of seeing it. You helped me to know when it was working and when to back off (and I assumed you would learn to take the cue to do the same). Together we reflected the thinking of those who were doing the teaching and the range of student responses. It helped release them to be open and honest and to push beyond what is normally "good enough" in a teaching situation but which is (for us) just too superficial. (Maybe I didn't tell you about how I was doing this because I hadn't realised it quite that way either; the trust also meant many things went unspoken and could have been misinterpreted. There is no doubt though that I learnt to do things in different ways because of the trust that was there.)

Through our self-study of our teaching of this subject we have learnt about our teaching about teaching and our students' learning about teaching in ways that we now conceptualize in terms of assertions that shape our practice.

Assertion 1: Start as if you're half way through the subject

We started the subject using an approach designed to encourage students to become immediately active in their own learning. In this way, we hoped to highlight the importance of student teachers "owning" their learning from the outset. We expected them to engage in intellectual risk-taking from the first session and, while for some this may have been quite confrontational, we also showed that we were prepared to engage in it ourselves.

It seemed that the accepted wisdom about encouraging risk-taking in the classroom is based on a building-up approach through developing an atmosphere of trust over time. We came to see that an atmosphere of trust could be established immediately if we showed that we were prepared to demonstrate our own vulnerability before asking student teachers to do the same. By trusting in the authority of their experience as learners (Munby and Russell, 1994), we hoped that student teachers would feel more comfortable and confident to contribute straight away. We believe that learners' experiences of learning are typically undervalued and that student teachers often expect to be told how to teach.

Through the initial experiences of the subject we hoped to demonstrate the value of trusting in, and responding to, the authority of learners' experiences, but this is not necessarily easy. The following example illustrates how this particular aspect of teaching about teaching might be grasped. Early in the course, Mandi conducted part of a session on classroom communication. What follows is her explanation of one particular aspect of that episode.

> As a relative newcomer to a lecture situation, I felt rather apprehensive about my role. My concerns were focused on content with less regard for what the students would be doing or feeling. I assumed the script of the format, lecturer speaks and students listen, with an occasional question from either. As part of the lecture, I drew a concept map on the white board with linking lines between the words. When I had finished the map, John asked "What are the lines for?" I had thought this was self-evident, so I hadn't described their purpose. I knew he knew what the lines were for too, so I figured his question was just to point out to me my assumption that the students would know what the linking lines were for, when perhaps they didn't. At the time, because I was so determined to get on with my intentions for the learning, I couldn't recognize the possibilities for others' learning. I quickly answered his question and moved on. Later, I saw that deviating from the plan to explain the lines or affirm the importance of questions of clarification during a lecture could have made this a teachable moment. I didn't pick up on the idea that we might capitalize on the moment as a teaching situation because, at the time, I was not comfortable to look. This incident illustrates to me that while the learning is in the experience, what is learnt does not necessarily happen on the spot, but can be triggered later by reflecting on experience.

This type of discussion could have been made public either at the time or in the debriefing. Such examples of thinking about practice illustrate the importance of critiquing the teaching in ways that might lead to genuine learning about teaching. We highlight this example to show how opening up for scrutiny the very issues that influence our own approach to teaching can be so important in helping our student teachers understand the pedagogical reasoning embedded in our practice. If the thoughts contained in the journal entry had been a conversation in the class, they would have offered valuable insights into teaching decisions and assumptions.

Assertion 2: Be confident to be responsive to possibilities in learning experiences

We began to realize that the most powerful learning for all of us often came from unplanned teachable moments (Van Manen, 1991; Hoban and Ferry, 2001). Rather than prescribing and controlling the learning experiences, we found it more important to create conditions for learning (Loughran and Northfield, 1996, p. 126). This let us highlight aspects of learning about teaching appropriate for the group (or particular individuals) at that time.

Responding to the needs of individuals as they arise means that real and meaningful problems of practice must be apprehended and responded to. Since such moments cannot be planned in advance, they require expertise on the part of the teacher educator to recognize a potential teachable moment and to make an on-the-spot decision about how or whether to respond. Considerable personal risk can be associated with such an approach because the outcome of the intervention is unpredictable.

MANDI: One incident immediately stands out for me: dealing with a latecomer during a teaching experience. At one level, this could be a simple superficial act, yet it was much more when it played out. Two students were up front teaching. When they had finished and were beginning to debrief with the group, you said to them "Do you remember what you did when Adam came in late?" They said that they didn't do anything. So you said "Why not?"

"Well it's not a real classroom so I don't need to worry about that stuff" was their response, yet you hit them with "What would you do in a real classroom?" When one of them started "Well I'd say … " you interjected and told Adam to go out and told Sally to say what she would have said to him if he arrived late. Adam looked a bit sheepish when he went out. (He has now been identified as a latecomer!) He had been quite happy just to slip in unnoticed and Sally and the other members of her group had been happy to let him do so.

So I can see what you are doing. Adam is now dealing publicly with being late. You're sending messages to the rest of the group about being late (they're supposed to be working together and supporting one another), but you're not berating him. But it's much bigger than that. You're saying everything here is part of the learning. Don't ignore stuff because you didn't think it was in the script.

When Sally starts to say "You're late … ", she stops and just looks embarrassed. "I guess I'd just say something like that." I noticed that no one else in the group stepped forward to help her out with more words. And yet you persist with her by asking her whether she would say anything else.

"Yeah, well probably", she offers.

Then you said "Adam go out again and Sally try to say all the things that you would want to say to him", Adam exits. Maybe it has turned into a bit of a game for him; now everyone is looking at Sally. (Glad I'm not up there; I can feel them thinking.) This scene is then played out twice more as you encourage (persistently!) Sally and her group members to say all of what they think they would say and at the same time questioning them: "Why would you want to say that?"

I watch this public "working through" of Sally's thinking along with the others. She is pinned and wriggling and clearly uncomfortable. You continue questioning. Eventually Sally says what she thinks and she also begins to ask questions about dealing with this or other situations. This is the breakthrough; here is where the learning through experience begins to really bite.

For me this has been more powerful than what the group presented in its teaching episode. I wonder if it has been for them? This is where it is not possible to plan, and yet these are the most powerful learning experiences.

As a teacher educator, the sense of uncertainty about how or when to inter-vene can be heightened and become a good learning opportunity enhanced through team teaching.

MANDI: Most times I really believed that you had planned in advance what was going to happen and that you knew what you were doing and why. I didn't attribute the same level of risk to your actions as I did to mine. I guess I assumed that you were actually taking few risks, because I assumed that because of your experience you more or less knew what was going to happen as a consequence of your actions in a class. It surprised me to find out later that you were unsure, that you felt uncomfortable and that you wished sometimes to have taken other decisions. Now I wonder "Is that how my teaching looks to my students?" Each week it became more evident to me that being responsive to possibilities is far more instructive than deciding what will happen and when. I need to trust myself more.

Assertion 3: An uncomfortable learning experience can be a constructive learning experience

Through our experiences of developing and teaching this subject, we came to see the value in creating uncomfortable experiences of learning: by publicly confronting assumptions about learning, we could extend the learning possibili-ties. We wanted to help our students be critically aware of significant features of their experiences so that they could better understand their perceptions of given teaching and learning situations. For example, in planning for their peer teaching, most student teachers spent a considerable amount of time and effort on *what* they would teach as opposed to *how* or *why* they would or would not use a specific teaching procedure.

This is to be expected, as their inexperience in teaching is inevitably driven by their initial concerns about mastering the content they want to *deliver*. As a consequence, their teaching is often focused on their front-of-the-class delivery and performance, limiting what they can see happening right in front of them. We wanted to push them beyond this perspective so that they might consider the why and how of their teaching. *We wanted to find ways to show them what they could not yet see.* Sometimes we did this by asking questions or making our observations explicit during the debriefing at the end of a peer teaching episode, encouraging participants to describe how they felt during the teaching. Sometimes we did this by confronting them with what was going on as they were teaching.

Making decisions about which approach to take, with whom, and what aspect of the teaching to highlight is risky and it cuts both ways. Not just their self-esteem was at stake, so too was our credibility as teacher educators. Students need to know that we genuinely care about them. It is imperative that we do not belittle or humiliate them, but, at the same time, we want them to feel uncomfortable enough about their practice to begin to examine the implications of their teaching decisions and actions.

Student teachers' planning often set the class up to play the familiar game of "question and answer", but they would not disrupt this game by asking challenging questions or changing the script (for example, giving an opinion that challenged the teacher). In one particularly memorable episode, as this script played out it was obvious that everyone was "playing the game", and when an uncomfortable situation arose for the group doing the teaching, the feeling became very real.

> Adam and Ben chose to teach the group about Buddhism. They had prepared a long and difficult text to explain Buddhism and they put it up for the class to read on the overhead projector.
>
> "How could anyone see that, let alone understand it?" I thought. "Yet no one is saying anything! Why are they all so polite?", I asked myself. "I can't read that!" I said aloud, sounding more aggressive than I actually intended. "It doesn't make sense!"
>
> Adam's response to this interjection was to read the overhead text aloud. John picked up on my intervention and pushed it along: "Yeah, what's the difference between Buddhism and Hare Krishna anyway?" Adam began a polite explanation but John interrupted: "Sounds stupid to me. Buddhism is dumb." Adam paused. Ben, his teaching partner, stood silent.
>
> "Come on, are you going to deal with me?" John continued. Adam and Ben did nothing. In fact, no one did anything. I wondered whether John had pushed this too far. What did he think he was helping them to learn about teaching? "Deal with me!" he repeated. But Ben and Adam didn't

seem to know what to do, where to look, or how to act. I could feel their anguish. A long and painful silence followed. Finally, a class member spoke up.

"That's inappropriate behavior, John. Stop it!" Claire had picked up on what was happening and she used the moment to show the others how a confrontation like this might be handled. The purpose had now been realized and Ben and Adam 'felt' what it was like to be in a confronting classroom situation. All of us had!

John's intervention was direct and persistent, pushing the boundaries of commonly acceptable teacher educator behavior. This incident highlighted for everyone how learning about teaching can be both confrontational and constructive. It also highlighted important differences about approaches to interventions that we were prepared to risk. Intervening in this way was not an option Mandi had considered or would have felt comfortable trying, but it provided a valuable opportunity to see what could be learnt when someone is prepared to take such a risk.

In his reflective report Ben described what he learnt as:

> Instead of thinking on our feet, we aimed to try to get through the lesson and stick to our plan … at the expense of the students' learning.

This episode was risky for all involved and is difficult to recreate in text; it is the *purpose* of embedding genuine learning in experience that we wish to highlight. A vicarious experience of a classroom confrontation could not be as powerful. The learning was real and was felt by all of us.

Assertion 4: A shared experience with a valued other provides greater opportunity to reframe situations and confront one's assumptions about practice

Where each of us saw possibilities for learning, we took action and accepted responsibility for taking that action. This was uncomfortable at times. Teaching with a trusted colleague meant that we felt a little braver to try things that we might not have tried alone. As we recognized potential learning experiences, we tried to tune each other in through verbal or non-verbal cues so that we could support each other and the students as we explored what the experience might offer. Sometimes this was realized in more traditional ways through reflection on experiences after an event. For example, in the third session the student teachers teach a pair of Year 7 students. Most are quite apprehensive, and we believe it is important to be available to debrief with them after the experience. Interestingly, on this occasion few students chose to talk with us for very long. This concerned John because he believed (from similar experiences in the Dip. Ed. program) that we needed to follow up this experience with the student teachers, both individually and as a group.

Later, as we discussed this issue, Mandi observed that the students had departed in small groups or pairs and that they seemed to be debriefing their shared experiences. Hence they did not need the teacher(s) to control or direct the debriefing. This was important in considering the learning from the student teachers' perspective. An opportunity to construct their own meanings by reconsidering what they had experienced was a viable alternative to hearing a teacher's perspective on what they had learnt.

Our discussion revealed how the meaning and status of knowledge gained through students developing understanding themselves was more powerful than anything we might have highlighted. Just as we had planned the curriculum and teaching so that their learning about practice might be enhanced through shared experiences, we too developed greater meaning by questioning practices and actions made possible through these shared experiences. Mandi's observation suggested that John might be operating in a way that diminished the value of the students' experience and reframed the situation so that practice better expressed the underlying principle of the experience.

New challenges: stepping out alone

The following year, I (Mandi) assumed the role as subject coordinator because John was on leave. We had analyzed our experiences together and developed useful frames for the purpose, approach and experiences of this subject, but I still felt uneasy. First, there were two additional staff members appointed to teach in the subject (enrolments had grown). Second, the understandings of practice that were being used to frame the subject in the second year had been developed through the previous year's experiences. How relevant would these be for new staff and students? Fortunately, one of the additional staff members, Pippa,[1] had co-taught with me in high school. She had shared numerous conversations with both John and me about the subject during the previous year and she was excited by the possibilities. The other staff member, Zoe, was an experienced and well-respected teacher educator who was keen to learn about the subject.

With the significant increase in student numbers, it was no longer possible to teach one big group. The only option was to establish two classes, although we organized the program so that all students began with a common session. Having to split the group into two classes was a disappointment; administrators who make such decisions seem to think in terms of efficient use of resources, not the quality of teaching and learning. In the end, Pippa and I co-taught one larger class while Zoe taught the second smaller class alone.

Because the subject rested on the teacher educators' preparedness to honestly, openly and publicly critique their own teaching, it was vital that we all discuss what this might mean in practice so that we could help student teachers see the purpose of this learning experience. The request was challenging; Zoe and Pippa were being asked to put their teaching up for public scrutiny as a means of encouraging their students to do the same, and also to trust that this would be a fruitful experience.

Explaining a subject that has goals rather than clear boundaries (Russell, 1995) is a difficult task because there is no neat set of curriculum notes detailing the weekly tutorial activities and expected learning. To some this might make the subject appear flimsy and unorganized. Thus it was important that the intended purpose of each part of the program be made explicit. I planned to meet weekly with Zoe and Pippa for this purpose, but time constraints intervened. Because Pippa and I shared a class, we often talked through our experiences; contact with Zoe became more a progress check on organization and administration.

This experience highlights the power of shared experience as a motivator for learning about experience (Assertion 4 above). Had Zoe been teaching with Pippa and me, it would have been difficult *not* to talk about teaching and learning issues. The first session we shared provided significant evidence of this! Because we were disconnected from Zoe's experiences after the first session, sharing and making sense of our experiences as a triad slipped off the agenda.

One important goal of the subject was to immerse students immediately in the kinds of experiences we intended for them, rather than building towards them slowly (Assertion 1 above). Thus we decided that, after a brief introduction to the subject, one of us would engage the student teachers in a twenty-minute teaching session and the others would debrief the session. We would then ask the student teachers to consider the effects of the teaching on them as learners. Since both Pippa and I felt comfortable and familiar with the process of unpacking another's teaching, Zoe was happy to lead the teaching session.

Here it is valuable to explore this session in detail, for what I learnt was representative of much that I learnt during the second year. Issues that I was unaware of came to light and I gained new insights. Having one of us prepared to demonstrate her vulnerability and show that we genuinely cared about the learners' responses gave students the confidence to engage in honest critique of their experiences of the teaching. An excerpt from my journal illustrates:

> What is interesting is that it feels to me like we are exploding the idea that creating a learning community in which students take safe intellectual risks takes a long time. One student commented at the end of the first session "I felt comfortable enough to say what I thought." The fact that we could create this learning experience together so quickly both surprised and excited me.

Although pleased that we could establish trust quickly, I was also acutely aware of the enormous difference between *discussing* the value of seeing our teaching through the learner's eyes and actually *experiencing* critique from the learners. I had not realized the significance of this until another teacher educator's practice was under public scrutiny. This new and challenging role for Zoe helped me understand that *learning through experience is hard work*, just as it had been for me and the students in the previous year. Being an experienced teacher educator does not make it any easier. In fact, I wondered whether being the teacher educator made the experience more difficult.

Zoe had chosen to teach about an issue of national social significance that had received a great deal of media attention. Her purpose was to have students experience and evaluate a range of teaching strategies that they might use in their future teaching of high school students, with the issue as a "hook" into the strategies. The effect of the teaching that emerged through the debrief was quite different from what she intended. Several students had not enjoyed her interactions with them and commented on this in the debrief. As the students described discrepancies between Zoe's intentions and their interpretations, I saw that our broader purposes for the students' learning were being realized powerfully, but I began to wonder at what personal cost to Zoe. I noted in my journal:

> When I heard students say in response to the teaching "I felt belittled when you asked us to write notes", and "I felt afraid to put my ideas forward when I heard how you responded to others", it was so powerful in helping me to know that we often do not genuinely hear students' responses to teachers' actions. It also reminded me (and I can't help wondering if we could have better prepared Zoe for this) how vulnerable a position the teacher is in. No matter how much we support the idea of professional critique, it can still be pretty demoralizing to hear what some students are actually thinking and feeling.

The fact that Zoe's teaching attracted feedback that she may have found hurtful caused me to reconsider our assertion that an uncomfortable experience for learning can be valuable (Assertion 3). *What are the acceptable limits of discomfort?* How would I know? Does it make a difference when it is the teacher educator experiencing the discomfort? I was surprised to find myself asking these questions because I had never expected to believe anything other than "What we expect of the learners, we expect of ourselves". I had been happy to apply that maxim in my teaching the previous year. In my new role as subject coordinator, I was reconsidering these notions in light of a different concern: *What were my responsibilities in relation to Zoe, in relation to the students, and in relation to the intent of the subject?*

While I understood that much could be learnt from confronting others with their assumptions about teaching and learning, I began to reflect on the delicate balance between exposing our vulnerability as teacher educators and maintaining students' confidence in our position as leaders. I recalled instances when John had struggled with decisions about how to debrief students after particularly risky interventions. Now I was beginning to better understand and feel that myself – through experience. At the same time, student experiences were strong:

STUDENT 1: You gave us an opportunity to see how a student's interpretation of a teacher's actions is not always synonymous with teacher's interpretation of his or her actions.

STUDENT 2: To examine the disparity in the range of experiences that students bring to class and to illustrate the sensitivity of students to teachers.

STUDENT 3: This session gave us an idea of what to expect in the course … .
We were shown how sometimes things don't go according to plan. Some
people will interpret things differently, as happened today, and this just goes
to show how conscious we, as teachers, must be of the instructions that we
do or don't give to our students.

This was a powerful experience for Zoe, one that preoccupied her thinking for
some time, particularly because she had never thought about her teaching in
this way. As I write about these experiences, I see how even experienced
teachers struggle to recognize the differences between what they intend to teach
and their actual teaching behaviors.

Growing in confidence

It became clear to me that my confidence in apprehending and responding to
teachable moments increased significantly during the second year of the course,
for several reasons. My experiences in the previous year helped me recognize
and work through potential learning situations. Also I felt confident taking risks
with Pippa because we had a shared understanding about purpose. More surprisingly, I believe my confidence grew because I was no longer working with John.
I felt more prepared to "be confident to be responsive" (Assertion 2) with Pippa
because of our relative inexperience in teaching about teaching in this way.

   I realized that too often I had been relying on John's experience to recognize
when and how to intervene. In some instances, then, working with a more
experienced other may limit learning because it is tempting to defer to that
person's decisions or to allow that person to lead. In hindsight the change in
responsibilities I assumed as subject coordinator also made me much more
mindful of the importance of modeling to Pippa possible ways of approaching,
and thinking about, teaching about teaching. This was another shift in perspective from the previous year and it raised a new teacher educator responsibility
for me. I realized that I needed to respond to Pippa's and Zoe's needs and
concerns, as John had to mine. Paradoxically, apart from creating opportunities
to talk (Assertion 4), it was difficult to find other ways to respond.

   Through working closely with Pippa when I was the subject coordinator, I came
to see that her initial expectations of the subject and her role in it were similar
to mine in the previous year. Our familiarity enabled Pippa to see the possibilities that the subject offered, especially the considerable freedom to explore
thinking about teaching. However, she was still faced with the challenge of not
knowing in advance what would come up in a session, nor how she might
prepare to respond. I recognized in her situation my own feelings from the
previous year. This encouraged me to step out and take some pedagogical risks
early in our classes; in some cases, what I did may have been motivated as much
by my desire to help her see things in practice as to help the students learn
about teaching.

   Pippa's familiarity with the subject may have amplified an unrealistic expectation that profound and public transformation in students' thinking would occur in each session. I think that she felt some sense of disappointment when this did not happen. While I shared this view to some extent, I could also see that we were having an impact on our students' thinking. We often found ourselves in conversations with students after class, discussing issues they had chosen not to raise in class but wished, instead, to pursue privately, thus illustrating that progress in teaching and learning about teaching occurs in different ways. This realization helped me to see new ways to respond to Pippa's needs. In Pippa I saw myself from the year before and, thus, I began to meaningfully reframe the situation.

Finally, although we may have assumed that things would evolve as they had the previous year, they clearly could not. Other things happened that were equally rewarding and our progress, although not necessarily bathed in public and profound experiences, was important and meaningful nonetheless. Through carefully reconsidering past experiences, I became more informed about anticipated outcomes and possibilities, even though the path to them was different. Through this growing understanding of my role as a teacher educator, I came to see how my pedagogy as a teacher educator had changed. As my understanding of teaching grew through these challenges, I recognized anew the importance of a pedagogy of teacher education.

A pedagogy of teacher education

Accepting responsibility for, and genuinely caring about, the interpersonal relations embedded in teaching is important in a pedagogy of teacher education, where there is a necessary synergy of learning between teacher educator and student teacher. Such an approach to, and understanding of, practice involves a recognition that:

- Responding to the learners' needs matters, and cannot always be predicted in advance.
- Possibilities for being hurt and making mistakes are real.
- Approaches to learning about teaching that a teacher educator hopes to encourage must be explicitly modeled and "felt".
- Knowing that different participants (teacher educators and student teachers) see different things in teaching–learning situations creates dilemmas in deciding what to highlight. The knowledge and practice of seeing what was once unseen needs to be framed and shared so that a knowledge base of teacher education practices can be better articulated, documented and disseminated.

Learning from teaching about teaching

This self-study has helped us to better understand teaching and learning about teaching as we have come to recognize that student teachers:

- Initially focus more on content than on teaching.
- Struggle to professionally criticize their colleagues and generally avoid difficult issues.
- Quickly move beyond a technical–rational approach to learning to teach when they are *personally* confronted by dilemmas in *their own* practice.
- Struggle, even in a trusting environment, to confront paradoxes in their own and their teacher educators' practice.

Finally, teacher educators need to see that telling is *not* teaching and that listening is *not* learning.

Conclusion

Learning about teaching must be embedded within meaningful experiences if such learning is to be more than a search for a recipe or the simple use of a teaching procedure. Teacher educators need to demonstrate their own vulnerability in teaching if they expect their student teachers to *consider* doing the same in their classes. Even when this vulnerability is displayed, *there are still differences between the teacher educator and the student teacher that can inhibit learning through these experiences.* Teacher educators and student teachers need to be open-minded in being prepared to apprehend problems in teaching and illustrate how reframing enhances understanding. These are difficult aspects of learning and teaching about teaching. We believe they are more sharply brought into focus when teacher educators involve themselves in self-study of their practices and use their learning about teaching to inform their pedagogy.

Note

1   Pippa and I co-taught high school science classes for one year. Our experiences of our shared teaching are documented in Berry and Milroy (2002).

References and further reading

Berry, A. and Milroy, P. (2002) "Changes that matter", in J.J. Loughran, I.J. Mitchell and J. Mitchell (eds) *Learning from Teacher Research*, New York: Teachers College Press.

Dewey, J. (1933) *How we Think*, New York: Heath & Co.

Hoban, G. and Ferry, B. (2001) *Seeking the teachable moment in discussions using information and communication technologies*, paper presented at the 32nd Annual Conference of the Australasian Science Education Research Association, Sydney, July.

Loughran, J.J. (1996) *Developing Reflective Practice: Learning about Teaching and Learning Through Modelling*, London: Falmer Press.

Loughran, J.J. and Northfield, J.R. (1996) *Opening the Classroom Door: Teacher, Researcher, Learner*, London: Falmer Press.

Loughran, J.J. and Russell, T. (eds) (1997) *Teaching about Teaching: Purpose, Passion and Pedagogy in Teacher Education*, London: Falmer Press.

Munby, H. and Russell, T. (1994) "The authority of experience in learning to teach: Messages from a physics method class", *Journal of Teacher Education*, 45: 86–95.

Russell, T. (1995) "Returning to the physics classroom to re-think how one learns to teach physics", in T. Russell and F. Korthagen (eds) *Teachers who Teach Teachers: Reflections on Teacher Education*, London: Falmer Press, pp. 95–109.

—— (1997) "Teaching teachers: How I teach IS the message", in J.J. Loughran and T. Russell (eds) *Teaching about Teaching: Purpose, Passion and Pedagogy in Teacher Education*, London: Falmer Press, pp. 32–47.

Schön, D.A. (1983). *The Reflective Practitioner: How professionals think in action*, New York: Basic Books.

Van Manen, M. (1991) "Reflectivity and the pedagogical moment: the normativity of pedagogical thinking and acting", *Journal of Curriculum Studies*, 23 (6): 507–36.

3 A balancing act

Self-study in valuing the individual student

Deborah Tidwell

Context for the study

As an educator, I first became aware of the importance of valuing the individual through my work with a very diverse population of children in a neighborhood school in an inner city. As an elementary teacher in the western portion of the United States, I taught children who came from a wide variety of linguistic backgrounds, social experiences, religious experiences, and family structures. As I grew as a teacher, I found that children's learning was deeper and more dynamic if they brought their own experiences, understandings and interpretations of events to the learning environment. In addition, such interactions provided me with a better understanding of the children themselves and helped me in my instructional planning and teaching. For example, when I taught map skills in a fifth-grade classroom in an inner-city neighborhood school (students were not bussed, but within walking distance of their school), the introduction to the development and use of maps came from using the students' own travel routes to and from school. Students were asked to provide a detailed description of the route they traveled to school in the morning and of the route they took going home. They were encouraged to include what they considered to be important landmarks and markers they used to know which directions to go. Students could also include drawings, photos or cuttings from newspapers to help describe their journey to and from school. The success of using their own lives in their learning of new information lay in the opportunity to connect school skills with life skills. Often students came to more profound understandings than the original curriculum had intended.

When these fifth-grade students shared their routes to and from school, they discovered there were many different ways to get to the same point. This helped in their understanding of the lesson's focus on a map as a bird's-eye view. They could see how all their varied routes could be presented in one picture. They also discovered that the route between their home and school looked very different going to school than going home, using different landmarks and seeing different perspectives of landmarks depending on their direction of travel. Their examination of their own experiences enabled them to realize complexities that went beyond the required curriculum on map skills to examine the role of perspective and context in making sense of their world. Indeed, I found the inclusion of students' own lives and experiences in the classroom a critical component to their success as learners and my effectiveness as a teacher.

Later, as a professor of literacy education with an interest in second-language learners, I found support for my earlier teaching experiences in works by educators such as Sleeter and Grant (1994), Collier (1995), Faltis (1997), Freeman and Freeman (1997), and Ovando and Collier (1998). These authors highlight the cultural and social contexts of education, where students must negotiate the learning environment. Successful learning includes each student's own experiences and realities. An effective teacher creates a learning environment that values students' differences. Instruction in such an environment provides for student choice, creates opportunities for students to connect their own experiences and knowledge with content to be learned, and requires the teacher to understand the role and context of students' personal lives (family cultures) in the learning process.

For me, then, the essence of effective teaching centers on the idea of valuing the individual. And herein lies the conflict. As a professor working with both undergraduate and graduate students, I am constantly challenged to incorporate individual ways of knowing into the larger context of my program's curriculum. My colleagues and I often struggle over these notions of academic rigor and individuation of a program. The notion of academic rigor is raised in higher education when too many students receive passing grades. A discussion often ensues over grade inflation and the lack of rigor in a program. I find this perplexing. In my experiences working with pre-service and in-service teachers, their decision to major in teacher education reflects their strong interest in teaching and their desire to make a difference in a child's education. This drive to become an effective teacher creates a classroom of pre-service teachers with a genuine focus on learning and also challenges me not only to provide knowledge about teaching but also to model how that teaching should occur. It is through this modeling that I address the individual ways of knowing in the content I teach. To me, this is true academic rigor. But this, then, creates a dilemma at the university level, where rigor is reflected more in the challenges a learning experience provides and where rigor is defined by limiting the number of individuals who can actually succeed.

The very premise of higher education defines participation through institutional standards and institutional norms. However, if students' own cultures are an integral part of their negotiation of the learning experience, then those cultures need to be reflected in the classroom. Equally as important, those students' sense of reality, ways of knowing, and ways of negotiating need to be honored. If effective instruction means valuing the individual, how is that negotiated in a university context? More specifically, if I find valuing the individual a critical part of effective teaching, how is this realized in my interactions with my students?

My interest in better understanding this connection between my teaching beliefs and my teaching practice served as the catalyst for the self-study described in this chapter. The outcome of this study led to a change in my understanding of the relationship of my teaching to my beliefs, as well as to a change in my teaching practice (Richardson, 1994).

The study

Development of the question

When first conceptualizing this self-study, I wrestled with the research focus. Initially, I planned to examine how I negotiate my teaching to incorporate students' individual ways of knowing within the context of a university setting. I believe so strongly in the value of including different ways of knowing in effective instruction that my initial question assumed the inclusion of such in my practice. But as I began to design the data collection, I realized that to assume that I was already incorporating students' different ways of knowing in my teaching was to sidestep a critical question. It became apparent that my first question was not *how do I incorporate* different ways of knowing, but *do I incorporate* different ways of knowing? Or, more importantly, *do I value* my students as individuals? This led to the realization that I needed to know more about my dynamics when working with different students. These dynamics would then inform me about what it is I actually *do*. To that end, my research focus changed not only my phrasing of the question, but also the very nature of my data collection itself. My research question then became: *How do I interact with students at an individual level?*

Design of the study

To answer my question I studied three cases representing three different levels of study at my university – the Bachelors program, the Masters program and the Doctoral program. Each case study tells a story of my interactions with a student, chronicled through journaling and instructional documentation (class notes, assignment/assessment records, and anecdotal records from one-to-one meetings with the student). Working with all three students on a near-daily basis provided ongoing face-to-face contact that helped insure the validity of my data gathering (Kirk and Miller, 1987). Data were examined for patterns and categories, which were then embedded within the story of each student and my work with that student. Patterns and categorical statements were then analyzed from the perspective of three tenets for valuing a student: student choice, connecting to student's previous experiences, and understanding/appreciating the student's own culture (Davidman and Davidman, 1997; Faltis, 1997; Ovando and Collier, 1998). The completed stories and their implications were then shared with a colleague for feedback, and were revised to reflect the colleague's insights (McNiff, Lomax and Whitehead, 1996).

The three students involved in this self-study (all given pseudonyms) were enrolled in three different courses during the same semester. Martin was an

African-American undergraduate student in a Bachelors of Arts program in education, taking his first methods course in reading and language arts. Karen, a European-American graduate student in a Masters of Education program in reading, was enrolled in a supervision practicum course. Ruby, a Chinese graduate student in a Doctoral program in curriculum and instruction, was enrolled in her first three hours of dissertation and writing her proposal.

The stories

Martin, Martin, where have you gone?

Martin arrived in my class late on the first day. I have never been one to focus on time; however, I noticed that he shuffled into class in an almost glassy-eyed daze and sat in the far corner at the back of the room. None of the students in class acknowledged his entrance nor paid much attention to him throughout the class period. This lack of attention to his presence continued throughout the semester. Martin was the only African-American in a class of twenty-eight students and one of only three males. The remaining students in the class were European-Americans. I was concerned about making this class a place where Martin would feel safe and welcome; I saw this as an educational equity issue (Davidman and Davidman, 1997). Since I organized the course around group interactions, each student chose a group to join. Martin chose a group that sat near him.

In an initial survey of interests, Martin stated that he had experience working with pre-school children for three summers and wanted to teach in Florida or Texas, working at kindergarten through third-grade levels. Under the category "something unique about you", he stated "I never give up on anyone". He explained that in his life experiences, people had given up on him when he knew he could do things. He had trouble following directions, but if people took the time to explain things to him, he did "all right". Martin worked a night shift at a local factory and got off work at 7:30 AM, with class beginning at 8:00 AM. Understandably, Martin had difficulty arriving in class on time. I offered to arrange for him to take a later class, but Martin insisted that this class time worked best for him.

At the onset of the semester, Martin experienced difficulty in completing assignments on time. The work he did submit often did not match the assigned task (for example, when he was assigned to write about the teaching he had observed in a third-grade classroom, he wrote about his impressions of the physical room). I set up regular meeting times with Martin to discuss assignments and his understanding of the class lectures, activities, and readings. I hoped these meetings would facilitate his success in my class and I tried to arrange times that he agreed would accommodate him. However, he began missing a number of classes and missing meetings with me as well. I asked for a more formal arrangement that involved the Student Support Services on campus. By meeting with me, with a Student Support Service adviser about his coursework, and through ongoing progress reporting, I thought the different perspectives and the concrete reporting would help Martin make sense of the course and of his progress. It did not.

My instructional guidance had focused on preparing Martin to succeed in college rather than on specific content about literacy. While class meetings focused on content and literacy processes, our one-to-one meetings and individualized attention during class time focused on student strategies (such as how to follow class directions or how to confirm his understanding of assignments). My underlying assumption was that he was not able to function successfully as a student. All of my attempts to facilitate his success focused on external guidance. While some internal guidance was nurtured through providing student strategies that he could implement himself, this was superseded by external guidance measures when I perceived he was ineffective in using these strategies.

My sense of frustration was realized in my journal notes discussing his "lack of effort" to come to talk with me, complete assignments, or attend classes and meetings. Group participation was an important part of the class, and with his constant absences Martin was unable to develop any sense of community with his group. In fact, when he attended class he rarely participated in group activities, preferring to listen and observe. I wrote conflicting journal entries that reflected my struggle with the notion of providing a classroom sensitive to cultural and knowledge differences "creating an environment for all students to learn", versus the more exclusive notion that some students are simply "not college material". My initial journal comments highlighted my interactions with Martin.

> *Week 1*   Martin asked to speak with me about taking my class. He seems concerned that I understand his schedule and know that he works just before class. Talked with him at length on course requirements; he seemed very interested. Would another class time work better for his schedule? Or maybe assignment dates can be changed.

As Martin began to show signs that he was not succeeding in my class, my journal entries reflected my struggle to make sense of the dynamic.

> *Week 3*   Martin late for class (3rd time). Assignments not ready. He seemed unclear about what was to be completed for class. I'm not sure I'm making the course content and requirements clear to him. Maybe if we meet weekly to discuss how he perceives what is happening in class I'll have a better understanding of how my teaching is coming across.

As the semester progressed, I perceived Martin as dependent on me for his success and not an independent learner.

> *Week 5*   Martin is not letting me know when he is confused. He appears to wait for me to instigate any conversations about his work .... I am

becoming frustrated over Martin's dependency on me to fix it or make it better for him. I want him to work independently on this, to take more initiative for his work and for our interactions when we meet.

> *Week 8*   … need to work with him on taking correct notes and on keeping and following a calendar of due dates.

However, Martin felt he was an independent learner, stating that he "preferred to work alone". He recognized that he was not keeping up with assignments, but he believed most of his work was of good quality. He believed his late assignments related to misunderstandings about what was to be done. As the semester progressed, I began to shift the responsibility for Martin's participation in class from myself as the instructor to Martin as the student.

> *Week 6*   Martin continues to be late for class and not turn in assignments. It's as if he is not making an effort to try.

> *Week 7*   Martin has missed our meeting to discuss assignments (which he did not do) – I don't believe he has read the assignments.

> *Week 8*   This is so frustrating! – how could he have not heard the class discussion and overview from the last two weeks?

Despite my frustrations, I constantly questioned in my journal whether Martin's voice could be heard (*Week 4*: "Can the students in his group hear his ideas? There didn't seem to be follow up to his statements." *Week 6*: "Do I understand what he is saying to me?"). My perception of him as a student may have clouded my view of what he did and how he performed. For the most part, Martin's voice came through in defense of his work and his attendance or in explanation of his performance. There were few events where his voice was initiated outside those contexts. My journal notes reflected my conflict over how to talk about what was happening with Martin.

> *Week 6*   I have talked with him on several occasions about his tardiness and about his late assignments (or no assignments)… .It seems as if he is unable to connect with his small group in class. But why? What is keeping him from being successful?

I related his poor performance to his inability to become a part of the community. Most of my initial journal entries put the onus for his poor progress on my inability to find the "right connection" for him. As the semester progressed and my continued attempts to help Martin remained unsuccessful, I began to explain Martin's progress in terms of his responsibility.

Week 6   Or is it that he does understand what I am saying but is just not completing the work. It seems as if he is unable to connect with his small group in class.

While I provided some choices for Martin (change to a later class time, pick help-session times that worked for him), most of the options I gave him were *faux* choices. This realization emerged from my self-study through the examination of my journals and through the reflective process of stepping outside the context of the moment and looking at the broader picture. It seems that within my "normal teaching", my reflection is often moment-specific and moves quickly from one negotiated moment to the next without the opportunity for extended time to step out of the moment.

It is the leaving of that moment-specific context through my self-study that actually provided me with different insights. It was through this stepping outside those moments when I wrote my journal comments about my interactions with Martin that I was able to look back at these issues of choice with a more critical eye and realize that I was using the term "choice" in very limited ways. For example, the help sessions for Martin were required (no choice); choice was only in his determination of the times he would meet. My journal did refer to Martin's frequent absences as his use of student choice. However, this was a very different use of the term *student choice* on my part, a use that placed the onus for failure on Martin (in a student-choice context). By the middle of the semester, Martin had missed five of sixteen class meetings and four of seven personal meetings with me. Martin withdrew from class at mid-term.

Wait for me, Karen, I have more to teach you!

Karen came to the reading supervision practicum course from a background in early childhood. This experience had given her a sense of confidence in working with children, and from the beginning Karen approached her practicum in reading tutoring supervision with enthusiasm. If anything, Karen reinforced the notion of higher education working best when students already fit the prescribed knowledge base. She knew how to be a student, how to take notes, follow directions, and complete tasks that had been assigned. In fact, she was so adept at being a student, at participating, that I found myself asking her to do less, to be less. I wanted her to slow down her take-charge approach to the class long enough to be able to see what I had to offer as the teacher.

Karen came from a family of educators. She grew up with the notion that school was a "fun" place. It is fair to say that the culture of school matched very closely the family culture in which she lived. Throughout her schooling, Karen had been successful. She talked of playing school as a child. In addition, Karen enjoyed working with people. She was very social and found the role of supervisor in a reading clinic "very comfortable". The students she supervised were quick to comment on her "warmth", stating she was someone that was "easy to talk to".

Karen seemed to already know what to do with supervision. While this was her first course in clinical supervision, her previous experiences with early childhood programs had provided her with many opportunities to supervise. My role as the mentor/instructor in her practicum quickly evolved into more of an observer and occasional sounding board. Rather than being pleased with her ability to supervise well and to become independent quickly, I found myself questioning whether I was providing appropriate instruction for her learning. If she appeared to have "nothing to learn" was this even considered "a valuable learning experience?"

My journal entries centered on the notion that any program of study in teacher education should offer courses that challenge the student and that provide new knowledge and understandings about teaching. Because of Karen's early childhood supervisory experience, she came to the practicum with knowledge about effective dynamics for supervision. She was also a very social person, able to talk easily with undergraduate students and able to relate her own experiences to their current clinic tutorial experience. In addition, she had a high comfort level for the multi-task assignments asked of her in this clinic supervision. In most semesters, my practicum instruction involved working with the student on becoming familiar with the many roles of a supervisor and in organizing the complex nature of the multi-task environment. However, with Karen my typical instruction was not needed. Because of this I questioned whether this course was of value to her, and it became an important goal for me to find ways in which this practicum would challenge Karen and provide her with new knowledge and understandings about teaching.

To my chagrin, I found myself abandoning the tenets for valuing a student (student choice, connecting to previous experiences, and understanding the student's own culture). Karen's success as an effective supervisor was related directly to her previous experiences in supervision of young children, the tight mesh between her own culture and the culture of higher education, and her choices and decision-making processes. I appreciated Karen's experiences and her enthusiasm for her work ("[Karen] is a positive addition to the clinic", "[she] is energetic and enjoys working with undergraduates"), I also felt a "need to direct her experience more closely", or "the practicum would become out of control".

It was this notion of control that emerged from my journal writings and my notes from staff meetings. In fact, I focused the remainder of the semester on two areas of the clinical experience that were new to Karen, the use of a practical argument frame (Fenstermacher, 1994) for discussing students' tutoring, and a unique system for taking anecdotal records. These were my choices, not hers, and related less to her previous experiences.

The very nature of this practicum (set within a tutorial program, working with pre-service teachers) suited Karen well. But I felt a need to provide instructional guidance. My weekly observations confirmed her effective work. In addition, I required her to meet with me regularly to discuss her weekly supervision in the tutorial program. At our weekly meetings, where Karen discussed her students' progress and her concerns, my notes consistently indicate that I would redirect her comments to her work with practical arguments and anecdotal records. In effect, I would ask her to "tell the story of her week", only to interrupt her story to provide my own thoughts and suggestions on how she could improve her use of practical arguments and anecdotal records. I was recasting her success in a way that provided me with an avenue to "teach". Yet throughout the semester my notes also conclude that Karen was "an effective supervisor". Karen completed the semester practicum with high marks from the pre-service teachers she supervised. In fact on the surface my overall records indicate that Karen was an excellent student in her supervisory practicum with no indication of my conflicts or issues. It was only through this self-study, examining more closely my own actions and reactions through the language of my records, that I saw the conflicts I felt and began to understand at a deeper level my need to define my role as an effective teacher through that which I taught.

Ruby lets me teach ...

A strong advocate of bilingual education and second-language acquisition, Ruby had worked with me for two years as a doctoral graduate assistant. Throughout those two years she had developed a literature base for teacher preparation of bilingual learners. In the process of developing this literature base, Ruby had become a strong advocate of bilingual education. With a Masters degree in TESOL (Teaching English to Speakers of Other Languages), she worked off campus as an ESL (English as a Second Language) instructor for new Chinese immigrants to the United States. As Ruby described it, her personal connection to ESL students' life experiences led her to appreciate the importance of maintaining the family culture and language in order to successfully acculturate to the United States. By maintaining the children's family culture and language while learning a new language and culture, she believed families were better able to stay intact. She saw on a personal level the need for language maintenance as integral to family survival ("[Ruby] stated her daughter must keep her Chinese to speak with her grandparents, to know who she is").

For this semester of my work with Ruby she was enrolled in dissertation hours, developing and defending her proposal for study. From the outset Ruby was passionate about her dissertation topic, studying the beliefs of parents who send their children to heritage language schools, where the language of their family or ancestors is taught. These schools are typically held after school or on weekends. As a Chinese national who was raised by parents involved in Christian ministry in China, Ruby brought to her study a strong desire to "do the morally correct thing" for learners. Her interest in bilingual education came from a belief that family and language heritage related closely to moral development and an appreciation of one's heritage and culture.

Journal entries of my work with Ruby reflect my desire to have Ruby develop a study that tied her own cultural experiences and beliefs to content studied in her doctoral program. ("[Ruby] could incorporate her work with new immigrants at her church with her bilingual studies"). However, I felt a need to provide instructional guidance to help Ruby balance her passion for her topic with academic rigor. This translated into ongoing discussions with Ruby about the reasoning behind her study, the narrowing of her topic, and maintaining a focus on that topic in her research design. Across my journal entries about Ruby I describe my meetings with very positive language and with an appreciation for her interest (for example, "Her passion for her work makes these dissertation meetings come alive!") and an appreciation for her need for guidance (for example, "I feel like I've really helped her today").

Over the semester my journal entries and one-to-one meeting notes reflected my perceptions of Ruby as someone who evolved from a student dependent on my confirmation of her work, to an independent researcher who felt a real ownership of and connection with (expertise in) her area of study. I saw my role evolve over time from instructor to facilitator ("I'm directing less now, she's really begun to take this project over!"). Because of her passion for her topic, Ruby's voice came through ("[Ruby] insisted that her introduction state that children must have the opportunity to connect with their own culture"). I attributed the success of her dissertation proposal experience to study of content related to her own life experiences and culture, a connection to her own moral purpose to education, in a forum that provided structure but encouraged student voice. In other words, Ruby's experience best reflected the tenets of valuing a student. Her voice was heard, she related to her own life experiences, and, indirectly, she was able to relate to her own culture. It is interesting to note that, in my journal entries, most of my enthusiasm for Ruby's work was found in my comments about being able to "facilitate her growth" ("Examples of writing a literature review seemed to have helped – Ruby rewrote her introduction using the research literature, she eliminated a lot of her personal opinion statements"). Apparently, Ruby provided me with the chance to be what I called a "real teacher", to be successful in a role that allowed me to inform, direct, and facilitate.

Summary

Through this self-study of my interactions with three students, I am able to better understand my own premises about what I believe to be effective teaching. I was intrigued and surprised when my notions of being a teacher emerged from the data. While I have been involved in several self-studies that examined my practices in teacher education, it was this particular study with a focus on valuing students that led me deeper into my own notion of self as a teacher. By examining my own language for writing about my teaching, I was able to see issues about the role of teaching and my roles as a teacher that I had not seen before. Across all three students, despite their academic level, there was a consistent need for me to be able to play the role of teacher. The teacher roles included being able to inform students (content), being able to direct students in some way (control), and being able to facilitate students (service). When these roles of content, control, and service in my teaching were compromised, I found the learning experience less effective. The description of teacher roles that emerged from the data provides an interesting conflict between what I say I believe and what beliefs emerge in my actions.

This contrast can create interesting dilemmas in my instruction when working with students who already know the information to be taught (Karen), work well independently (Karen), or decline the services I wish to provide (Martin). This insight serves to inform my future teaching. Given that I want to create an environment where students use self as a premise for learning, being aware of the roles I create as teacher will help me change my teaching and thus the learning environment for my students. I can now use this awareness of my need to be a content provider, a controller, and a service provider in my thinking about my teaching.

Martin elicited conflicting views within my own thinking about the broader question of the purpose of higher education. His struggle to follow the coursework or to attend class led me to question my belief of university as an environment that should be shaped for all students. Should university be a unique environment for students possessing institutionally preferred ways of knowing? Or perhaps the issue is one of culture versus quality. Was Martin's lack of success due to cultural conflicts he found at university? Was he capable of better quality work but unwilling to make the effort? While I attempted to provide Martin with what I considered many "opportunities to succeed" in my class, were they really opportunities for him? Whatever the reason, he was unable to be successful. His lack of success emerged from the data as a progression from a teacher/teaching issue to a student/learning issue. By the time Martin dropped out of the class, I had relabeled his learning problems as student choice. This particular case remains problematic for me. It was much easier as the semester progressed to rely on the argument of "rigorous program" and "poor student choices" to explain Martin's failure. His story poses unanswered questions about the nature of higher education and accessibility to learners. For me, this notion of valuing the individual is a bit of a slippery slope. Did I provide genuine access for Martin that he chose not to partake of, or were my attempts at access so narrowly defined as to prevent Martin from participating? I don't know, but these enigmas of "rigor" and "access" will certainly continue.

Karen, as an extremely successful student, raises questions for me about when and how I value students in my class. Does my need to provide instructional support to my students override my desire to provide an instructional environment that values students? Karen's story best demonstrated my somewhat contrived role of teacher. This was the most intriguing and surprising finding in this self-study. My sense of self as teacher is clearly shaped by what I believe I "should" do as opposed to what perhaps really needs to be done. It is my hope that my awareness of this will make a difference in my future role as teacher. The most immediate way to make this happen will be in my reasoning behind my teaching actions. Through this awareness of my need to "be the teacher", I now can look at my actions and, ideally, think about my actions before acting in a way that values the student's own experiences and knowledge, incorporating that knowledge and experience into the learning experience.

With Ruby, my desire to create what I considered to be a successful learning environment was most closely realized. I attribute most of the success to a combination of familiarity (we had known each other for two years) and the fortunate combination of Ruby choosing a research topic that brought together her previous experiences, her current life experiences, and her academic/professional goals. However, it is interesting to note that a key reason I felt most successful with Ruby was that she allowed me to play all the roles of teacher: informing, directing, and facilitating. Questions emerge. Is it possible for me to relinquish these roles? Can I find a way to teach without relying on authoritative stances? The roles emerging in this self-study seem to be ones that I create in response to what I need, as opposed to roles that develop naturally in response to interactions with students and their needs. My charge, then, is to be able to step away from these self-imposed roles and move toward teaching roles that emerge naturally through my interactions with students. Toward this end, I can begin by using this newfound awareness in my reflection and decision-making for my teaching practice.

What I find most fulfilling, intriguing, and difficult about this type of self-study is that it requires me to get very close to my own teaching and to my own thinking. It forces me to ask questions that are not always easy to answer, and this can be a painful process. As a teacher educator, I spend a good part of my time instructing students about ways of teaching that can make a difference for learners. But often these ways of teaching, these beliefs about practice, are grounded in strong theoretical premises that, in some contexts, may be difficult to realize in practice. This is due, in part, to the organization and structure of higher education, such as large class sizes that often limit getting to know students or interacting well with students. An even larger constraint to realizing these practices is the mythical notion of professor, subscribed to by students and professors. The pre-defined roles of "professor" (expert, lecturer, authority) often create conflicts with teaching that values the individual student.

Self-study provides me with a frame for examining those compelling contexts for my teaching practice, for asking those good questions. Equally important in self-study is bringing in the voice of colleagues to confirm or oppose my findings. It is that collegial nature of self-study that creates a sense of community that is both unique and powerful. In this self-study, the collegial voice was instrumental in helping me see the context of my teaching. By sharing the compiled stories with a colleague who had been involved in reflective practice in a different field, I enabled him to confirm and question patterns and labels. This was particularly helpful in thinking through the role labels I saw emerging in my data. Questioning led to re-examining data and patterns, confirming those patterns, and finally reconstructing roles to reflect a clearer explanation of the dynamics involved.

So what do I do with this information about my practice? I plan to use the knowledge I have gained from this study to continue examining the notion of effectively valuing students in my teaching because these are issues that are important to me in my teaching. The next step will be to see if, by being aware of my need for contrived roles of informing, directing, and facilitating as a teacher, I can use that awareness to make a difference in my teaching so that my teaching can appropriately support the learning of all my students, not just those students who fit comfortably into my existing conceptualization of the roles of a teacher.

References and further reading

Collier, V.P. (1995) "Acquiring a second language for school", *Directions in Language and Education*, Washington, D.C.: National Clearinghouse for Bilingual Education.

Davidman, L. and Davidman, P.T. (1997) *Teaching with a Multicultural Perspective: A Practical Guide*, 2nd edn, New York: Longman.

Erickson, F. (1986) "Qualitative methods in research on teaching", in M.C. Whittrock (ed.) *Handbook of Research on Teaching*, 3rd edn, New York: Macmillan, pp. 119–61.

Faltis, C.J. (1997) *Joinfostering: Adapting Teaching for the Multilingual Classroom*, 2nd edn, Upper Saddle River, NJ: Merrill.

Fenstermacher, G.D. (1994) "The place of practical argument in the education of teachers", in V. Richardson (ed.) *Teacher Change and the Staff Development Process: A case in reading instruction*, New York: Teachers College Press.

Freeman, Y.S. and Freeman, D.E. (1997) *Teaching Reading and Writing in Spanish in the Bilingual Classroom*, Portsmouth, NH: Heinemann.

Glover, M.K. (1994) "Providing time for flowers: a curriculum vision for the twenty-first century", in A.D. Flurkey and R.J. Meyer (eds) *Under the Whole Language Umbrella: Many Cultures, Many Voices*, Urbana, IL: National Council of Teachers of English, pp. 295–308.

Kirk, J. and Miller, M.L. (1987) *Reliability and Validity in Qualitative Research: Qualitative Research Methods Series*, London: Sage.

McNiff, J., Lomax, P. and Whitehead, J. (1996) *You and Your Action Research Project*, London: Routledge.

Ovando, C.J. and Collier, V.P. (1998) *Bilingual and ESL Classrooms: Teaching in Multicultural Contexts*, 2nd edn, Boston, MA: McGraw-Hill.

Richardson, V. (1994) "Conducting research on practice", *Educational Researcher*, 23 (5): 5–10.

Sleeter, C.E. and Grant, C.A. (1994) *Making Choices for Multicultural Education: Five Approaches to Race, Class, and Gender*, 2nd edn, New York: Merrill.

4 Opposites attract

What I learned about being a classroom teacher by being a teacher educator

Joseph C. Senese

Introduction

Ten years ago I left a high school English classroom to become an assistant principal at Highland Park High School, in a suburb of Chicago. An important influence on my growth in this new role involved establishing the Action Research Laboratory (ARL), a model professional development program that applies the principles of collaborative action research to teacher education (Senese, 1998). My position as an assistant principal has further evolved so that I now specialize in working with staff on curriculum, instruction, assessment, and staff development. But the deeper I plunged into my administrative duties, the further I drifted away from student contact. I felt a compelling need to get back to my roots as a teacher.

In the Fall semester of the 1999–2000 school year, I taught English for the first time in eight years. By teaching a semester class in British Literature to senior high school students for the last two years, I have discovered that I am not the same English teacher I was ten years ago. My intervening roles in the ARL as a teacher educator, staff developer, and facilitator have significantly influenced how I teach high school English. Because I work in a high school and not in a university, my role as a teacher educator is different from the role of university teacher educators. However, I believe that what we learn about teaching and learning by studying ourselves as teachers, whether in pre- or in-service programs, is of value to all of us. Consequently, I use the terms "teacher educator" and "staff developer" interchangeably.

Aim of the study

Before I ventured into administration, I had been a successful teacher. I could easily recall what it was like to teach high school English, and I remembered that students routinely told me that they enjoyed the classes I taught. Yet I also knew that I had grown in my beliefs about teaching and learning, and had developed in my understanding of what learning looks like. I had not had the opportunity to put my beliefs and knowledge of teaching into practice for the last eight years. I wondered if my skills would be up to the challenge.

By no means had I done something as simple as a U-turn by re-entering the classroom. I had long believed that my primary job as a teacher was to make my students independent of my instruction and of me. I had strongly subscribed to providing students with multiple opportunities to learn, with choices, and with creative outlets. But as often as I turned the curriculum over to the students, I had still maintained control of it, doling out pieces as I saw fit, gauging how much was good for them, and allowing them to move forward only in measured steps. That was not how I acted as a staff developer.

In this self-study I set out to discover the ways that performing one job (as administrator) had influenced how I performed the other (as teacher). I posed the question: *What have I learned about myself as a staff developer (teacher educator) that has changed me as a high school English teacher?*

Constructivist influences as a staff developer

Since I last taught English, I had been deeply influenced by the learning theory referred to as constructivism. I had attended workshops, heard speakers, and read books and articles about constructivism. I embraced constructivist thinking as a way to amalgamate and deepen a set of beliefs I already held. But if I were truly to teach in a constructivist way, some of the control I had had as a teacher would now be wrested from me. The literature told me that I could provide students with opportunities for learning, but I was in no way responsible for anyone learning anything. My primary job as a teacher was to create the environment that would allow students to learn in their own ways. Other than providing a loose structure for this to happen, my charge as a teacher needed to be redefined so I could encourage students in their own pursuits and ultimately relinquish control to them.

In my administrative role I was already enacting this credo as a staff developer. Ironically, I was doing a double somersault. I had adapted the literature about teaching in constructivist ways to the work I did as a staff developer. Now, eight years later, I needed to reverse that process and re-apply it to teaching students.

Of all the work I had done as a staff developer, the establishment of the Action Research Laboratory in the Spring of 1995 probably signified the apex, because it so fully involved putting my beliefs about learning and change into practice. I acted as a facilitator who provided the opportunities and resources for teachers to investigate, through action research, how best to teach their students. The teachers in the ARL chose their areas of inquiry, collected data, made decisions based on that data, and wrote about their experiences. Although I undoubtedly had some influence on their work (providing resources, literature and experiences that I thought would enrich and inform them), I always tried to stay in the background. When a team of ARL teachers first met to discuss how to put their own beliefs into practice, they were clearly annoyed that I did not "lead" them. I always turned to their thinking, the results of their action research, and their experiences as a way of inviting ownership in the process. The following reflection, written two years after starting the ARL, provides a backward glance into my actions.

In the ARL the teachers themselves are developing their own competencies to solve problems, research their ideas, and meet the needs of their students. It really cannot be any other way. After all, the teachers are the ones who are breathing life into the projects of their research. The decisions they make have to make sense to them and have to feel right to them. As a facilitator my rightful place is in the background.

I have said to teachers in various contexts that I do not pretend to be an expert nor do I have the answers, but "I can sure ask good questions". Although the statement may sound flippant, I truly believe that as a facilitator my role is to provide the structures and environment that will allow the teachers to grow at their own rates. The most I can do is to make a suggestion, but even that I do rarely.

The greatest tools I have as the facilitator of the ARL are the abilities to focus my listening and to place questions carefully. By listening to what the teachers are saying about their research, their backgrounds, their knowledge-base, or their experiences, I can help to make connections or observations. I can also act as a process observer, paying attention to the flow of the talk and offering a question or summation to help put things into focus. After we had been meeting for about six months, I observed to Team #2 that I would often say very little over the course of the morning; they initiated the conversation and directed their talk to each other. After all, they knew what they wanted to know and they knew who in the room was facing the same issues. Relegating me to the background was the greatest compliment I could have received as a facilitator because this showed that the teachers themselves had taken ownership of their learning.

I subscribe to a constructivist philosophy both in and out of the classroom. Therefore, in the ARL I try to create a learning environment for the teachers, one in which they are comfortable, encouraged to ask questions that are truly meaningful to them, to take risks, to dream of the ideal, to reflect, and to posit solutions. I provide the agenda, the articles for discussion, and the structure in which they can pursue their own work.

This year's participants reinforced my perceptions. In response to a question about the role the facilitator played in their professional growth, teachers gave these responses:

- You had this insistence that we really define what it is that we wanted to do and how we wanted to go about doing it … you forced us to come to our own conclusions and to be problem-solvers. I guess, in other words, you asked us to practice what we're preaching in our own learning. (Bryan Ott)

- You would jump in with this little comment here or there, never say very much, but just enough to kind of trigger us ... back on the focus of where we're going. (John Gorleski)
- I thought that first of all you established an environment and a place, then let us take ownership of it ... you really allowed us to construct what our time together would be. (Paul Swanson)
- You never seemed to have a personal agenda, and I just felt [that] you were the source of information and some resources we needed at times. You were a source of encouragement and support. (Lauren Fagel)
- You have structured things so that we can share what we are doing with other people in the school. (Christine Hill)

In addition to my own experiences, professional readings shaped and reinforced my beliefs. Wheatley's *Leadership and the New Science* (1992) has been quite influential in my transition from an efficient, hard-working administrator who could "get the job done right" to a constructivist thinker and doer. I reflected on its influence on my administrative style in a journal entry in the Spring of 1998:

> Wheatley's writing has struck a chord in me. Because of the ideas presented in this book and reinforced in her latest book, *A Simpler Way* [Wheatley and Kellner-Rogers, 1996], I have learned to be more open to the moment, to look for possibilities, and to adapt to changing situations more than ever before in my life.
>
> The Action Research Laboratory, too, has been based in part on Wheatley's application of the new sciences, especially in her thinking about organizational change. The Action Research Laboratory was designed to be a slight disturbance in the school system that would make the system, by self-reference, readjust itself. That theory fuels my role as creator and facilitator in The Action Research Laboratory as well as assistant principal.

Senge's *The Fifth Discipline Fieldbook* (1994) has also shaped my thinking about staff development. In the same reflection cited above, I also wrote:

> The thinking about organizational behavior in *The Fifth Discipline Fieldbook* has had a significant impact on my development as an assistant principal ... [and] has provided me with a framework for creating programs at the high school.

My growth as a teacher educator was well documented as I synthesized data about school programs and my role in them. Looking back over the last six years, I am intrigued by how I measured my own growth. I took the palpable things, the products that could be pointed to and enumerated as evidence of the growth that had taken place inside. I am not so sure now that there is a correlation. I do not deny that the artifacts signify something important, but they can only hint at the development of my self as a teacher and administrator, much less as a person. I have become much more interested in exploring the issue of how my growth as a staff developer has influenced me as a high school English teacher.

Method of study

This self-study developed from several sources over the course of six years. To track my own growth as a staff developer, I have revisited data used to analyze the work of the teachers who are members of the ARL. The data included qualitative analyses of their yearly written reports and interviews that I had conducted with them. These sources provided a rich vein of information about my interactions with ARL teachers and the organization that I created to support their growth. My own reflections, coupled with professional readings, have led to a greater awareness of how I created structures and a nurturing culture in which teachers could grow professionally. These reflections and analyses have offered considerable information about my own growth and, subsequently, the influence of that growth on my teaching. As I taught my English course over the last two years, I noticed how I put my beliefs and experiences as a staff developer into practice with my students.

In this elective English course, I applied my beliefs about learners based on constructivist principles: ownership of content, choice of methods for learning and assessment, useful activities based on personal goals and beliefs, shared inquiry, social processes, reflection on learning practices as well as content, and production of varied and rich outcomes (Senese, 2000). I monitored my own growth and reactions through notes, artifacts and conversations with students and other teachers.

I have taught the class twice now and each experience has been unique. True to a strong belief in constructivist learning, I adapted the class to the needs of the students who were in it. Therefore, the experience for each student each year was individual. Additionally, the students in the course shaped the class each year. To differentiate the experiences, I refer to them as BritLit 00 and BritLit 01.

Outcomes

Three axioms, each containing overtones of tension and even irony, have emerged from my role as staff developer and now play a significant role in my venture as an English teacher.

- Go slow to go fast.
- Be tight to be loose.
- Relinquish control in order to gain influence.

Each axiom is counterintuitive, and the tension inherent in each rises from the opposing forces at play. Understanding and employing these opposing forces in the proper perspective is key to helping teachers grow professionally and also to helping students grow academically.

Each of the axioms has greatly influenced me as a teacher educator and now as an English teacher. However, the axioms signify more than a change in behavior. They suggest a development of personal beliefs and, in that way, signal a change in nature. Influenced by systems thinking (Senge *et al.*, 1994), organizational theories based on the new sciences (Wheatley, 1992; Wheatley and Kellner-Rogers, 1996), and constructivist principles (Brooks and Brooks, 1993; Caine and Caine, 1997a, 1997b), I can trace changes in my behavior to changes in my beliefs and values. These have affected my own attitudes and behaviors, and have influenced how and why I interact with others, both adults and students. This self-study, therefore, is an iterative process, beginning and ending with my own self-awareness and growth, and ultimately having a critical impact on others with whom I come into contact. I first address how I employed each axiom as a staff developer and then describe how the axiom played out in my role as a classroom English teacher.

Go slow to go fast

In the ARL, I have learned that to produce significant results I have to allow people to grow at their own pace. This requires giving them enough time to accept responsibility for their own professional development. For example, before teachers are ready to collect data, they need to want to find something out that a data collection can illuminate. My experience in "going slow" has shown that, once they have accepted the responsibility for their own growth, teachers make progress at an accelerated rate so that they are able to "go fast".

Because this axiom had played out so truthfully in the ARL, I applied the same axiom to the British Literature course to allow for individual learning styles and personal pace. Therefore, in both BritLit 00 and BritLit 01, the atmosphere in the course was relaxed and unstructured. Without a formal curriculum, students chose their own books, set their own timelines, and read at their own pace. They formed their own literature groups and created their own assignments. When they were ready to make a firmer commitment to the process, they could, but they were not pressured to "perform" in class. Students commented often about the freedom they experienced in the class and how much they enjoyed the wide variety of choice they had in reading literature, writing assignments, and becoming involved.

I allowed students this unprecedented kind of freedom because, in this instance, they were unlearning years of school behavior. At quarterly conferences in both years of the class, some students felt that seventeen-year-olds were not ready to take on this kind of responsibility. Evidence from student conferences and surveys showed that most students were prepared to take on the responsibilities of self-direction, but some were not.

My most pressing difficulty throughout the semester involved determining how loose a structure these students could comfortably work in without me losing them. I now believe that in BritLit 00 I allowed them to flounder for too long at the start of the semester. I had surmised that they would know how to organize themselves into teams according to interests and that the class would naturally flow from that. It did not work that smoothly.

If asked now, students would probably say that they floundered for an entire quarter, but the indecision actually lasted about two weeks. During that time, students came to class each day and argued about how to organize themselves, how to choose a piece of literature, how to get started, and how to act as a team. We entered a vicious circle, unable to move forward. At the end of the third week, I stepped in and forced them to choose a piece of literature that we would all read. I would act as the "teacher" and construct daily lessons for them, but this would only be the starting point, a way to give us the push we needed. It would also indicate to me their skills in English. They gladly agreed. I had learned that I needed to go slow, but more structures needed to be in place for students to make the most of the situation. This ties directly to the second axiom.

The second time around, in BritLit 01, I used the curriculum written by the BritLit 00 students (http://www.d113.lake.k12.il.us/hphs/curriculum/senese/-index.html). They had written into the curriculum a period of introduction in which the teacher conducted class. This certainly made the class more comfortable at the start for the BritLit 01 students. Although they appreciated the slow approach to this newfound (and confusing) freedom, many students revealed that they felt we had worked together as a class for too long. They were eager to delve into the curriculum in their own ways much sooner. As imperative as it was to "go slow", students in BritLit 01 felt they could "go fast" much sooner than I had anticipated.

Be tight to be loose

The significance of this axiom was clear to me in my role as a staff developer, yet it somehow escaped me in my role as a classroom teacher. As already noted, the structure of the course was loose. Students enjoyed the freedom but not all were prepared to make productive use of it. In the ARL, teachers agree to certain frameworks before they join. Teams of teachers must represent three different subject areas. Teachers must collect data. Teachers meet for a full school day once a month, off campus. Teachers make a commitment to "get the word out" about their research and the ARL through publication and presentation. I have noted that in this voluntary professional development program no teacher has shirked these responsibilities. Teachers may negotiate deadlines or take extra time to accomplish something, but they do adhere to the guidelines that make the ARL.

As a professional development program, the ARL has never been the same from one year to the next. The guiding principles of collaboration, experimentation, a basis in research, and teacher empowerment remain constant, but the ways in which various teams meet those goals is always evolving. By adapting our practices to the needs of the participants, the ARL has remained a viable and evolutionary program while maintaining its integrity as a force for teacher professional development and for school change.

Although counterintuitive, the logic behind the ARL is that the more freedom participants are given to construct their own meanings, the more structure they create. Conventional wisdom would say that given freedom to determine their own professional development, teachers would evolve in chaotic, unpredictable ways, losing sight of organizational goals and going off in their own directions. In fact, good staff development does appear chaotic and unpredictable, but tight, clear program goals keep the teachers aligned to the purpose of the organization, which in turn strengthens their impact on the system as a whole.

Making this play out in an English classroom was more complex. In BritLit 00, one problem loomed greater than any other. It was even mentioned by students who rated the course highly: *the need to balance the choices and freedom with structure and accountability.* Interviews with students revealed that each individual had a personal concept of what that meant. Some thrived, others faltered. It appears that the greatest asset of this course was also its greatest liability. When I pointed out to students that they could impose their own structures and standards for their performances, they balked. As one student said, "If it doesn't come from you, it doesn't seem real."

The familiar system of teacher-directed instruction had taken its toll. After my first experience teaching the course, I knew that I needed to offer more guidance and, especially at the start of the course, more structure in which students could make decisions and take charge of their learning. Once they had the structures in place, they might proceed more smoothly through the course. Improved accountability was one area of the curriculum that had to be addressed.

Consequently, BritLit 01 was more tightly structured. After all, these students actually had to follow the curriculum designed by the BritLit 00 students. Given initial direction and a semester plan for what was required of them, students enjoyed the freedom to form their own groups or work alone, to choose their own literature and to share their learning in their own ways. To address the need for accountability and to assign first-quarter grades, small groups of students acted as review boards. Students had to present to a group of peers what had been accomplished in the first quarter and then, using the rubric we had designed together, assign themselves a grade. While they appreciated the opportunity to present what they had learned to their peers, they were uncomfortable 'grading' each other. They suggested that they provide a grade to me privately and then leave it up to me. We did not use either of these systems for the second quarter. I reverted to having students write a reflection of what they had learned in the semester and assign themselves a grade based on the criteria under the rubric.

When students chose the literature to read, they had a tight structure designed by the previous year's students. They had to read at least one piece of literature from each literary genre (fiction, non-fiction, drama, poetry). They were intended to read much more than that, but this was defined as the minimum. Unfortunately, some saw the minimum as the goal of the course and did exactly that amount of work. Many, however, expanded their reading based on their interests. For the future I need to find ways to encourage them to use the tight structure as the framework from which to expand their reading and writing and not as the objective of the class.

Relinquish control in order to gain influence

Distinguishing a difference between control and influence has been a hallmark of the ARL. Teachers in the ARL are in charge of their own professional development and know how they need to grow. My strong belief in teacher self-direction and autonomy allows me to step back and take the role of facilitator in the ARL. I make a conscious effort not to direct teachers in their action research. When appropriate or when asked, I will offer an opinion, make an observation, summarize a conversation, or ask a question, but the teachers truly control the process. Because teachers accept the fixed structures of the ARL, they slowly accept responsibility for their own learning. It does not come naturally or quickly. Teachers are no more accustomed to deciding their professional development path than students are used to deciding what to learn and how to learn it.

It is no coincidence that ARL teachers are working to be published and to present the results of their action research. If this were not a personal goal for these teachers, all my prodding or organizing as the facilitator of the program could not make it happen. The fact that every Summer these teachers write a four- to ten-page paper with numerous attachments in order to document their professional growth and their students' growth demonstrates their commitment to their own development as a way to help students and to contribute to their profession.

These teachers have taken the responsibility for their own professional growth as researchers. Without a facilitator, some processes might take a little bit longer or the communication might not be as efficient, but the work would still get done. Teachers who make a commitment to research because it produces palpable results in their work and in their students' performance will sustain themselves. There is no going back. They do not need someone telling them what to do and when to do it, but they do need someone who can offer suggestions and support when appropriate. In the final analysis, participation in a collaborative research community has made the teachers in the Action Research Laboratory at Highland Park High School self-reliant and self-confident.

This axiom is potent in that it emphasizes that any learning that happens in the classroom is *not* about the teacher. Years of teaching taught me to separate responsibility for the learning in the classroom from me personally. I cannot control student learning; I can only influence it.

In approaching a classroom of seventeen-year-olds, I wanted to provide the same opportunities for individual growth and personal accountability as I had for ARL teachers. As a way to relinquish control to the students in my British Literature course, I did not grade them, test them, or provide a curriculum for them. In both years of the course, student satisfaction in learning in an atmosphere that allowed them to construct their own meaning through personal learning was generally high. Students expressed a strong appreciation for taking charge of their learning and sometimes exhibited more ownership of their learning.

In end-of-semester surveys of BritLit 00 students, sixteen of twenty-three students (70 per cent) mentioned that they most enjoyed or appreciated the freedom that the class gave them to direct their own learning. Clearly they embraced the tenets of constructivism: constructing their own meaning in personal ways. In the same survey, students listed what they had gained from the course. They were able to name the literature they had read, secondary sources they used to illuminate the literature, and the writing they had done. They also made specific references to the use of technology for learning and communicating, a goal of all English curricula at the high school. One student in particular was able to articulate how she gradually began to appreciate the larger goals of the program:

> It has been said that our curriculum is a living document, one that will go on and be revised and reworked and hopefully appreciated by many. The curriculum was just a project when I first started, but once I understood the greater idea behind the class, it had a pulse. The pride I feel from doing that is far greater than that of a good grade, it is the type of pride and sense of accomplishment that will propel me through life and bring me an overall sense of happiness. That, to me, is success.

Her ability to intuit an understanding of the constructivist principles applied in creating this curriculum speaks loudly to the significance of this learning theory. Not all students, however, had this experience. A minority of students (two students or 9 per cent of the class) rated their experience as very low (below 5 on a scale of 1 to 10), complaining of a lack of direction and frustration with their classmates and the teacher.

The final product that BritLit 00 students created was a live presentation to assessors from outside the school to explain the curriculum that they had written and to share how it had played out during the semester. Assessors remarked that the presentation showed depth of understanding of the content of the course as well as high student interest in continuous learning. One student, who chose to continue his study of British Literature in a second semester comprising independent study with me, put it this way:

> In Aldous Huxley, I found an author that I can say I actually enjoyed reading. This has never happened to me before … . Looking at this, I can honestly say that this class has motivated me to be more of an independent student and has brought the "love", or whatever you would like to call it, to

me, something I never felt would happen ... . I want you to know that I have found a new passion for a skill that once drove me crazy, reading.

To address the need for personal accountability, for the BritLit 01 class I designed (with the advice of the class members) a public poster session as their final examination. Students created posters to demonstrate their learning over the course of the semester. They invited the high school staff, university professors and parents to their "examination", and thirty-five people attended. During the eighty-minute exam periods, visitors interacted with students who shared their learning. The response to this format was positive both for students and for visitors. This "real world" exhibit allowed them the freedom to express their learning in various ways, while still requiring each student to be accountable for producing something to display and explain.

All ARL teachers have encountered difficulties in measuring the learning that occurs in a non-traditional setting. To deal with this complication, I stay in contact with all the British Literature graduates and will continue to monitor ways in which the class may have changed them. I also save any correspondence they send me, such as this one:

> I just wanted to contact you with an updated e-mail address and also to let you know that one of my teachers is one of those who plays "guess what I'm thinking" and while I never thought about it before, after being in your class I really thought about how infuriating it is for me.

A longitudinal study will help to determine the influence the course may have had on them.

Advancing our knowledge

Wheatley (1992, p. 21) observes that what we perceive as shapeless or chaotic really contains patterns that we may not be able to see without the advantage of distance in location or time. She points out that only when we near the end of our lives can we perceive the patterns that were there all along. I accept that I am still becoming and my perceptions are limited, but I am able at this time to generalize a little from my experiences.

From being both a teacher of high school students and a teacher educator, I have learned to accept and welcome the contradictory nature of interactions in teaching and learning, especially when one person is in a position of authority. My work as a staff developer has provided a cohesive philosophical framework for my work as a teacher of high school English. Conversely, my experience as an English teacher has helped me as a teacher educator by reinforcing my conceptions about constructivist learning situations.

Oddly enough, I can best summarize my experience by referring to an episode of a popular American TV show, *Seinfeld*. In this particular episode, George discovered that his instinctive predisposition to speak or act was always the wrong thing to do. He accidentally discovered that he could get what he wanted by saying or doing the *opposite* of what he felt like saying or doing at that moment. His friend Elaine told him to do the opposite of his inclination as a rule of thumb. Once George adopted this thinking, his life turned around. He appeared more appealing to others, found successes in his work and love life, and became happier.

If opposites truly do attract, then over the last two years I too have learned to take Elaine's advice. Either as a teacher educator or as an English teacher, when my tongue wants to speak, I have learned to remain silent. When my role as staff developer or teacher demands action, I wait. When I become impatient, I slow down. My intuition has become counterintuitive! Taking this route has freed me to become a better listener, a more perceptive learner, and a fairer coach. I find myself better able to synthesize experiences for others. I am free to take the balcony view, to embrace the whole, and to view the horizon.

I have learned that secondary school students are not all that different from adults. Time and again I have noted the similarities between the behaviors of students and teachers. We differentiate learning theory and teaching practices for adults but, if we expect students to grow into adulthood, they need to encounter experiences that they will have as adults.

I have learned that the system(s) in which we work control and shape our behaviors, no matter what role we have adopted. When given opportunities for self-direction, all students and teachers hesitate. In general, our school systems do not encourage independence or exploration for either students or adults. Although we profess a mission to free students to learn, the message we teachers send is that students cannot learn without a guide, someone who will not only plan the route but also interpret the experience for them. When students do not easily mold themselves to how a class, a school, or an experience has been structured for them, they often struggle. Our systems need to allow for variations, individualization, and experimentation to get at the marrow of learning. This is as true for students as it is for teachers. No one can tell someone else what any learning experience will mean. Learning will always be as unique as the individual experiencing it. By developing an awareness of ourselves as learners (self-study) we can truly learn to see what we can be.

References and further reading

Brooks, J.G. and Brooks, M.G. (1993) *The Case for Constructivist Classrooms*, Alexandria, VA: Association for Supervision and Curriculum Development.
Caine, R.N. and Caine, G. (1997a) *Education on the Edge of Possibility*, Alexandria, VA: Association for Supervision and Curriculum Development.
—— (1997b) *Unleashing the Power of Perceptual Change: The Potential of Brain-based Teaching*, Alexandria, VA: Association for Supervision and Curriculum Development.
Lambert, L. *et al.* (1995) *The Constructivist Leader*, New York: Teachers College Press.
Senese, J. (1998) "Action!", *Journal of Staff Development*, 19 (3, Summer): 33–7.

—— (1999) *The action research laboratory as a vehicle for school change*, paper presented at the meeting of the American Educational Research Association, Montreal, April.

—— (2000) *British Literature, Highland Park High School*, http://www.d113.lake.k12.il.us /hphs/curriculum/senese/index.html.

Senge, P. *et al.* (1994) *The Fifth Discipline Fieldbook*, New York: Currency Doubleday.

Wheatley, M.J. (1992) *Leadership and the New Science*, San Francisco, CA: Berrett-Koehler Publishers.

Wheatley, M. and Kellner-Rogers, M. (1996) *A Simpler Way*, San Francisco, CA: Berrett-Koehler Publishers.

5 Self-study as a way of teaching and learning

A research collaborative re-analysis of self-study teaching portfolios

*Lis Bass, Vicky Anderson-Patton
and Jerry Allender*

Teaching in a minefield.

The books still aren't in. The computers are down today? The copier is down? Can't do the lesson I planned because they didn't get it last time. Adjusting the curriculum standing on one foot. Half did the homework so they need to be doing something productive while the rest catch up. (I turn.) But some of them really need help. (Turn again.) If only I could sit beside each one while they did their work ... like my mother did when I needed it, like I did with my kids, but these students are also so different because we never needed it like this. A word here, praise, a good idea there, a careful reprimand.

I move so fast and each move is pregnant with possibilities for winning or losing. When I miss it, I see in their faces that I failed to find exactly the right word to make us connect. Self-study is part of my constant self-regulatory activities: what did I do or say, did it work, did I miss a chance, can I make it up the next time I see that student?

(Lis' teaching journal)

Introduction

Self-study is part of a wave, a sea change in the world of research. This wave no longer rises with positivist assumptions, no longer accepts that truth is the result of careful statistical analysis. No longer is our depiction of learning or 'best practices' based on numbers, for what we have learned from those numbers is to distrust them. We find ourselves asking what is the nature of the learning that the numbers describe. And, when force-fed *best practices*, we ask: "In whose hands? In what context? In whose interest are those glowing insights?"

Self-study suggests that our understanding of teaching and learning derives from contextualized knowledge, by a particularly reflective knower in a particular teaching situation. Thus a single teacher in a classroom may be both the beginning and the end of research. Yet questions arise: How does one mediate solipsism? How can good work be valued beyond the individual involved? And how does change occur?

We (Lis, Vicky and Jerry) have been involved in a variety of self-studies, functioning as critical friends. For this chapter, we changed the focus of our research collective to re-analyze our previous self-studies. Lis and Vicky had mentored self-study teaching portfolios with teachers who were graduate students and then created their own teaching portfolios, while Jerry had inter-woven his teaching stories with his students' stories (Allender, 2001). We now believe that the process of self-study, in particular using a collective of critical friends and representing our teaching stories through creating alternative repre-sentations, produces valuable learning about teaching.

This re-analysis provides a description of the varieties of self-study we have engaged in and illustrates the learning for each of us. This chapter also reflects our insights into how changes in awareness, interactions with critical friends, and creative engagement can lead to changes in practice.

Mentoring graduate student self-study teaching portfolios

Together, we (Vicky and Lis) assigned our graduate students self-study teaching portfolios as the cumulative assignment in our teacher education classrooms. We introduced self-study (Hamilton, 1998; Loughran and Northfield, 1998) and used teaching portfolios (Freidus, 1998; Lyons, 1998; Shulman, 1998) to scaffold the self-studies (Gipe, 1998; LaBoskey, 1998).

The portfolio structure required gathering artifacts, reflecting on them collaboratively, and creating representations. First, students wrote personal narratives about their development (their creative and teacher self for Vicky, and a literacy biography for Lis). Next, the students articulated their teaching values. Vicky and Lis structured reflection on the students' teaching practice though journal starters, group activities, and individual reflection activities (often based on teaching artifacts such as their students' work, lesson plans, interviews, and so on) for discussion. Students also experienced classrooms other than their own. With mentoring from their collaborative groups and Vicky and Lis, the students developed sub-questions to help personalize and focus their teaching portfolios (Grant and Huebner, 1998). At the end of the semester, students presented their teaching portfolios through a variety of media: poetry, short stories, personal essays, posters, scrapbooks, big books, drawing, collage, found objects, video, and music.

Introducing the studies to the research collective

Vicky's and Lis' self-study teaching portfolios

While we mentored student portfolios we developed our own self-study teaching portfolios. During the process, we also met with Jerry as a research collaborative. The portfolios were a multi-faceted self-study project that resulted in a paper describing the process and some preliminary reflections (Anderson-Patton and Bass, 2000). We presented our work at the Castle conference (2000), including five pieces:

1   a dialogue that represented the process students went through while creating their teaching portfolios (based on Vicky's and Lis' teaching journals, students' comments, and pieces of student writing);
2   students' artifacts – selections from their teaching portfolios;
3   meta-narratives (our version of their stories);
4   alternative representations (a collage and a drawing) of our self-studies; and
5   the paper.

Thus our portfolios used drama, narrative writing, academic writing, and graphic arts to present our self-studies. These we brought to the research collective.

Jerry's narratives

Eight years ago I (Jerry) decided to enliven my teaching by writing stories with my students about their experiences in an undergraduate course, *The Art and Science of Teaching* (a course I had taught for thirty years). While writing and interweaving the course with stories written by students, I widened my skills for supporting the development of relationships with and among the students in class. As I worked, I realized I had to broaden my empathy enough to write others' experiences so that it felt true to everyone. One thing the writing did was to heighten my awareness of what might be frustrating my students. The stories were not written to solve their tension, but to mark it and respond with some thinking that could lead to small shifts in subsequent planning and in ongoing classroom behaviors. Another insight was that I began to teach in order to get good stories for the book. It felt strange but, upon consideration, it was more than ethical; it was a great strategy for inventing. After all, good stories require not only a beginning, middle, and end, but more importantly a dramatic tension that is significant in transformative learning as well as writing.

These stories became my self-study (Allender, 2001). This work was particularly enlightening to me because the stories revealed the same classroom events from both the teacher's and the students' points of view. This storying, and re-storying, influenced my teaching in subsequent semesters. I brought these experiences to the research collective for re-analysis.

Our current study

After completing these self-studies and formally presenting them (Vicky's and Lis' at a conference and Jerry's as a book), we met regularly to reflect on the impact of this research on our teaching practice and ideas of self-study. Vicky has used self-study teaching portfolios in five subsequent semesters since the original study and Jerry spent a semester as a participant observer in Lis' writing class. This added data to our discussions of how self-study impacts on teachers and teaching development.

The three of us spent a semester meeting weekly to discuss these impacts. Together we believe that self-study changes us in a cyclical fashion. Also, because the value of a self-study is most immediately and best judged by the researcher, each author relates personal learnings. Finally, the conclusions we draw represent our collective sense of the nature of self-study work.

A self-study cycle

We learned that small shifts of awareness were made visible through the self-study process. These shifts had significant, though subtle, impacts on how we taught. Throughout this process, we noted how working with critical friends helped make visible these shifts and pushed reflection to reflexivity. This current re-analysis has deepened our conception of self-study as a creative and personally meaningful method. Our research collaborative concludes that self-study is an emergent and creative process, that change in practice necessarily integrates change in self, that self-study requires a collective, and that self-study's version of professional growth challenges the developmental model that implies that teachers improve simply with experience.

The following reflections note shifts of awareness that were significant for us as teacher-researchers. These shifts resonated as meaningful learning and constitute the results of our personal self-study work. We also believe they constitute a form of data for examining self-study.

Lis

I have been teaching remedial reading and writing on urban campuses for eighteen years and currently chair a county college skills department.

Shifting my sense of self from that of teacher to that of teacher-researcher

I thought I hated research. I now realize that the obstacle was my stereotypical view of research as unethical. I did not want to do unto students what I saw being done. My cynicism stemmed from a background in social survey research where results could be very close to what whoever funds the study wants.

Self-study took away my straw-man version of research and challenged me to do something meaningful. The value of the study was to be judged by all the participants. Nobody funded it; no particular conclusion was desired; no prescribed set of protocols had to be followed. I could trust myself, with help from my collaborative, to keep relationships primary.

My awareness has shifted. I now see myself as a researcher and I am learning all the time. Learning about teaching energizes me and, more importantly, instills a sense of agency. I became a teacher because I liked learning and teaching. I no longer fall into the teachers' lounge complaints about students because the drive to understand student resistance reduces my cynicism and because self-study supports the idea of personal agency: I have the power to change the situation.

Additionally, as a researcher I am suddenly part of a larger community. There were books and articles I had to read and people in my collaborative to talk to about them. Then conferences appeared and presentations had to be put together. People listened and critiqued my work. A teacher-researcher is a member of an intellectual community that classroom teachers are often isolated from. The self-study community has become important to my ideas and growth.

Shifting my sense of working with others on my teaching

There has been a strong shift from being protective of my independence (the four walls of my classroom were my kingdom) and being distrustful of others' advice (I have had a couple of evaluations that bordered on the bizarre) to inviting one of my colleagues (Jerry) into my classroom for a whole semester. Now I do not even flinch when inviting graduate students and adjunct faculty to observe my classes. Whatever they see is important for conversation and learning. And my observation of other teachers has become less stressful for me (and for them) because I do it as a critical friend, not an administrator. That is, I let the teacher set the priorities and I serve as a pair of eyes in the room, not to judge but to give feedback.

I now believe that teachers must maintain personal agency in order to change their teaching. Giving advice, evaluating other teachers, is a different process when I believe that change is primarily an internal process. Teachers might want to change superficially, but only when they experience the change as integrated into who they are as people, as consistent with their values, only then do I believe that they will feel that their small moves are inherent in classroom interactions.

My journal recalls a conversation in which I was becoming irritated with Jerry. Although he had promised that the self-study would adhere to my research agenda, the conversation kept harking back to two areas important to him. First, teaching was about relationship (life was about relationship!). Second, everything should connect (one lesson to another, learning always to one's life blood). I had a nice lesson plan: lively, engaging activities varying every fifteen to twenty minutes so no one got bored, and a great deal got done. He wanted to talk about his things: Could I have made the grammar lesson connect to the pre-writing activity? Could I have gotten more blood out of the students' discussion of the writing topic? I was so annoyed. He was riding his hobbyhorse and it did not matter that I agreed with his teaching values: he needed to see what a nifty class I had created.

My irritation was a sign that our worldviews were colliding enough to push my thinking. I had chosen to work with Jerry because I did agree with his teaching values. My annoyance was the simple self-absorbed desire to be patted on the back. Better than compliments though is the learning that can come when I open myself up to actually looking at my teaching. Yes, I am a competent teacher, but I invited him into my classroom to help me think about my teaching and to make it better. I have come to see that compliments alone do not lead to learning.

Academia trains us to be critical; friendship teaches support. How then does one become a critical friend? I have often been made to feel distraught by the nature of academics: each person riding their hobbyhorse. When people are asked to respond at conferences, their responses are more about their perspective than what they saw. When dissertation committee members enter orals, they often ask only how the work relates back to their area of interest. But what if we learn to work with this tendency instead of just harping on about it? A good self-study collaborative should cause a clash of worldviews – making reflection reflexivity. In order to have critical friends, I have to open myself up and become less defensive.

> Reflexivity ... often pits different representations, ideas, assumptions, and worldviews against each other. Reflexivity asks us to turn these conflicts back on ourselves so as to uncover, study, analyze our views and assumptions in response to engagements with an 'other' – another text, idea, culture, or person.
>
> (Gradin and Carter, 2001, p. 3)

The self-study process – talking, writing, reflecting, and articulating my teaching with others – makes me more confident. I can be less defensive when I accept that others will see my teaching from their perspectives. In doing so, they provide me with multiple ways of looking at what I do, but I must be able to retain agency, be who I want to be, and still hear them.

My shifting sense of what teaching means: from teaching content to teaching students

Before class:

Today I abhor teaching. Why can't I write novels, stay home, work in my bathrobe, and not have to see anyone? I'll get a mindless drone job and ...

After class that same day:

I love the show. I wonder if there's a science fiction reality that we haven't been able to quantify wherein people are nourished by others' attention. The students look at me and suddenly I am awake, alert, aware, articulate, and having fun. They feed me. I wonder if little energy quarks fly out of their eyeballs. Note to self: if universities do become totally on-line, remember to quit.

(Lis' teaching journal)

Teaching remedial students is hard (so much harder than teaching graduate students). These students are so needy, so close to the surface, so close to giving up. Every word, every interaction, is significant. Chronic absences, chronic lateness; who does homework at home? And everything must be noticed: "Hey, you made it to class on time today – great!" I turn to the student who is writing of her uncle who died of AIDS; oh my goodness, in the conclusion she just added that he left his wife and new baby infected too (her aunt and baby cousin are dying). Then Roberto can't understand the computer (still!) but he looks almost sixty and – patience with him, for him – but not with Edward, that's it. I turn off Edward's screen, take him into the hall and tell him coming to class high won't cut it. Denial – I say it's not me who pays the consequences, just try being straight for a couple weeks. Shanda's essay is carefully organized: nine examples of why her boyfriend can be considered abusive, divided equally under three subcategories of abuse – physical, emotional, and mental ("Oh girlfriend, what are you going to do!" and "Which examples go under emotional abuse and which under mental abuse? Are they different categories?").

My students want to be known, attended to, given a chance, given help, given praise, to have the experience of doing something right in school. Please! – they plead with me. They want to succeed, to be told they are smart, competent, can do it. Damn if I don't think some of them would be happier with well-paying factory jobs (but the factories are gone). Teaching is this huge fight against poverty.

I turn off a student's screen (I need his attention for ten minutes). He says "I'm not doing anything." I turn the screen back on and see he is in the middle of a sentence, look at him, and quietly say "You must think I'm an asshole to lie so blatantly." He says "What's your problem? I was just kidding."

I am different: white, female, Jewish, middle-class, and educated. I must be careful not to inculcate these students with the racism and anti-working-class bias of the system that diminishes them, but I must inculcate them with some of the values of the institution or they won't survive. I find leftist materials, anti-racist materials; empower voice! There is so much they don't know! There is so much I don't know! I mess up; I asked the nine-month pregnant student when she was going to drop the baby (instead of when the baby is going to drop). Animals drop babies. I apologize. I learn. I do self-study so that I might teach these students, and so I can sleep at night.

Articulating my focus – the concept of transformative learning

Working with a collaborative of critical friends has helped me articulate what can be seen through my lens. I hold a belief that learning changes people. Superficially, a college education is precisely for the purpose of transforming my working-class students into middle-class workers. But I am not Henry Higgins forcing assimilation. My assumption is that there is transformative learning that helps us to be ourselves: clearer thinking, more empathetic, competent, and moral.

Vicky

I have been teaching creativity courses with undergraduate and graduate elementary education students for nine years at West Chester University.

My shifting awareness of what it means to own creativity

When I wrote my dissertation about creative teachers, one of the primary things I discovered was how important it is to nurture one's personal creative outlet. The teachers I interviewed all had organized ways of expressing their creativity that they practiced throughout their lives. Self-study alerted me to the fact that I had stopped playing the piano when I came to the United States from New Zealand. So I began to take lessons after a ten-year hiatus and had to struggle with my confidence and competence. I realized that I have high standards because I was classically trained and I hear every uneven passage. I also feel exposed when I play because for me music is about emotion: I feel people can hear straight to my heart and I am not used to being so open. Plus I never get enough time to practice so I never feel truly competent; the expert I *should* be. I get frustrated when I cannot play things as I used to. Yet as I master each new passage I feel joy, a sense of accomplishment, and inner peace. I think playing improves my life in many ways.

I cannot ask students to attend to their creative voices and to foster creativity in their teaching if I am ignoring my internal creative voice. Owning my creativity makes me more authentic with my students. I have also discovered that for me meaningful learning requires integration and transformation of my personal and professional selves. I want to know my students as *whole* beings and I am most interested in facilitating real life learning. Utilizing teaching portfolios that require alternative representations was an excellent tool for me to invite students to explore and connect their personal creativity with their teaching. Self-study allows me to integrate my personal and professional selves, and examine how they influence each other – I am doing what I require of my students.

My shifting awareness of anxiety: acknowledging it, mining it, and accepting what I cannot change

Through self-study I have learned to pay attention differently to anxiety in my teaching. I have moved from minimizing it or trying to take care of students' anxiety, to acknowledging and examining it directly. Anxiety is an important clue that issues and insecurities are being tapped. Now I tell my students and remind myself that anxiety signals an opportunity to take a risk, to use the energy, and to try something new.

The first semester I implemented teaching portfolios I was filled with anxiety because the process was new. Undoubtedly the students and I fueled each other's anxiety, although I resisted the temptation to tell them exactly what to do, which is what they wanted. Instead, I acknowledged the anxiety and reassured students that developing their self-study teaching portfolios was an emergent process. Five semesters later I am more confident implementing the self-study teaching portfolios, counterbalancing some of the anxiety inherent in the process.

Early this semester, my imposter anxiety was ignited by a student's inquiry: "Were you an elementary school teacher?" My internal voice clicked on – oh no, I have been found out; now I will lose all credibility! The truth is I have done many different things with children but no, I never taught an elementary class every day for a year. Then again, I have never considered myself an expert. I am teaching about ways to stimulate creative thinking and expression in the classroom. While I do not know the curriculums the students are teaching thoroughly, they do. I offer different perspectives and help teachers to problem-solve, to understand their own teaching, and to consider where creativity fits into their curriculums. Through my self-study I see this anxiety shift from a defensive posture to an acknowledgment of students' ownership of their teaching.

My shifting awareness of process-centered learning

Both the creative process and the self-study process are emergent. In our research collaborative we do some work, discuss it in our weekly meetings, reflect more, and then write, discuss, and reflect further; all the while our teaching is being affected. My teaching then is an emergent changing process. I cannot control the learning process that will unfold for my students. I make predictions based on previous experience about what I think will happen and where the content will take us, but as I strive to be authentic and responsive to students' needs I have to be open to what emerges. Through the constant self-monitoring and reflection of self-study I have learned that the more I give up the illusion of control, the smoother and more effective I can be. The students and I enjoy class more when I step back and guide rather than control and direct.

Self-study keeps me reflecting on what I do and trying to understand how I influence my students. Acknowledging and approaching my teaching as an emergent process keeps me authentic, open to change, and energized.

My shifting awareness of owning my self in the classroom

In the beginning of this semester, I had an older white male student who quickly let his skepticism of creativity be known. He declared that "creativity is subjective" and not relevant in his inner-city classroom of poor minority students. In an instant, I felt and owned my defensive response. Instead of ignoring this student's responses or becoming directive and imposing my ideals upon him, I acknowledged his position and tried to empathize with his teaching struggles. I invited him to talk about his experiences further and tried to find a way for him to join pieces of the content with his experiences.

The more I know myself through self-study, the more available and open I can be with students. The biggest shift in awareness and change in practice has been in my response to *challenging* students. The process of reflecting with Lis and Jerry each week has helped me to develop a capacity to listen carefully and to embrace differences more comfortably. I am practicing widening my lenses with my critical friends and this gives me more confidence to be open with students' differences. It's not easy to recognize and own my biases, -isms, and entitlements; however, in struggling with these issues my classroom becomes a rich microcosm for real life learning.

My shifting awareness of ways collaboration empowers personal voice

Like therapy (with a good therapist), self-study (with good critical friends) forces me to peel away the layers of my self and figure out how they color my teaching. Yet I am uncomfortable focusing on self – my personal history and culture have taught me that this is indulgent. The research group, however, is a legitimate place to explore my self in the context of teaching. I feel pulled in many directions (mother, wife, teacher, friend, daughter, and so on), but our work is a space for me and my growth ripples out and affects others. In fact, I think my self is re-appearing through self-study.

Now I encourage my students to explore self through their teaching portfolios and small group collaboratives. I provide more time for students to discuss how the content fits with their personal and professional experiences. I require more personal writing through the personal narrative, struggles, and creative process papers. I have shifted my focus in class from the group as figural and the self as ground, to the self as figural and the group as ground (although there remains fluidity in the relationship and balance). I am finding a stronger and more confident personal voice through our collaboration.

Jerry

I was a professor of education at Temple University for thirty-six years, now retired.

Seeing my entitlements: shifting to listening

I noted that after one collaborative meeting I was troubled because I wondered whether I had pushed my colleagues with questions that were inappropriate. Even assuming that Lis and Vicky will take care of themselves, I knew that how

I function in interpersonal space is quite driven. I've gotten better at asking students probing questions, but I have not thought to apply this skill to my family, friends, and colleagues. It seems to be attached to my male, white, educated entitlement. Typically, this entitlement has to do with possessing intellectual knowledge that one is sure must be communicated strongly to others – what one finds in the arrogance of professordom. Eschewing that kind of arrogance, because it does not fit with my humanistic values nor press for supporting lively respectful relationships, I get a picture of myself as having another kind of arrogance: knowing oh so surely when inner probing lacks in adequate depth and authenticity. And I give myself license to say so whenever I feel this disjunction. Oops.

Where does acknowledgment of my entitlement come from? In part, reflecting with critical friends helps me see where my talking produces others' silence and where my being quiet supports others' conversation. Lis' political commitments (critical theory) have explained how I was able to be a humanist and remain somewhat oblivious to certain issues (the student body brought issues of race and multiculturalism to the class so that all I needed was to make a safe space for it). Gestalt psychology and my daughters in particular have also given me a handle on the mechanisms of being silenced. Even so, seeing one's entitlements is difficult. Ironically, trying to work with privilege is the hardest challenge I have faced.

In my classes with my students, I had come to recognize the error of my ways, but otherwise I see in this insight that I sometimes act clueless. Whereas in class I trust the process, outside of class I am very pessimistic that the people in my life will get to where (I think) they need to get (without my help). Oops again. I need to broaden the range of my experience with listening more, trusting more, and interrupting less. My drive to express the profound has not lowered much; I simply have learned to accept it and sit on it without undue discomfort. I liked the results in my classes, and I want to see what happens in the bigger world.

I think I will be happier if I encourage myself to back off more. The obvious irony is that as I trust others more, I will trust myself more. Applying this to the personal in the classroom means that there is plenty of need and room for probing and depth. But it needs to be guided gently, respectfully, cautiously, and with a strong belief in the integrity and agency of others, by committed work with critical friends. And it has to be a two-way road that reflects balance between the self and others. Self-study is about voice, for the self and other, not about Truth.

Self-study as a way of teaching and learning

Self-study appears to us as simply the way our professional lives should be – continually filled with meaningful learning. Odious (and too often true) comparisons concerning salary and status make teachers feel undervalued, but self-study responds by attending closely to teachers and their students. Self-study re-centers research and grounds it in classroom practice, using the language of teachers rather than the distancing voice of erudite theoreticians. Also, collaboration is rare in the academy's competitive environment, in the hustle of too little time and too many demands. But, in the company of others who care about us and about good work, we can know the comfort of support and the challenge of learning. In a world of big buzzes, self-study friends listen carefully to small shifts, which is how, we believe, changes in teaching occur.

We think self-study came along at the right time. Self-study provides an ameliorative to the despair of post-modernist relativism with the right to value contextualized knowledge. We are now asked as thinkers to not just sustain and protract a state of doubt (Dewey, 1933), but to develop flexible resilience because there is no certainty. The authority of knowing the Truth does not support our position as teacher anymore. Still, we must wake up tomorrow and face our classrooms with both the constancy of the sun rising and the awe of a new day.

The keys to the kingdom

Working with others is crucial and annoying. Moving beyond simple reflection into a collision of worldviews firmly places all knowledge into a particular context. It is perhaps too easy to think reflectively, for humans are well equipped with defense mechanisms to justify their actions rather than challenge them. Reflexivity, wherein worldviews clash from the input of critical friends and theory, can push reflection past defensiveness into transformative learning.

Personal agency is enhanced when it is our different perspectives that are valued. We have noted how privilege and entitlements, unless directly addressed by the person and critical friends, can interfere with one's ability to attend to others – reducing others' agency and one's ability to learn and accept challenges. We rarely challenge our privileged status until we try to empathize with its negative impact on others. This move, from reflective to reflexive thinking, is valuable for grappling with issues of identity as well as the trials of collaboration.

Like good therapy, knowing better one's points of vulnerability gives more conscious control over defensive behaviors that do not work in a classroom or anywhere else. Self-study provides a form for practicing a valuable kind of self-monitoring; critical friends with alternative views temper it. Critical friends get to know each other's reactive points and blind spots, and hopefully learn when to support and when to challenge. As Bullough and Pinnegar note, the "self-study researcher has an ineluctable obligation to seek to improve the learning situation not only for the self but for the other" (Bullough and Pinnegar, 2001, p. 17). Authenticity, integrating the professional and personal, and practicing personal/professional agency in a supportive context, has positive ripples in terms of one's ability to remain flexible with and for others.

The self-study experience teaches us about emergent learning processes. Trusting process learning comes from experiences and the self-study experience parallels other types of process-centered learning, such as learning to write, to be creative, and to teach. We carry our experiences from the self-study colla- borative to our classrooms. Challenging ourselves to represent our research creatively, using portfolios or stories, also is an emergent process that necessarily engages the self. Involvement with self-study teaches one that all learning is better when integrated with self, and collaborating with critical friends is a good reminder of how central issues of identity and relationship are for learning, even when we as teachers want to focus on delivering curricular content.

Students become crucial informants in self-studies. Every question a student asks, and every indication of frustration, becomes a point to reflect upon what was missed, where needs were not met, and where teaching could be improved. Like the aliens in Jane Wagner's play (1985) who, when they first go to a theatre, accidentally watch the audience rather than the performers, self-study teaches us to attend to and decode our audience, reminding us that students are central to research about teaching.

What a great way of life. Many of us became teachers because we loved learning and self-study challenges us to continue to learn. We became teachers because we loved discussion and ended up isolated in our classrooms, but self- study connects us to caring, conscientious, and critical friends, and to a larger, worldwide web of research. Self-study offers us research that puts us in touch with who we are, what we do, and how we change – to consciously be working on ourselves so that we are agents in our daily lives. Finally, self-study creates a vision of ourselves as flexible, open, and creative; we can work with our defen- siveness and vulnerabilities; we can grow as we continuously learn to teach.

References and further reading

Allender, J.S. (2001) *Teacher Self: The Practice of Humanistic Education*, Lanham, MD: Rowman & Littlefield.

Anderson-Patton, V. (1998) "Creative catalysts: A study of creative teachers from their own perspectives and experiences" (doctoral dissertation, Temple University), *Disser- tation Abstracts International*, 59/06, 1998.

Anderson-Patton, V. and Bass, L. (2000) "How well did we structure and model a self- study stance? Two self-studies of imposing self-studies using teaching portfolios", in J.J. Loughran and T. Russell (eds) *Exploring the Myths and Legends of Teacher Educa- tion: Proceedings of the Third International Conference on Self-Study of Teacher Education Practices, East Sussex*, Kingston, Ont.: Queen's University Faculty of Education, pp. 10–14.

Bullough, R.V., Jr and Pinnegar, S. (2001) "Guidelines for quality in autobiographical forms of self-study research", *Educational Researcher*, 30 (3): 13–22.

Dewey, J. (1933) *How we Think: A Restatement of the Relation of Reflective Thinking to the Educative Process*, Boston: D.C. Heath.

Freidus, H. (1998) "Mentoring portfolio development", in N. Lyons (ed.) *With Portfolio in Hand: Validating the New Teacher Professionalism*, New York: Teachers College Press, pp. 51–68.

Gipe, J.P. (1998) "Self-study of teacher education practices through the use of the faculty course portfolio", in M.L. Hamilton (ed.) *Reconceptualizing Teaching Practice: Self-study in Teacher Education*, London: Falmer Press, pp. 140–6.

Gradin, S. and Carter, D. (2001) *Writing as Reflective Practice*, New York: Longman Publishing Group.

Grant, G.E. and Huebner, T.A. (1998) "The portfolio question: The power of self-directed inquiry", in N. Lyons (ed.) *With Portfolio in Hand: Validating the New Teacher Professionalism*, New York: Teachers College Press, pp. 156–71.

Hamilton, M.L. (ed.) (1998) *Reconceptualizing Teaching Practice: Self-study in Teacher Education*, London: Falmer Press.

LaBoskey, V. (1998) "Have five years of self-study changed teacher education?", in A.L. Cole and S. Finley (eds) *Conversations in Community: Proceedings of the Second International Conference of the Self-Study of Teacher Education Practices*, East Sussex, Kingston, Ont.: Queen's University Faculty of Education, pp. 1–5.

Loughran, J.J. and Northfield, J. (1998) "A framework for the development of self-study practice", in M.L. Hamilton (ed.) *Reconceptualizing Teaching Practice: Self-study in Teacher Education*, London: Falmer Press, pp. 7–18.

Lyons, N. (ed.) (1998) *With Portfolio in Hand: Validating the New Teacher Professionalism*, New York: Teachers College Press.

Shulman, L. (1998) "Teacher portfolios: A theoretical activity", in N. Lyons (ed.) *With Portfolio in Hand: Validating the New Teacher Professionalism*, New York: Teachers College Press, pp. 23–38.

Wagner, J. (1985) *The Search for Signs of Intelligent Life in the Universe*, New York: Harper Collins.

Part II

Studying teacher educators' roles and responsibilities

6 Guiding new teachers' learning from classroom experience

Self-study of the faculty liaison role

Tom Russell

Introduction

This self-study reviews five years of work in a role created by a major structural change in the pre-service teacher education program at Queen's University. Initiating a career-long process of learning from experience through reflective practice was a major goal of the change. As a result, an extended practicum experience of ten weeks now occurs early in the eight-month post-degree program.

The supervisors of this practicum are referred to as Faculty Liaisons – faculty members teaching a section of a "field-based" course intended to support and enhance learning from classroom experience. The Faculty Liaison role calls for a broad array of activities, including supporting teacher candidates in a range of subjects, consultation with experienced teachers in whose classrooms the candidates are placed, explaining the purposes of the revised program structure, fostering school–university partnership, and guiding teacher candidates through the development, enactment and reporting of a personal action research project in the final weeks of the practicum placement. Candidates are normally placed in school cohorts, and each Faculty Liaison's section usually contains candidates from several schools.

Sarason (1996) often raises the issue of whether a change achieves its intended goal and, as he would predict, the culture of our pre-service program changed far less than the actual structure. Reality soon demonstrated the sheer impossibility of a Faculty Liaison being all things to all people, especially when so few seemed to understand, in practice, the reasons for change.

For this self-study an action research methodology was chosen and conducted in the period 1999–2001 with the goal of better understanding teacher candidates' expectations of their Faculty Liaison. This chapter summarizes and interprets what I have learned from my own efforts to perform the new role of Faculty Liaison. Data collected in university classes, school meetings, and course evaluations are examined to better understand expectations of both new and experienced teachers. Comments from research interviews with principals concerning school–university partnership provide additional perspective. Attention is also given to the conduct of self-study within a larger organizational culture that is not similarly engaged in self-study.

Context of the study[1]

After a pilot project with sixty volunteers in 1996–7, the pre-service teacher education program at Queen's University shifted dramatically in 1997–8 for all 600 new teachers pursuing our eight-month post-degree certification to teach in the province of Ontario. A major feature of the revised program structure is an early extended practicum that initially ran for fourteen weeks (from the opening day of school in the first two years, 1997–9) but now runs for ten weeks in the first half of the program. Teacher candidates attend classes at Queen's for the month of September and then teach through October, November and December, with a two-week return to the university in November. The role of Faculty Liaison is intended to connect this school placement to the rest of the program.

I was active and enthusiastic about the potential of the Faculty Liaison role. Linking practice with theory is a longstanding personal interest that I believed led naturally to reflective practice and learning from experience. A major feature of the new role is the requirement that a Faculty Liaison work across all subjects in secondary schools. The issue of faculty members observing in classrooms outside their subject specialty remains a significant tension as the new structure moves into its fifth full year in 2001–2, and it highlights the issue of whether a teacher educator's loyalty is to a subject, to the process of learning to teach, or of necessity to both.

With the clarity of hindsight, I realize that there were many moments when I tended to assume that simply being in the school was the basic requirement for success in the new role, both in the eyes of those learning to teach and in the eyes of the experienced teachers to whom the teacher candidates were assigned. Personal experience and self-study of that experience have taught me how much more complex the matter is. My efforts to learn the Faculty Liaison role have taken me to six different secondary schools, and my longest relationship with one school was four years. Working in at least two schools each year readily reminds me that each school is unique, offering a particular climate and culture that has significant effects on a teacher candidate's practicum experiences and earliest professional learning. One of the goals for the new program structure was an enhanced sense of school–university partnership (see Osguthorpe *et al.*, 1995), an elusive and amorphous quality that is frequently sought and infrequently achieved. I hoped to be able to facilitate the development of the partnership that could be so productive for both university and school. Principals and teachers were consulted in the development of the new program structure, but that consultation faded rapidly under the strain of the first full year of "putting our new theory into practice".

As we begin the fifth year, we continue to tinker with the structure as we also attempt to re-examine and re-define its underlying assumptions and our collective beliefs about learning to teach. Predictably, teacher educators are no better at changing their practices than are teachers anywhere else. The years since 1997 have been turbulent for our organization (Russell, 1999). Thus it is in the light of both my personal experiences of the Faculty Liaison role and the organizational turbulence around how people learn to teach that I have attempted to study my own learning of the role. The pressure to reframe my understanding of the role comes from many sources, including shifting feedback received on course evaluations and my own sense that I could do better.

The complexities of practicum supervision

It is important to recall that in many pre-service programs, school supervision is readily and conveniently delegated to graduate students and adjunct faculty members. Creating a new role that is crucial for program success and then assigning that new role to regular faculty members is a unique and potentially risky step. Perhaps more than anything else, I regret that there has been no collective will to share and study the learning of this role. Other faculties at Queen's University expect us to enhance our *research* profile as a faculty, yet teacher candidates and schools alike expect us to enhance our *teaching* profile. While the quality of our teaching is largely invisible to the rest of the university, that quality is readily apparent to teacher candidates and experienced teachers in schools. Thus the Faculty Liaison role moves academics from a research environment into a teaching environment, yet the organizational reality is that we are expected to excel at both teaching and research to please our two quite different audiences.

Compounding the situation further are the well-documented complexities of practicum supervision. Richardson-Koehler summarized some of the issues clearly and succinctly:

> The role of the university supervisor is ambiguous at best, and that role in relationship to the expectations for the cooperating [associate or mentor] teacher is even more confused … . The degree to which the university supervisor can affect the classroom practices of student teachers, given the structure of the experience, is questioned by supervisors themselves … I felt that as a supervisor I was not affecting the student teachers' classroom practices very much … . Short observation and feedback sessions once every two weeks do not constitute adequate supervision.
>
> (Richardson-Koehler, 1988, p. 32)

Apparently when we changed the structure of our pre-service program, we created a role that was more than crucial to successful change. The role also had a deeply entrenched history of complexity and limited success. As Richardson-Koehler (1988) explains, new and experienced teachers alike have a great deal of faith in learning from experience. Our Faculty Liaison role was intended to shift candidates' views of how one learns from experience.

Changes over time

When the Faculty of Education changed the structure of its pre-service teacher education program in 1997, significant new features included an early extended practicum experience (fourteen weeks) accompanied by two field-based professional studies courses (PROF100 and PROF190–1). The Faculty Liaison teaches the second of these courses and the major assignment for secondary candidates (who take PROF191) is an action research project carried out in the final weeks of the early extended practicum. Having appeared to be successful in the Faculty Liaison role in the first two years, when practicum placements began on the opening day of school, I was unprepared for the practical consequences of the change that occurred in 1999. Candidates no longer began their school placements on the first day of the school year; instead they arrived in schools at the start of the fifth week of school, after three weeks of classes at the university. This change represented an early effort to respond to organizational turmoil about how people learn to teach. Most of my colleagues appeared to believe that the pre-service program must begin with substantial time in university classrooms.

I appeared to be virtually alone in arguing against this change, which struck me as having *powerful epistemological significance*: Beginning the program in schools (after a week-long orientation period at the university) with support from Associate Teachers and a Faculty Liaison was a powerful way of demonstrating how one learns from experience. Most teacher candidates seem to have little or no sense of what it means to learn from experience, yet this learning goes to the heart of the constructivist reforms that many argue are needed in our schools and in our teacher education programs (Featherstone, Munby and Russell, 1997; Richardson, 1997). Thus, over the period of this study (from 1999 to 2001), PROF191 began not in the schools but in the familiar university classroom setting.

Over a nine-week placement in 1999–2000, I managed seven full-day visits to each school, although only two visits were officially required of me. The official requirement is set to control costs of sending Faculty Liaisons to the many Associate Schools located several hours or more from the university. Inevitably, faculty members must make decisions about where to invest their limited time. Candidates seemed to appreciate my presence, but over time did not always find my efforts matching their expectations. The following year, 2000–1, proved different yet again. Political turmoil in Ontario's secondary schools led many teachers, and in some cases entire schools, to withdraw their agreement to accept a teacher candidate. Many of the candidates originally assigned to the two secondary schools I was to work with had to be reassigned to a range of local schools, making it impossible to visit each candidate's school as frequently as I had hoped. To summarize, each of the five years has been unique, even though there has been only one formal structural change – shifting the start of the early extended practicum from the first day of the school year to a point four weeks into the school year.

Focusing the self-study

Several issues that were obvious before beginning the study have proven to be complex and demanding:

- A Faculty Liaison's primary commitment appears to be to the teacher candidates learning to teach, yet each candidate works with one or more experienced teachers. How are a Faculty Liaison's commitments balanced and how is time best distributed between beginning and experienced teachers?
- What actions by a Faculty Liaison are most useful in linking practice with theory, when teacher candidates can be expected to have very strong loyalty to their practicum experiences?
- Is the Faculty Liaison's limited time best spent with candidates individually or in cohort groups, in the classroom observing lessons or in conversations about overall progress?
- If a sense of genuine school–university partnership is desired, and if the Faculty Liaison is visible in the school intermittently over a period of ten weeks, how does that Liaison monitor and foster a sense of partnership?
- What is the Faculty Liaison's role in explaining to teachers the revised program structure and the role of the early extended practicum in helping candidates learn to teach?
- What data can best inform a Faculty Liaison about the value of time spent with those learning to teach and with those who receive teacher candidates into their classrooms?

The Faculty Liaison role, in theory and in practice, links to a broad range of issues in teacher education. None of these questions has a simple answer, and each question calls up fundamental premises about how people learn to teach.

The central question that emerged for me was: *How can I help each candidate improve the quality of professional learning during the early extended practicum?* Although this central question focuses on candidates, a second question was always prominent in the background: *How can I help to improve the quality of the professional relationship between this school and the Faculty of Education at Queen's University?* My self-study, then, is based on an action research design with a view to documenting and understanding each individual's experiences of learning to teach. Even though I have had informal discussions with individuals about the Faculty Liaison role, I did not identify someone who could serve as a long-term "critical friend" for this self-study.

Data from 1999–2000

To help the thirteen candidates in 1999–2000 better understand their first action research experience, I explained that I would conduct action research of my own to better understand *my* contributions to *their* professional learning. Some showed little interest in providing me with "backtalk" (see Schön, 1983, pp. 295–307 for a discussion of reflective conversations with the situation), while others were quite willing to do so. Their data and our discussions seemed positive and I took away many interesting ideas for the following year. One major theme seemed to be "one size does not fit all" – tailor your approach to each individual's situation and personal characteristics. The data-gathering process was not as comprehensive as I had hoped; some people simply did not contribute. In addition to my personal impressions of my work as a Faculty Liaison, I have three sources of data from those I was teaching:

1   Free responses to specific aspects of my work, obtained after six weeks of teaching.
2   Free responses, obtained at the end of the course, to the headings "Strengths", "Weaknesses", and "Suggestions".
3   Numerical ratings on standardized statements in the formal university-wide course evaluation process, completed at the end of the course and reported to me four months later.

Responses after six weeks

A selection of the free responses after six weeks in schools indicate the suggestions that I found most interesting. Although these are responses to several aspects of my work, they indicate that most candidates place greatest value on my watching them teach full lessons and providing detailed comments and suggestions. This expectation appears to come naturally to most teacher candidates.

- Observing our teaching is critical. I would actually appreciate even more feedback (positive/negative) about your observation of our teaching styles, content, classroom management, etc.
- Very valuable to have you observing.
- It is only parts of a lesson that you watch – the whole lesson would be better. Nice to have another person's input to help out in improvements.
- Great! Made me stop and think/reflect on what was happening. Usually just go through the motions of daily grind but it was nice to try and make some sense of it.
- Try to come to see the "meat" of a lesson. Provide constructive criticism on observation sheets. Ask the associates how it's going, and get feedback from them.

Responses at the end of the course

These themes at six weeks persist in the "Suggestions" offered to me at the end of the course.

- Positive reinforcement is as much, if not more, beneficial than negative reinforcement – tell us what we are doing correctly or offer suggestions for improvement.
- Provide more concrete techniques to implement. (Want to benefit more from your knowledge.)

• I think it would be great if you could meet with us before and after you come to watch us teach. I know that this would be difficult to do since you have several candidates to work with in a limited amount of time, but I really think that this idea might be worth considering. Sitting in for one class does not always let you know what is really going on. By meeting with us ahead of time, we will have the chance to let you know what we have done with the class up to that point, and fill you in on various situations that might be going on. We can also let you know where we plan on going with the class so that you can see the "Big Picture" when you are visiting our classrooms (instead of just a "snapshot").

• Read the person, see what they want out of you, prevent both being frustrated. Keep being so positive and interested. I have enjoyed all our conversations and all of your help.

Course evaluation results

Course evaluation data are different by their very nature. There are eleven standardized statements on the university's course evaluation form, and on four of these my personal averages were below the faculty-wide average:

2 "Overall, this instructor is an effective teacher."
4 "The instructor showed sensitivity to the needs and interests of students from diverse groups."
9 "The course was well organized."
10 "The instructor presented material clearly."

It is difficult to interpret the low average on statement 2 because there is no way to distinguish between my on-campus classroom time and my in-school time with candidates. I assume that the responses to statements 9 and 10 refer to my on-campus classroom time, and the low scores here probably reflect my personal difficulty adjusting to the change from 1997–9, when candidates and I got to know each other in the school context rather than in the experience-free atmosphere of the university. I am at a complete loss when trying to interpret the meaning of the low score on statement 4.

Data from 2000–1

In the second year of this self-study, my section of PROF191 had fifteen members. The political turmoil in schools that year meant that these candidates originally destined for only two secondary schools were placed in six different schools. Visiting as often as I wanted to became physically impossible. One school accepted eight candidates, including six officially assigned to me. When this group of candidates scheduled a regular meeting time, a program specification that had never been achieved in my schools in previous years, I elected to attend that weekly meeting as often as I could, simply to try to understand what that meeting could contribute to candidates' professional learning. Inevitably, I saw those eight candidates much more frequently than the four who were both members of my class and assigned to a school. With such a range of schools, I did not attempt to collect comments after six weeks of teaching as in 1999–2000.

In response to the data gathered in 1999–2000, my most deliberate change in practice was to observe full lessons and insist that time be found to discuss them. I left it to each candidate to invite me at a time that seemed personally appropriate. In some cases this strategy was effective, and my observation of one candidate had a dramatically positive effect on subsequent teaching, an effect quite at odds with Richardson-Koehler's (1988) discouraging portrayal. In other cases my observation probably came too late in the practicum; in two instances the request to observe was never made. My personal preference that people begin to take charge of their own professional development allows me to tolerate such a result. For this second year of my self-study, the course evaluation data are the main data source. The free-response comments offered by candidates also provide interesting insights.

Course evaluation results

This time, only two statements attracted an average well below that for all courses in the program:

5   "Grading was a fair assessment of my performance in this course."
9   "The course was well organized."

When the course evaluation forms were completed there had been no grading, and six out of thirteen respondents to statement 5 indicated "not applicable", while two more neither agreed nor disagreed. Statement 9 applies to our classes at university, and I accept their judgment as I continue to develop effective use of classroom time before the extended practicum. (The political circumstances in 2000–1 led to rearranging the program so that almost all meetings of this course occurred *before* practice teaching began – hardly a "field-based" course.) To my considerable surprise, one statement was scored well above the mean:

8   "My interest in the subject has been stimulated by the course."

Interpreting this unexpected result is assisted by free responses to the question: *Do you have any specific suggestions for improvements to this course?*

- This course should primarily be focused in the Winter – maybe a short prep sometime in the Fall, but most in Winter.
- It would be good to have more classes post-placement. Also, two visits from professor (for those of us who are reluctant to invite visitors into the classroom).

- This course is more important to me now than before we started the placement. Learning about other experiences and strategies is extremely important to put into my practice.
- I think this course needs to be longer; I only started to benefit from it.
- We should spend the six weeks of this class either during or after the practicum rather than before. It is a shame to have to "squish" all of the real STUFF into two classes at the end. The idea of Action Research might be planted after four or five weeks of teaching, so that the candidates will have to look for points of "inquiry" in their style of teaching.
- It would have been more useful to have this class following some practicum experience.
- This course is more useful when coming back from our practicum rather than having it in the first six weeks of the program.
- Time should be more evenly spread amongst the practicum schools.

I draw encouragement from these responses, which suggest that the pre-practicum classes were less productive than my interactions with candidates in their schools. It also appears that my time in schools was helpful in stimulating their interest in action research, which is certainly one purpose of the course and one of the unique program experiences that is made possible by the ten-week length of the practicum. Observing full lessons was a productive move on my part, and one person's acknowledged "reluctance" to invite me in to observe suggests that I should next year study the effect of required visits to all candidates. Numerous references to more time for the course in the Winter term are novel, surprising, and compatible with my personal preference for constructing professional learning from experience.

Studying one's practice over time is complicated and confused by inevitable variations from year to year. In 2000–1, in response to the political turmoil at the start of the year, candidates attended six weeks of classes before teaching and then did not return to the university for the usual two weeks midway through the ten-week practicum. Thus twelve of the fifteen scheduled hours occurred *before* the practicum began, and the group had only three hours to share their experiences of action research. This concludes the reporting of data from candidates in the period 1999–2001; I turn next to data about school perspectives on the role of a Faculty Liaison.

Relevant school perspectives on partnership

Three school principals agreed to be interviewed for another research project that also considers the issue of school–university partnership. The two secondary school principals have paid close attention to the revised program structure and provided comments that reinforce the point that there are high expectations when a Faculty Liaison moves from the university into the school. Their comments help to extend issues already raised in this self-study. Principal

1 speaks strongly about the research/teaching tension and about the relation-ship not just of theory to practice but of practice to theory.

P1:   I got a very clear message, at least when we were beginning the pilot project, that what the Faculty believes it's supposed to be doing as a Faculty is to study education. It studies education and educational theory and does educational research. Its purpose is not to train teachers. Well, people in the schools think that McArthur [the Faculty of Education] is supposed to be training teachers. The people who are attending McArthur and the people who stamp the qualifications record cards might assume that what McArthur is doing is training teachers.

P1:   The problem, as it is with any partnership, project, business or institution [is that] if you're not on the same page from the point of view of what your goal is [and] what your basic beliefs are, then you're going to have trouble. And the Faculty of Education and the schools are not on the same page. The point is that theory informs practice and practice informs theory. If you don't have the two things working together, then there's no point to it.

Principal 2 speaks even more directly about the importance of the Faculty Liaison role:

P2:   There's no question that the key to this Associate School concept is the Faculty Liaison, the link to Queen's and how they handle that job. I think that makes or breaks this program. If the school gets used to seeing that professor, if there's some indication that there's a little bit of give from Queen's to the school as opposed to the other way around, just that little perception can go a long way. In the pilot stages of this program, there were a couple of schools that the teachers just got turned right off of the program. And I would put most of the blame on the professor looking after that school, because there was no understanding that this was a give-and-take partnership. The teachers viewed it as Queen's unloading responsibilities on the schools while the professors, instead of being in the schools with their students, were having free time. We know that's not true, but that was the perception in some schools. But in schools where the [Faculty Liaison] really did own the thing, and really was actively engaged with the staff of that school, even if it was just to be in the school one day a week going from class to class and talking to teachers, the perception is completely different. Where that professor also attends a staff meeting or two just to be part of the organization, then there's a sense that there is some structural connection.

P2:   We understand that we have a professional obligation as teachers to support our future colleagues, however that responsibility is realized. Queen's has to somehow create the perception, at least, that they view the schools as part-ners, [that our taking teacher candidates is] not something that's owed to them, but something that they're privileged to have.

These two principals emphasize the importance, interrelationship and interdependence of time spent in schools, of balancing research and teaching, and of conveying a meaningful sense of partnership. These interview excerpts contribute usefully to my own sense of the importance of studying my performance and understanding of the role of Faculty Liaison.

The following concluding statements from a report by Weiss and Weiss reveal that these principals are not alone in their sense of the importance of school–university partnership and collaboration. These findings also emphasize that university courses, early teaching experiences, and supervision by a Faculty Liaison either unite or conflict in the overarching goal of providing the best possible preparation of new teachers.

> A re-conceptualized meaning of supervision is needed to support new teachers in becoming reflective practitioners. The new definition of supervision at Crossroads PDS includes reconfigured supervision roles and relationships. The PDS is beginning to challenge an embedded traditional "top-down", hierarchical paradigm, with the student teachers at the bottom as passive recipients of training. Student teachers are experiencing professional development occurring in a community of learners that fosters collegiality among professors, principal, teachers and student teachers. They are taking active roles in the learning process, roles that are reflective and responsive to children's needs in a school culture that expects teachers to take leadership.
>
> (Weiss and Weiss, 2001, p. 145)

The Reflective Supervision Model that has emerged at this PDS illustrates one way that professors, principals, and teachers might work together to create a trusting, collaborative school culture that supports reflective teaching and reflective supervision.

So what? Learning from and about self-study

On a private level, an individual self-study has an audience of one. It would be simple enough for me to gather up my course evaluations each year and plot a plan of action for the next year. Making my self-study public in this chapter generates three new audiences, but it also does much more. One audience for this chapter consists of those I will teach in PROF191 in the years to come; their seeing my questions and dilemmas may make it easier for them to help me work with them. A second audience consists of my colleagues in education at Queen's and teachers in our Associate Schools; their seeing my questions and dilemmas may help all of us move forward in developing the Faculty Liaison role that has been thrust upon us in structural (but not cultural) change. Finally, a third audience consists of those teacher educators around the globe who may read this chapter and find similarities to and differences from their own roles and their efforts to better understand and improve their practices. As I conclude this chapter, I am acutely aware that forcing myself to move from the private to the public level has generated many layers of further understanding that I would not have reached at the private level.

This self-study has forced me to reconsider my early premise that visits to schools to observe pre-service candidates are, in and of themselves, valuable to all concerned. School visits are made with the best of intentions, yet we have little evidence of the impact of a faculty member's school visits on candidates' professional learning or on the school–university relationship. We would be foolish to assume that visits are good, in and of themselves. Spending more time in schools does not automatically contribute to candidates' professional learning, but *time spent in schools is a fundamental base on which broader goals and relationships can be constructed.*

In Chapter 9 of this collection, Chuck Myers asks whether teacher education can go beyond the familiar and longstanding "telling, showing, and guided-practice approach to teacher education". His characterization of teaching in this way reminds me of one of the fundamental possibilities that is easily overlooked in the PROF191 course. Instead of telling candidates how to teach, showing them what that teaching might look like, and then guiding their practice in schools, PROF191 has the (unrealized) potential to *alter a fundamental tradition of teacher education.* The course puts teacher candidates into a school for an extended period of time, early in their program, and it puts faculty members into schools with them. If that faculty member focuses on the process by which candidates learn from experience, there may develop unique opportunities to explore the interplay of practice and theory, both with individuals and with the school groups. Seen in this light, the Faculty Liaison role can provide unique opportunities for teacher educators to gain firsthand experiences related to the question: *How does teaching experience change teacher candidates' understanding of how they learn as professionals?*

One of my purposes in this self-study is *to model professional learning in ways that support candidates just beginning to understand the nature and challenges of professional action and learning from experience.* Caught between theory and practice, I have struggled with the question: *Should I be doing just what the candidates expect me to do?* My response is now affirmative. As recent candidates indicated, and much as the clinical supervision literature has always recommended, observing full lessons and meeting soon after for discussion can be very productive. Perhaps if I can meet that apparently central expectation, I can then give greater attention to professional learning from experience. Nevertheless, there is much more to do beyond meeting candidates' expectations.

While experience is powerful, learning from experience is far from automatic, perhaps because all levels of formal schooling pay little attention to learning from experience. Candidates' initial mind sets now seem even stronger than I realized. The course is meant to be "field-based" and about learning from experience, yet much of its formal meeting time occurs before experience begins. These issues take me back to a set of contrasting assumptions that I have developed over the last ten years (Russell, 2000, pp. 231–9). My personal biases about teacher education are obvious in Table 6.1 when I cast the Transmission premises as "barriers" and the Interpretation premises as "frames" (Barnes, 1976, pp. 139–45). I believe that in the first two years of our restructured program, starting in school on the opening day after a brief orientation period stimulated most candidates to adopt an Interpretation view of their professional learning. When the decision was taken to abandon the first-day-of-school experience to provide a three-week introduction at the university, the impact may have been even greater than I anticipated. Classes at university inevitably reinforce a candidate's default predisposition to the Transmission view of teaching and learning to teach.

This self-study of my own efforts to learn the role of Faculty Liaison over a five-year period has been productive both practically and conceptually. By seeking comments on my role from those in my school groups, I have come to understand better the assumptions I was initially making more by default than by decision. Principals' comments on the school–university relationship prompt me to continue to spend more than the required minimum time in schools. Over the last two years I have made specific changes to how I spend my time in schools and I will make further changes in the coming year. At the same time,

Table 6.1 Contrasting views of the nature of learning to teach

Transmission view of learning to teach	Interpretation view of learning to teach
BARRIER 1: Teaching can be told.	FRAME 1: Teaching *cannot* be told.
BARRIER 2: Learning to teach is passive.	FRAME 2: Learning to teach is active.
BARRIER 3: Discussion and opinion are irrelevant.	FRAME 3: Discussion, opinion and sharing of experiences are crucial.
BARRIER 4: Personal reactions to teaching are irrelevant.	FRAME 4: Personal reactions to teaching are the starting point.
BARRIER 5: Goals for future students do not apply personally.	FRAME 5: Goals for future students definitely must apply personally.
BARRIER 6: "Theory" is largely irrelevant.	FRAME 6: "Theory" is relevant.
BARRIER 7: Experience cannot be analyzed or understood.	FRAME 7: Experience can be analyzed and understood.
OVERALL: When others tell me how to teach and I watch experienced teachers, then my learning is automatic and I easily become a good teacher. Teaching experience generates a steady progression to *mastery* that is largely unaffected by the students who pass through classes.	OVERALL: Good teaching requires constant effort to bring my actions in line with my goals for my students' learning and my own professional learning. Teaching is an inherently unstable activity that requires building and maintaining a unique and *dynamic relationship* with each new group of students.[2]

studying my learning of the new Faculty Liaison role has refocused my attention on the multiple and challenging tasks that the role permits and invites.

To close this chapter, I return to the issues I posed at the outset. My most compelling insight is that teacher candidates, experienced teachers, and Faculty Liaisons can be expected to approach supervisory interactions with "default" assumptions driven by unexamined personal experiences. At the outset, self-study is a way to bring such assumptions to the surface; over time, self-study is a way to keep one's focus on the goal of extending our professional understanding of what it means to learn from experience in the classroom and school settings. With that long-term end in view, genuine partnerships may emerge from a base of significant time spent with candidates and experienced teachers, unpacking not only observations of candidates' teaching but also our fundamental premises about teachers' professional learning.

Notes

1   The research reported here is supported by the Social Sciences and Humanities Research Council of Canada as part of the 1999–2002 study *Understanding Program Change in Teacher Education: Sharing the Authority of Experience*. Suzin McPherson helped in data-gathering and literature review, and also contributed her perspective as an associate teacher.
2   The contrast between "mastery" and "dynamic relationship" was provided by Garry Hoban of the University of Wollongong during an invited visit to Queen's University, 18 January 2001.

References and further reading

Barnes, D. (1976) *From Communication to Curriculum*, Harmondsworth: Penguin.

Ethell, R. and McMeniman, M. (2000) "Unlocking the knowledge in action of an expert practitioner", *Journal of Teacher Education*, 51: 87–101.

Featherstone, D., Munby, H. and Russell, T. (eds) (1997) *Finding a Voice while Learning to Teach*, London: Falmer Press.

Osguthorpe, R.T., Harris, R.C., Harris, M.F. and Black, S. (1995) *Partner Schools: Centers for educational renewal*, San Francisco, CA: Jossey-Bass.

Richardson, V. (ed.) (1997) *Constructivist Teacher Education: Building a world of new understandings*, London: Falmer Press.

Richardson-Koehler, V. (1988) "Barriers to the effective supervision of student teaching: A field study", *Journal of Teacher Education*, 39 (2): 28–34.

Russell, T. (1999) "The challenge of change in teaching and teacher education", in J.R. Baird (ed.) *Reflecting, Teaching, Learning. Perspectives on educational improvement*, Cheltenham, VA: Hawker Brownlow Education, pp. 219–38.

—— (2000) "Teaching to build on school experiences", in R. Upitis (ed.) *Who Will Teach? A case study of teacher education reform*, San Francisco, CA: Caddo Gap Press, pp. 221–34.

Sarason, S.B. (1996) *Revisiting "The Culture of the School and the Problem of Change"*, New York: Teachers College Press.

Schön, D.A. (1983) *The Reflective Practitioner: How professionals think in action*, New York: Basic Books.
Weiss, E.M. and Weiss, S. (2001) "Doing reflective supervision with student teachers in a professional development school culture", *Reflective Practice*, 2: 125–54.

7 Learning about our teaching from our graduates, learning about our learning with critical friends

Sandy Schuck and Gilda Segal

Introduction

We commonly assume that after graduation neither the teacher educator nor the beginning teacher has anything more to offer one another. This chapter presents a study in which this assumption is challenged. One focus of the chapter is on what we, as teacher educators, learnt about our practice by examining the experiences of our graduates when they began teaching. Our learning illustrates to us the value of self-study of teacher education practices continuing after graduation. We gained new understandings about how our practice had been effective in facilitating our graduates' development of philosophies of teaching and learning that reflect recent research findings in our discipline areas of mathematics and science education. At the same time, we learned how our practice could be modified to take more account of the realities of the school context.

On a second level, the process of self-study is examined. As two colleagues who work well together and trust each other, we did not expect our roles as critical friends to be problematic. However tensions arose for us, and we share those experiences and consider the dilemmas that self-study can pose.

Overview of our self-study

We both teach in the four-year Bachelor of Education (Primary) course at our university; Sandy teaches mathematics education and Gilda teaches science education. Keen to study our practice as teacher educators, we felt that by inquiring into the experiences of our graduates when they started teaching, we could gain real insight into the value of our practice for these newly qualified teachers. Reform movements concerned with approaches to the teaching and content matter of mathematics and science have strongly influenced our practices as teacher educators. We were interested in how, if at all, our graduates would manage to implement the reforms that they had studied and experienced in our classes.

We asked beginning teachers who had been our students to participate in this study and share their experiences with us. What they told us became our data, collected through journal entries and reflections from them, through workshop sessions in which they shared their ongoing experiences and through our weekly telephone conversations with them. We also explored ideas by keeping reflective journals ourselves. We then considered the data by sharing the findings with each other and discussing what they meant. In this way we were setting each other up as critical friends who would help each other to explore the meanings of the data and consider how these meanings might lead to reframing of our practices. Ultimately, we hoped that our findings would allow us to come to conclusions that would enhance our practice with other student teachers in our subjects.

This chapter discusses two aspects of the study. First, we challenge a common assumption that after graduation neither teacher educator nor beginning teacher have anything more to offer each other. We have learnt a great deal about our teaching through our interactions with beginning teachers who are graduates of our teacher education subjects, and the beginning teachers reported that they found the contact with us to be an invaluable means of support in their first year. However, an unexpected outcome of the study was that we also learnt a great deal about the difficulties of being critical friends in a self-study and of critiquing and advising each other. Being a critical friend to someone engaged in self-study is not necessarily easy or unproblematic.

A context for learning about mathematics and science education

The preparation of teachers of mathematics and science in Australian primary schools has always been problematic because of the prior experiences of prospective primary school teachers in these areas and their associated attitudes and beliefs about the nature of these subjects. Generally the subjects enjoy different statuses in the primary school curriculum: time honoured, in the case of mathematics; relative newcomer, in the case of science. For science, this differing status allows primary teachers who lack confidence to teach science to dispense with regular teaching of the subject (Appleton and Kindt, 1999), while the perception of the primacy of mathematics often leads to methods of teaching that emphasize procedure over understanding (Schuck, 1996).

The literature of mathematics education shows that many primary school teachers and prospective primary school teachers see mathematics as a fixed and sequential body of knowledge that is most effectively learnt by rote, algorithmic and repetitive procedures (Wilcox *et al.*, 1992; Mayer, 1994; Schuck, 1996). Burton (1996) suggests that much of what is taught in school classrooms as "immutable mathematics" is in fact a body of facts and strategies that were developed in a particular context and as an expression of the social norms of particular times and places. She suggests that the teaching of "immutable mathematics" has led to widespread marginalization and failure for its learners.

Burton's views are shared by many mathematics and science educators (Ernest, 1991; Dengate and Lerman, 1995). Science too is frequently taught didactically as a fixed body of knowledge without regard to its uncertain origins (Seddon, 1991) and is usually accompanied by a formula-like scientific method for investigation. It is against this quantitative view of the nature of knowledge and its accompanying alienation for many that the reform movements in mathematics and science education have evolved.

In Australia, calls for reform have been reinforced by recommendations of the Discipline Review of Teacher Education in Mathematics and Science (Speedy, Annice and Fensham, 1989) and the Curriculum and Standards Framework: Mathematics (Victoria Board of Studies, 1995). The reforms are embedded in alternative philosophical and epistemological understandings about the nature of the disciplines themselves and how they might be more effectively taught and learned. It is in the context of these reform initiatives that our teacher education courses in mathematics and science take place.

Our beliefs as teacher educators

Both of us bring to our teaching strongly held convictions that learning is a socio-cultural activity, mediated by group interaction and a need for learner autonomy. We recognize that along with the need for students to actively construct knowledge in a learning community, they also need to be aware that there are consensually accepted aspects of knowledge that hold true in particular communities. As teacher educators in the areas of mathematics and science education, we have constantly worked with the challenges of helping our student teachers to grapple with the nature of mathematics and science, to improve their attitudes towards these subjects, and to enhance their conceptual understandings of mathematical and scientific phenomena. Over the years we have tried a number of different interventions in the mathematics classroom (Schuck, 1997; Schuck and Foley, 1999) and in the science classroom (Segal and Cosgrove, 1992; Segal, 1999a) aimed at improving student teachers' attitudes and changing their conceptions of these subjects. Self-studies of our practices over the years (Schuck, 1999; Segal, 1999b) led us to develop what we saw as successful strategies for helping student teachers to appreciate different visions of the two subjects, to try out different approaches to those subjects, and to gain confidence and enjoyment from their teaching in these areas.

Both of us are aware that conceptions of successful mathematics and science teaching in primary schools are often in conflict with our notions of teaching in these subjects and that when students are on teaching practicum they often revert to the supervising teacher's views of the "correct ways" to teach. Students often return to our classes to inform us that reform views of mathematics and science education are not matching "the reality" – that is, the classroom in which they had been placed. Consequently, we felt that a logical extension to our understanding of how our practices were elaborating student teachers' views and approaches to teaching mathematics and science would be to examine what happens to our students on graduation and placement in primary schools.

Learning from our graduates

At the time of this study, students at our university could qualify with a Bachelor of Primary Teaching after three years and could then choose either to start teaching or to complete a fourth year and gain a Bachelor of Education. For those who went on to study in the fourth year, an induction period existed in which, as qualified teachers, the students took responsibility for a class for a period of seven weeks (as Associate Teachers). They then had an opportunity to deconstruct their experiences with their lecturers at university.

As we were eager to examine the value of our subjects and their underlying philosophies for our students once they started teaching, we approached our final year students and those who were going on to the fourth year of study. We included Associate Teachers in our study because we felt that their experiences would provide a natural bridge between our study of our practices as university educators and our study of the experiences of the beginning teachers. At the time of asking (towards the end of their third year of study), more than twenty students indicated their willingness to participate in the study. The numbers dropped to twelve at the start of the school year, when some graduates did not receive job offers and others felt that the context in which they would be teaching would not be suitable for the study. Some volunteers who did join the study initially were simply overwhelmed by the challenges of being a beginning teacher and did not have time to devote to the study. Of the twelve remaining, one volunteer then took up a teaching post overseas and suggested we communicate by e-mail, but this proved to be more difficult than she had thought so she withdrew from the project. This left eleven participants, seven of whom were graduates of our three-year teacher education program and in their first year of teaching, and four of whom were in their fourth year of the course and who participated in the study during their Associate Teacher period. All participants were female.

Of the group who were in their first teaching position, six of our seven volunteers taught in state schools and the remaining teacher taught in a Catholic systemic school. Two of the schools were in low socio-economic areas and the remainder were in middle-class areas. All of the beginning teachers taught early childhood classes (ages 5 to 8). Of the four Associate Teachers, two taught the lower age groups and the other two had senior primary classes (age 10 to 12). Two of the teachers did not have an opportunity to teach science during the period of the study, and this situation itself was a finding with implications, as the teaching of science is mandated in the primary school curriculum.

How did we learn from our graduates and Associate Teachers?

In the first two terms of the school year we held four workshops in which we discussed the project, issues arising, life histories of the beginning teachers with regard to mathematics and science and any critical incidents. We recorded the workshops and transcribed relevant parts of the discussion. Initially we asked the beginning teachers to maintain reflective journals, on a weekly basis, in which they would document critical incidents and current practices in teaching mathematics and science. We very quickly found in discussion at the workshops that most of them found weekly journals difficult to maintain due to time constraints. One did maintain her journal through our suggestion of dictating her thoughts to a tape recorder. Most, however, preferred to have us phone on a weekly basis so they could reflect on the week's happenings in the telephone conversation. We recorded, in writing, the essence of the conversations and after each phone call we wrote reflective notes on the issues that had arisen. The Associate Teachers were more able to sustain the maintenance of a reflective journal, but they too were happy for us to phone them while they were in the schools.

Throughout these varying contexts for data collection, participants were asked to describe their experiences in teaching mathematics and science, including reflection about the success of their lessons, problems, the rationale for choosing a particular model or approach, constraints, challenges, facilitatory factors, and any critical incidents that occurred during these lessons. Thus data collection was designed to inform us about both the challenges and the constraints that beginning teachers face in teaching mathematics and science.

Interestingly, our method of collecting data on the experiences of the beginning teachers and Associate Teachers became an interactive one, in which they could ask us for ideas or get support or sympathy from us. Consequently, the phone calls became much more than merely methods of collecting data. One student preferred to keep a journal and did not want to speak to us during the project. She also did not attend the workshops, as she was teaching and living in another town about 150 km away. We did not feel that we managed to build a personal relationship with her in the same way that we had with the other teachers, and we were not able to offer her any support in her first year as we respected her desire not to communicate with us as part of a two-way process. However, with the other beginning teachers we found that the nature of our project, which we had originally envisaged as being solely to contribute data for our self-study, expanded dramatically. It became a study of mutual benefit to all of us, a research design that happened quite serendipitously.

We were aware that beginning teachers might not want to be completely frank in conversation with us about any perceived shortcomings of our subjects. Consequently, towards the end of the year and after we had ceased contact with the beginning teachers, we employed an external research assistant to conduct interviews with each of the participants to assess the role of the study and to elicit more information from the beginning teachers on how we could have enhanced their preparation to be teachers of mathematics and science in primary schools.

Through the workshops, weekly phone calls, journals, and interviews, we examined the experiences of the eleven teachers. We did so during the first two school terms of the year, as we felt that these beginning terms were the ones in which the beginning teachers would need most support and would also most frequently encounter issues of concern to them. Throughout our study, we used our notes in informal discussion between the two of us, and on these occasions we discussed the issues arising and probed each other's rationales for our approaches in our university classes. The two of us also started keeping reflective journals, but stopped doing so very early in the research.

Gathering, reflecting upon and analyzing these data, we anticipated, would enable us to think deeply about the effectiveness of our practice in preparing our students for their future roles as primary school teachers of mathematics and science. Discussions between the two of us on the meaning of the data collected were anticipated to be the stimuli for framing and reframing our current practices as teacher educators.

What did we learn from our graduates and students?

We analyzed our data through a grounded theory approach (Segal and Schuck, 1999) and found that our analysis of the data was enlightening for our practice. For example, we felt that our views and positions had been influential in reframing our students' views of mathematics and science teaching. We noted that most of the beginning teachers had embraced our socio-cultural views of teaching mathematics and science, and were keen to put into practice their beliefs about how mathematics and science should be taught. However, we observed some large barriers to the reforms. The major barrier was that, generally, the school context interrupted their implementation of teaching in new ways. For example, one of our beginning teachers did not teach science to her class simply because the school had appointed a person to teach science to all classes at the school. Other barriers were that some of the beginning teachers were uncertain of the ways in which they could implement the socio-cultural philosophies they had developed during their study with us.

We quickly came to understand that the tension between school realities and beginning teacher ideals often created a great deal of frustration for the new teachers. Some difficulties that beginning teachers had were issues that we had raised in our classes – for example, the lack of resources in many of the schools, or the secret appropriation of resources by other staff members. Other major difficulties that the beginning teachers mentioned were related to school contexts with which we had not dealt explicitly in our subjects. These difficulties included specific dilemmas in classroom management, the requirement to teach from another teacher's program, and lack of time for science teaching and hence little increase in expertise and self-confidence in science teaching. These findings were important in suggesting ways that we could reframe our teacher education practices. We became aware that far more discussion of the school context was needed in our subjects, that more integration with school-based experiences would be helpful, and that we needed to deal more effectively with issues of resource management, negotiation with other staff members, and behavior management in the context of our own disciplines.

Fortunately though, some of the teachers were able to enjoy considerable freedom of choice in implementing their preferred pedagogy, making use of resources at hand, or using experiments and activities undertaken at university. They found that they had a substantial knowledge of approaches to mathematics and science teaching, that they had developed deep and thoughtful personal teaching philosophies, and that the intervention entailed in our project was both helpful and supportive.

Implications of our findings for our self-study of practice

While beginning teachers had generally embraced our views and philosophies regarding the socio-cultural nature of mathematics and science learning, they found that holding such views often led to conflict between the ways in which they wished to teach and the school culture. We focus here on such constraints experienced by the beginning teachers, because our joint reflection on the constraints led to greater learning about our teaching practice. We illustrate this through two mathematics examples.

> Sarah was extremely concerned because she desired to teach mathematics in investigative ways that were directed by the individual levels and abilities of the students. She was eager to have them work collaboratively and with concrete objects that were part of their environment. However, the staff at her school had decided that each student was to work from a commercial workbook that parents would purchase at the beginning of the year. Given that the school was in a low socio-economic area, the outlay by parents for the book was regarded as quite significant and Sarah consequently felt obliged to work through a page of the book each day so that parents could see it was being used. This left her no time to do other mathematics with her students. Sarah felt highly frustrated that she was not able to help her children learn in ways she felt would benefit them and this was a major cause of concern to her through the study. It led to significant feelings of frustration and perceptions of failure as a teacher.

It appeared to Sandy, as one of Sarah's mathematics educators at university, that such feelings were exacerbated by the emphasis that we had placed on investigative work in the mathematics subjects at university. In our classes, our eagerness to move student teachers away from the deeply held views of mathematics with which they had entered the program led to our emphatic suggestions of new ways of teaching. Constraints in using these new ways were not highlighted in our classes. The lesson in this for teacher educators is to be aware of the constraints of the classroom, the primacy of the school community in educational decision-making, and the need to prepare student teachers to avoid self-blame for circumstances beyond their control.

Jane, in her weekly conversations with Gilda, kept talking about the difficulties she was having with her mathematics groups. Gilda approached Sandy for clarification of this issue. Gilda felt that there was a certain lack of flexibility in Jane's view of the use of groups and wondered how this issue had been approached in class. Sandy informed her that there was a strong emphasis on working in groups, as Sandy's personal beliefs were that children learnt through interactions in a learning community or group. This question, however, prodded Sandy to re-examine her approach to group work in her mathematics classes.

What both of these examples illustrated clearly to Sandy was the need for her to discuss more carefully the possible constraints existing in the classroom. Setting up cases such as the ones above to discuss in class might help beginning teachers develop the ability to be more flexible and respond to the context of their particular school.

In science, two examples illustrate how this study has informed Gilda's practice. The first concerns the role and use of student-centered activities.

Although all of our participants explained that their preferred (idealistic) teaching and learning philosophy for teaching science was student-centered and activity-based in small groups, it was evident from our data that they attributed different shades of meaning to the function of student-centered activities in science. For example, Deanne proudly reported that her class had enjoyed a variety of science activities, but she did not seem to be concerned with the development of any science concepts during those activities.

Gilda now understands more clearly that we needed to employ multiple strategies in class to challenge the assumption of some of our students that as long as the children are having fun, they are developing conceptual scientific understanding. A second example of learning for Gilda about her practice involves the use of firsthand experiences in teaching.

A beginning teacher (Rose) found that implementing the lessons that she had been excited about at university led to difficulties in managing her Year 1 class early in the year and also led to her curtailing all hands-on experiences for the children in Science for most of the year. As Rose told us, "I think it was one of the first experiments I did. It was an experiment

> in which objects floated … . Since that [time] I have been a bit apprehen-
> sive about doing, like, group experiments. I just do an experiment out the
> front and get the children to participate that way.

For Gilda and other science teacher educators, there is a strong message here.
We need to caution our enthusiastic student teachers that they need to plan
how to gradually implement the alternative teaching strategies that have
excited them at university. Without much experience of teaching science and
technology during their practica in schools, and without much opportunity to
observe experienced primary teachers teaching science, there is certainly a
danger for enthusiastic beginners if they try to achieve their ideals too early.

Thus a major finding for both of us in this self-study is that the practices we
use in teacher education classrooms appear to be seamless and unproblematic to
our student teachers, and that the situation changes when they try to implement these same practices in the school context. As teacher educators we need
to make explicit the problems, contexts, and realities of the school classroom in
the activities we do with our student teachers. For both of us, this lesson has
already been taken into our current classes. Future self-studies would be valuable in assessing how this reframing of our teaching assists beginning teachers.

Another finding for us arose from the interactions we had with each other.
We have been colleagues in the same program for seven years, and we had
become friends as well as colleagues when we both were on sabbatical at the
same overseas university. This project was the second one on which we had
collaborated, and we shared an interest in self-study. We felt we were able to
question each other's practices, as we had developed a working relationship
built on shared experiences, interest in enhancing our teaching, and a strong
trust in each other. We anticipated that this questioning would encourage individual reflection on practices that we might otherwise have taken for granted,
as they were deeply entrenched in our belief systems. However, when we
analyzed our experiences in this self-study, we found that we had unknowingly
created tensions and anger in the other person through our frank and honest
attempts to be critical friends.

Learning from each other in a self-study

When we started preparing a conference presentation (CASTLE Conference
2000) on this self-study, we became aware of the tensions we had created for
each other in our roles as critical friends. In writing about the study, we had
chosen incidents to discuss and analyzed the reactions and discussion we had
shared when first raising these incidents with each other. When preparing our
presentation, Gilda noticed that Sandy was getting more and more tense, but
was unsure how what she had been saying was generating this tension. When
we stopped and talked about the situation over a friendly lunch, we discovered

that Gilda, too, had experienced some tension and been upset at comments that Sandy had made earlier.

We had felt that to be genuine researchers in this self-study we should document our thoughts and feelings, as well as any critical incidents that arose as we worked on the study. We also thought that it would be important to share our reflective entries in our journals with each other, and that these might be valuable sources of data for us. So, after an initial meeting with a colleague who we were going to ask to facilitate our workshops, we agreed to write about the incident and share it with each other. In an attempt to be totally honest, one of the issues Sandy raised in her journal was her discomfort at the way Gilda had adopted a novice stance with our colleague. She felt that Gilda had portrayed us as beginners in the area. She even indicated that this was typical of the way Gilda usually interacted with people, and that she did not like being included in the way Gilda was framing our roles. Feedback can be very confronting, hurtful, and surprising when it is unexpected, and Gilda found the incident extremely unpleasant. While not indicating to Sandy how hurt she was, she did suggest that journal writing and sharing was very difficult, and we did not raise the idea of such writing and sharing again.

> My feelings were not disturbed by your recognition that I was interacting with our colleague in that manner. I knew that was the way I usually behaved – deferring to someone that I thought had more experience than I had. What disturbed me was that you did not like this aspect and it was quite a deeply ingrained part of the way I am. So in writing your journal in that way, to me, you were criticizing me personally in a very deep and meaningful way. I think I have put that behind me. I now recognize that I have found your feedback helpful in that now I do try not to portray myself in a negative way in conversations.
>
> (Gilda's journal)

It is worth noting in this first example that the result of being totally honest with each other in the critical friend role was that one partner was extremely hurt by the comments of the other. This hurt arose, even though we were trusted friends who worked well together.

A second incident occurred during our preparation of the conference presentation. Where Gilda had challenged Sandy over her teaching about group work in the mathematics classroom and Sandy had found that useful in prompting her to think more carefully about her approaches to group work, when it came to reporting this incident for other teacher educators to read, some apprehension arose on Sandy's part. She agreed to record both incidents noted earlier, in the paper being prepared, but had some misgivings about their presence. When preparing the presentation, Gilda made some suggestions as to how these incidents could have been avoided. We agreed that she would raise these suggestions at the presentation. We then moved on to other examples set in the science teaching context. However, in response to Sandy's critique of these incidents, Gilda felt that Sandy was not responding to accurate representations of what had occurred in the science classes, and so rejected the critique. This led to frustration and some anger on Sandy's part. The following interchange that was recorded from our conversation about the issue explains the incident further.

SANDY: You know, Gilda, I feel as if I am opening up and exposing myself and giving you the impression that I am not a good teacher and you are being quite critical of me, but I do not feel you are reciprocating this openness. I feel very vulnerable about what I have written in the paper, for example, about groups and your querying our practice – you appear in my mind to come over as the expert and me as the novice bumbling along. Similarly, your comments here about Sarah's problems appear to be quite critical of my practice, where I have looked at our data as indicating common problems to solve rather than criticize your practice. While I am eager to assess my practice and improve it, I do feel quite confronted by some of our interactions.

GILDA: I actually feel quite helpless to interact with your feelings here. I had no idea that you were feeling vulnerable about what you wrote in the paper. I certainly do not think of you as a poor teacher, and have never thought of you in this way. Similarly, I have no intention of coming across as the expert. I have very little knowledge of your practice in maths education. In saying this, I suspect that you will not be happy, as you will see it as a self-defensive comment – perhaps it is, but I do not apologize for it. I see the need to be self-defensive if I feel I am misunderstood. We need to discuss the ways we have handled our interaction here in more detail, and perhaps can return to that soon …

One thing though that I must admit to you is that I do not feel vulnerable about discussing my practice in science education for this particular study. I do not feel this study touches me as personally as you appear to feel it touches you. It may be that you have sensed this detachment on my part and that is adding to your feelings about our interactions.

We have four science education subjects and the science educators share responsibility for preparing and coordinating those subjects. Some of our participants were not in my classes at all and some were in two of the four subjects at most. I do feel a shared responsibility for our science education course and feel that I have learned a great deal from our study that I can take back to improve our course. To me, though, that is different to my personal practice as a science educator and the feedback that I receive directly from students in my classes and it is very different to the personal feedback you gave me in your journal about the way I converse with others.

SANDY: Well, we too share our responsibility for our subjects and I too had only taken one or two of the participants in our study and then for only one or two of the four maths education subjects and not for others. However, it is the conversation about our teaching that makes this personal.

By the way, I did not realize the extent to which you had found our sharing of our journal entries to be so upsetting. I thought we had found a point of disagreement and the journal entries brought it out in the open for discussion. So I was not sensitive to your reactions until this discussion. I did not feel that I had made a very personal comment, but more of an observation of how we perceived ourselves differently. I am quite disturbed that it upset you because I pride myself on being sensitive to others' feelings and trying to avoid confronting people.

When I heard what you said [about the incidents in mathematics education], I felt a little confronted but I realized that the nature of self-study is like that. However, when we came to talk about the issues arising in science education, I felt that you were only presenting the data in ways that showed the students' deficiencies and not those of your teaching. Hence my outburst.

GILDA: While we were preparing our dialogue for presentation, I could see that you were disturbed by some of the things I was saying, but I could not really understand the reason for your feelings. After you explained how you felt, I could see the damage I was doing in continuing to defend myself, but I did not have the skills to know how else to continue the conversation. In trying to explain my position in our conversation, I was making things worse. I now know you thought that I was protecting myself for our presentation while leaving you in the vulnerable position.

Implications of being a critical friend

The incidents above highlighted for us the notion that being a critical friend in a self-study is rarely simple and straightforward. Loughran and Northfield have developed a framework for the development of self-study of practice in which they argue that it is "working with an important 'other' that matters" so that the individual conducting the self-study is pushed to explore areas that might be uncomfortable (Loughran and Northfield, 1998, p. 7). They suggest that individuals need a lot of self-confidence to conduct self-studies, and that the results of a self-study are often challenging and discomforting. Our study certainly supports this view. However, we would like to expand on this issue because we feel that the discomfort experienced by having a critical friend might well dissuade teacher educators from conducting self-studies. Further, if dissemination of such studies is viewed as important, and we have argued elsewhere that it is (Schuck, 1999), then situations such as the one described above need to be resolved. Again, we point out that a resolution of sorts was arrived at in our situation, because we are such good friends and trust each other. This trust allowed us to raise issues with each other that others, with lesser relationships, may (would) not.

The question, then, is "How can you be a critical friend without alienating the person you are advising?" We suggest that the following elements of a critical friendship are essential if the self-study is to be effective and valuable for the teacher educators involved:

- Building trust is an essential first step in establishing a critical friendship. Without trust, the person being critiqued may wonder about the other person's agenda or be unable to discuss any disquiet that might be felt.
- For a critical friendship to be highly effective, both members should be partners in the self-study. They should be prepared to share, on an equal basis, the incidents and critiques arising from their practice. Having one person as the researcher and the other as the critiquer makes the partnership unequal and the different statuses that inevitably occur do not promote honest reflection and reframing of practice.
- Critical friendship needs to be tested in a private way before it is disseminated to a wider audience. Many of us have different capacities for being critiqued, depending on the purpose and audience for the critique. Open and honest discussion about the purpose of the critique is helpful in this regard.

What have we learnt from this self-study?

Studying our practice through the continuation of relationships with our graduates has been extremely beneficial. It allows us as teacher educators to experience "reality checks" in that it is extremely easy to suggest approaches and excite students about new ways of teaching if the constraints of the classroom and school are ignored. If we are to support our students past the graduation ceremony, we need to be able to help our students develop strategies for working within school constraints without having to give up their ideals and philosophies. Significantly, the opportunity to work with beginning teachers in their context provided us with opportunities to develop strategies ourselves for dealing with specific situations.

In addition, discussion with each other about issues that the beginning teachers raised provided us with the need to justify our practices to each other or become aware of the limitations of these practices and ways in which we could modify them. Further, an awareness of the impact of our critiques on the other researcher led to an appreciation of the need for sensitivity in acting as a critical friend. The study allowed us to analyze the role of the critical friend and develop ideas about the aspects of such a friendship that appear to be essential for effective self-study. For the record, we are still close friends, both socially and professionally, and we are working together on a number of projects.

References

Appleton, K. and Kindt, I. (1999) "Why teach primary science? Influences on beginning teachers' practices", *International Journal of Science Education*, 21 (2): 155–68.

Burton, L. (1996) "Mathematics and its learning as narrative – a literacy for the twenty-first century", in D. Baker, J. Clay and C. Fox (eds) *Challenging Ways of Knowing in English, Mathematics and Science*, London: Falmer Press.

Dengate, B. and Lerman, S. (1995) "Learning theory in mathematics education: Using the wide-angle lens and not just the microscope", *Mathematics Education Research Journal*, 7 (1): 26–36.

Ernest, P. (1991) *The Philosophy of Mathematics Education*, London: Falmer Press.

Loughran, J.J. and Northfield, J. (1998) "A framework for the study of self-study practice", in M.L. Hamilton (ed.) *Reconceptualising Teaching Practice: Self-study in Teacher Education*, London: Falmer Press.

Mayer, C. (1994) "Mathematics and mathematics teaching: Changes in pre-service student-teachers' beliefs and attitudes", *Proceedings of MERGA 17 Annual Conference: Challenges in Mathematics Education: Constraints on Construction*, Lismore: MERGA.

Schuck, S. (1996) "Chains in primary teacher mathematics education courses: An analysis of powerful constraints", *Mathematics Education Research Journal*, 8 (2): 119–36.

—— (1997) "Using a research simulation to challenge prospective teachers' beliefs about mathematics", *Teaching and Teacher Education*, 13 (5): 529–39.

—— (1999) *Driving a mathematics education reform with unwilling passengers*, paper presented at the Annual Meeting of the American Educational Research Association, Montreal (ERIC Document no. ED 431 734).

Schuck, S. and Foley, G. (1999) "Viewing mathematics in new ways: Can electronic learning communities assist?", *Mathematics Teacher Education and Development*, 1: 22–37.

Seddon, T. (1991) "Rethinking teachers and teacher education in science", *Studies in Science Education*, 19: 95–117.

Segal, G. (1999a) "Innovation in primary science teacher education: Taking responsibility for learning through computer-mediated communication and classroom interactions", in S. Schuck, L. Brady, C.E. Deer and G. Segal (eds) *Challenge of Change in Education: Symposium Proceedings*, Sydney: Change in Education Research Group (CERG), pp. 318–30.

—— (1999b) *Collisions in a science education reform context: Anxieties, roles and power*, paper presented at the Annual Meeting of the American Educational Research Association, Montreal (ERIC Document no. ED 431 733).

Segal, G. and Cosgrove, M. (1992) "Challenging student teachers' conceptions of science and technology education", *Research in Science Education*, 22: 348–57.

Segal, G. and Schuck, S. (1999) *"I don't really feel guilty about science at all. No-one does it!" Primary teachers teaching science in their first year of teaching*, paper presented at 30th Annual Conference of the Australasian Science Education Research Association, Rotorua, New Zealand.

Speedy, G., Annice, C. and Fensham, P. (1989) *Discipline Review of Teacher Education in Mathematics and Science*, vol. 1, Canberra: Australian Government Publishing Service.

Victoria Board of Studies (1995) *Curriculum and Standards Framework: Mathematics*, Melbourne: Victoria Board of Studies.

Wilcox, S., Lanier, P., Schram, P. and Lappan, G. (1992) *Influencing Beginning Teachers' Practice in Mathematics Education: Confronting constraints of knowledge, beliefs, and context* (Research report 92–1), East Lansing, MI: The National Center for Research on Teacher Learning.

8 Framing professional discourse with teachers

Professional Working Theory

Mary C. Dalmau and Hafdís Guðjónsdóttir

Introduction

This chapter has a dual focus. First, we describe our development of a process that facilitates the articulation and discussion of Professional Working Theory with teachers – a process based on the dynamic interaction between "practice" (what teachers do), "theory" (how they understand what they do), and "ethics" (why they do what they do). We conclude the first section with an outline of the expanded discourse on teacher professionalism initiated by teachers as they discussed their "Professional Working Theory". Second, we describe and critically reflect on the self-study through which we developed this approach to Professional Working Theory. In this latter stage we raise questions about the nature and purpose(s) of self-study and the contribution of self-study (and practitioner research) to knowledge creation in education.[1]

We have spent many hours with educators in Iceland, Australia, and the United States in a variety of teacher education, school improvement and research contexts.[2] As educators reflected on their professional roles, and worked to re-vision and recreate their practice, four questions emerged:

1 How is teacher practice informed by theory and ethics?
2 How does reflective practice lead teachers to new knowledge and theoretical understandings?
3 Where does such discourse fit into the multi-tasked professional lives of the teachers?
4 How can teachers' voices be strengthened in national and international educational discourse?

Consideration of these questions is critically important to the preparation of teachers for complex and evolving professional roles.

> A significant body of circumstantial evidence points to a deep systemic incapacity of US schools and the practitioners in them, to develop, incorporate, and extend new ideas and teaching and learning in anything but a small fraction of schools and classrooms.
>
> (Elmore, 1996, p. 1)

The situation depicted by Elmore has been described in many countries. A constant thread in the literature emphasizes the dilemmas facing schools, the resilience of the *status quo* in education, and the importance of the capacitation of teachers in the face of "fundamental and difficult challenges to their practice, their conception of themselves as teachers, and their sense of professional reward and satisfaction" (McLaughlin and Talbert, 1993, p. 246).

In their review of teacher research in the last decade of the twentieth century, Cochran-Smith and Lytle (1999) identify three different conceptualizations of the roles and work of teachers (summarized in Guðjónsdóttir, 2000, p. 67).

Perspective 1

Teachers as technicians: Teacher technicians are consumers and receivers of curriculum and teaching materials grounded in university-based research. They learn from others about their profession and are skilled transmitters of information developed by others (Sykes, 1990; Van Manen, 1991; Jóhannesson, 1992; Cochran-Smith and Lytle, 1993).

Perspective 2

Teachers as professionals: Professional teachers are recognized as the creators of learning, assessment, and curriculum at the classroom level. They share a body of professional knowledge related to teaching and learning, and curriculum development. Professional teachers are mentors of new teachers, and perform important roles in school reorganization and governance. They participate in and create professional development with their colleagues (Duckworth, 1987).

Perspective 3

Teachers as reflective practitioners: Reflective teachers are curriculum developers, decision-makers, and consultants. They participate in and critically reflect on school restructuring and educational changes. They are inquirers, analysts, and activists who weave reflection into their professional role, and improve their practice by collecting and analyzing data from their daily practice (Handal and Lauvås, 1982; Anderson, Herr and Nihlen, 1994; Zeichner, 1994; Loughran and Northfield, 1996; Darling-Hammond, 1997).

Teachers are much more than "recipients [and implementers] of knowledge generated by professional researchers" and presented by teacher educators; they are reflective professionals with the theoretical, pedagogical, and critical abilities to contribute to teaching and learning, and the regeneration of schools (Cochran-Smith and Lytle, 1993, p. 1).

Professional working theory

Teachers' rejection of theoretical explanations may be an indication of their concern about the abstraction of theory (in teacher education and pedagogy) from the issues they face in their experience of education. The challenge in teacher education is to draw out teachers' theoretical backgrounds from their daily experiences, and introduce them to the skills and resources that will enable them to critically reflect on their practice together. We believe it is critical that such professional dialogue permeates all aspects of initial and continuing teacher education, and that the facilitation of this dialogue is an essential aspect of reflective practice and the professional capacitation of teachers (Handal and Lauvås, 1982, 1987; Rizvi and Kemmis, 1987; Ainscow, 1991; Dalmau, Hatton and Spurway, 1991; Kincheloe, 1991; Ross, Cornett and McCutcheon, 1992; Day, Calderhead and Denicolo, 1993; hooks, 1994; Apple, 1995; Bertrand, 1995; Chaiklin and Lave, 1996; Hargreaves and Goodson, 1996; Hargreaves, Earl and Ryan, 1996; Freire, 1998; Slee, Weiner and Tomlinson, 1998; Smyth, 1999).

Handal and Lauvås (1982) conclude that implicit or "practical theory" is behind everything teachers do or wish to do in their teaching. They use the model of a pyramid to describe a personal theory built on theory-based, practice-based and ethics-based arguments. Whitehead (1993) uses the term "living theory" to describe the way teachers build knowledge and theoretical understandings based on their perceptions, descriptions, and interpretations of their own educational practice.

We use the term "Professional Working Theory" to symbolize professional understanding that evolves through the constant interplay of professional knowledge, practical experience, reflection, and ethical or moral principles. Explicit Professional Working Theory is developed through systematic and comprehensive critical reflection and collegial dialogue, and also contributes to the construction of professional identity, the creation of professional knowledge, and the development of collegial approaches to practice. The Professional Working Theory process outlined below offers teachers (and academics) an opportunity to frame their reflection on the living theories implicit in their practice.

The Professional Working Theory (PWT) instrument and process

Mary (an Australian) and Hafdís (an Icelander) first worked together in teacher education at the University of Oregon in 1996–7. We taught collegial collaboration, school improvement, and teacher research to groups of pre-service and practicing teachers over three years. In our first year we introduced a framework that assisted teachers in describing their practice to one another through the development of individual and group profiles. Through iterative reflection on outcomes (in our preparation sessions, with class participants, and with our collaborative review group), we extended this initial activity to the creation and use of the "Professional Working Theory" (PWT) instrument.[3] In the second year, with a new group of students, we continued to use the framework and incorporated the dialogue thus engendered into our teaching/learning approaches.

The early versions of the PWT instrument contained:

1   an introductory overview,
2   a page each for "Practice", "Theory" and "Ethics" entries, and
3   space to develop a personal statement.

Figure 8.1 illustrates for us the interrelatedness of these three components and the idea of constant movement.

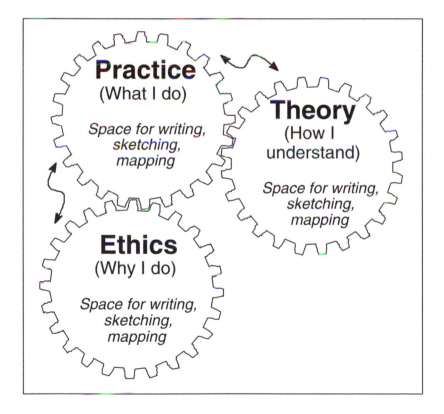

Figure 8.1 Scope of Version 1 of the PWT instrument (1997–8)

Using this graphic, we described each of the areas in terms of the teachers' professional work, and the meanings and beliefs that informed and motivated their practice:

Practice: Teachers' experience of their professional work and roles, including teaching, assessment, evaluation, collaboration with colleagues, and relationships with students and parents.

Theory: The way teachers understand and relate practice to theory. Teachers' explanations of what happens in the classroom, their theoretical frameworks, and their methods of relating self-understanding and reflective practice to theory.

Ethics: The way teachers explain the reasons behind their practice. It relates to their beliefs and values about the world, and reflects what they are becoming and what they want to be as teachers.

The open spaces (for writing, drawing, and/or concept mapping) and the stimulus questions were designed to help users to systematically explore each of the areas (see Attachment 1 for an example from the work of an Icelandic teacher).

As we began to use the instrument with more teachers, we found that, while the process supported more systematic and informed dialogue about their work, the discourse remained bounded by the classroom walls. Kincheloe (1991) found that research challenged teachers to confront the relationship between social theory, educational theory, and classroom practice. Could this not also be true of our process of individual inquiry?

In response to early use of the instrument, we modified it to encourage the inclusion of perspectives from beyond the classroom. The new version included three levels of reflective questions to support the relational analysis of experiential, systemic, and socio-cultural factors (1. Close/local; 2. Medium distance; 3. Broad/societal). Table 8.1 shows the topics around which we developed these reflective questions for the three sections of the instrument (practice, theory, and ethics), and provides an example of the reflective questions for the practice section. This process was challenging. However, as teachers used the extended PWT instrument to frame their reflections and their discussions, they began to build connections between implicit and explicit (or formal) theory, and between lived experience and socio-cultural and political influences.

How have teachers used the PWT instrument?

As innovators, teachers expanded our vision of how the PWT instrument (and process) could be useful to them. The following examples illustrate how teachers used the instrument to support the comprehensiveness and depth of their professional reflection.

Table 8.1   Three levels of reflective questions

	Close/local	*Medium distance*	*Broad/societal*
Practice	What do I see happen in my daily work?	What directly affects what I do?	What broad connections am I aware of?
Theory	How do I explain what I do?	What are the immediate sources of my understanding of what I do?	What theoretical frames of meaning form the basis of my understanding?
Ethics	What are my personal ethics and values? How are they visible in my work?	What are the sources of my ethics and values?	What are the cultural, societal impacts on my ethics and values?

The reflective questions below are taken from the Practice section of the instrument. (See Attachment 1 for the PWT contents and an example of one teacher's response.)

	Close/local	*Medium distance*	*Broad/societal*
	What do I see happen in my daily work?	**What directly affects what I do?**	**What broad connections am I aware of?**
	e.g.	e.g.	e.g.
Practice	• What does my day look like? What did I teach?	• What "rules" affected what I did today?	• What does my town/my state/my country expect schools to do?
	• What methods/ approaches did I use?	• What local/state/federal policies or legislation did I follow?	• What societal issues do I see in my school (e.g. beliefs about outcomes for different groups; relationship between school and work/school and taxes) and how do I see these reflected in my practice (e.g. priorities/curriculum/ assessment)?
	• What spontaneous teaching did I do?	• Which other professionals/adults did I interact with?	
	• How did I respond to students? Did I treat some students differently?	• How is authority and power configured in my work situation?	
	• What made me proud/satisfied/happy? What troubled me?	• How did these things affect what I did today/this week?	
	• What relationships were great? Difficult?		
	• What did I learn today/this week? What data did I collect?		• What are the powerful groups in the community? How do their priorities affect schooling?

Describing their approach to teaching

Individual teachers analyzed and described their professional practice in general (answering questions such as "How is my teaching going this year?", "What is my overall approach to students? ... to Special Education? ... to teaching Spanish?").

Reviewing a particular aspect of their work

Individuals and teaching teams explored and analyzed particular aspects of their work (answering questions such as "How did this science unit go?", "When I developed this English unit was I thinking about the different groups of students in my class?", "What is my approach to preparing students with disabilities for college?").

Communicating with others and supporting collegial dialogue and collaboration

Teams of educators structured communication in ways that minimized the influence of role-power and supported the inclusion of a range of perspectives. For example, a general educator and a special educator who planned to team teach a unit described and shared their professional working theories, and composed a team profile to support their work together; faculty groups or working teams within a school or district used the framework to create a discussion of the teams' overall approach at the beginning of the year or at a staff retreat.

Framing participatory research

Teachers and teacher educators expanded and systematized inquiry into their practice in school/university faculty partnerships.

Teachers used the instrument individually and in groups and built new understandings through questioning and dialogue, and academics or counselors interviewed them and participated in the conversation. These different approaches enabled all to learn with one another in research and professional learning programs.

What we learned

The PWT approaches support new forms of theoretical dialogue with teachers. Although it was difficult to move beyond the parameters of the classroom, framing the discussion (with the PWT instrument) and supporting the dialogue process effectively extended the scope of our discussions. What was most exciting was that the process enabled the teachers and ourselves to participate in situated theoretical dialogue in ways that we had not hitherto experienced. The ensuing discussions began a shared process of knowledge generation that incorporated and went beyond the teachers' ability to frame the discussion of their Professional Working Theory in new ways. Three areas were important:

1   identification of critical elements in the dialogic process itself,
2   new understanding of teachers' professional roles, and
3   implications for teacher research and research with teachers.

Critical elements of the process

The quality of the discourse did not reside in the PWT instrument itself, but in how and why it was used. Our emerging summary of the critical elements in the process includes the items below.[4]

Integrating action and reflection related to the "real" work of teachers at all times

Teachers' reflection and the ensuing discourse usually began with teachers' descriptions of their daily work and was grounded in the interplay (dialectic) of theory, action, and dialogue.

Respecting and incorporating "unique knowledges"

Asking individuals to describe their unique knowledge, understandings, beliefs, and skills (individual profile) and combine this with others to form a group profile provided a firm basis for cooperation and nullified many potential competitive or power struggles.

Sharing the "what" and the "why", as well as the "how to"

By articulating the nature of the process and our reasons for using it, we enabled teachers to critically review the PWT and adapt the process and instruments to their situations while maintaining essential elements.

Encouraging users to look for "data" rather than "judgments"

This rather metaphorical usage of these terms encouraged teachers to express "what is" (what they can see, hear, describe – for example, "My preferred working style is to work to deadline") rather than "what should be" (what they have learned, believe or think should happen – for example, "Groups work best when everyone works to deadline").

Visually and conceptually framing the description, analysis, and dialogue

The use of an instrument such as the PWT framed the reflection and discussion in several ways: (a) conceptually (parameters, relationships, awareness of stereotypical thinking), (b) multiple modes of presenting information (visual, mapping, textual), and (c) making data visible in ways that can be shared (to enable the shared exploration of the meaning).

Keeping a holistic approach

The structure of the instrument helped participants to recognize the interplay of factors that are often dichotomized or simply ignored ("reflection and action", "practice, theory and ethics", and "felt experience and socio-cultural/historical factors).

Critical relational analysis grounded in practice

The process always began by asking participants to visualize and reflect on their experience of practice, and the reflection and dialogue always returned to this core. However, the iterative use of the PWT process over time and in dialogue with others invited the teachers into a reconstructive process of critical relational analysis.

Raising consciousness about issues of power and the impact of power on knowledge generation

The reflective questions and the learning environment encouraged users to explore situations in which power relationships affected decisions about what is "true" and "good". Discussions of the concepts of collaboration, reaction, resistance and oppression (Freire, 1993), and "unique knowledges" supported the process.

As we continued to work with teachers in this way, their discussions of their professional identity changed. They were no longer seeking simple psychological explanations for their roles as "teacher", but situated their identity in their individual and collective professional action of the community.

Reframing our understanding: six integrated roles of professional educators

The teachers began to recognize and articulate a range of professional roles that went far beyond the simple concept of "teacher as technician" (Cochran-Smith and Lytle, 1999). They taught us about the unique knowledges and contributions of the teaching profession in our communities, and their perceptions encapsulated much of the earlier discussion of teacher professionalism. This process of critical reflection confirmed them in the belief that they are a professional group that contributes to the development of unique knowledge about pedagogy and the environments of learning. Together we identified roles that articulated the scope of their professional identities and practice.

Pedagogues and experts in teaching and learning

Teachers share a body of knowledge about teaching and learning. Whenever teachers meet, they continue the "never ending" professional dialogue with their colleagues.

Reflective and critical problem-solvers

In the classroom, teachers continuously respond to students in the process of teaching and supporting learning for each individual. Outside the classroom, independently and in collegial groups, teachers reflect more formally on events of the school day and plan action.

Researchers and change agents

When teachers wish to understand a practice in more depth or plan systematic or long-term change, they use a variety of assessment, evaluation, and practitioner/action research processes to collect data, analyze and interpret findings, and plan action.

Creators of knowledge and theory builders

In the process of reflective practice and educational research, teachers build new understandings of learning, teaching, and educational change.

Writers and adult educators

Teachers publish and provide adult education both formally and informally. They publish their research in professional journals, write curriculum texts, speak at conferences, and develop educational programs for parents and other teachers.

Authoritative voices in the community

Teachers' voices are heard in their local communities and beyond. Formally and informally, teachers' opinions are sought about educational issues, learning and educational improvement. Teachers provide the "good news" about student learning – often in pessimistic and critical environments (Guðjónsdóttir, 2000).[5]

Implications for teacher research and research with teachers

Teachers tend to interpret situations in ways that reinforce existing perceptions, unless explicit and collaborative processes are established for "making tacit understandings explicit" and for "considering alternative forms of reference" (Loughran and Northfield, 1996, p. 182).[6] The PWT instrument became one such process, assisting them to recognize the problematic in the familiar, raising their awareness of social and cultural influences on their work, and allowing them to see relationships with one another and with the larger community of education in a new light.

We extended our use of the PWT to our research. Hafdís used the PWT as the stepping-off point and the ground for a year-long study of responsive professional practice with six Icelandic teachers (Guðjónsdóttir, 2000), and Mary used a similar process with teacher co-researchers in a study of learning and change in education (Dalmau, 2001). We are excited by what we learned with these teachers, and by the teachers' enthusiasm for the studies and the research process. We are eager to continue to explore the usefulness of processes such as the PWT to action and teacher research, and to the discourse through which teachers participate in the creation of professional knowledge and the development of collegial approaches to practice.

Five years of collaborative self-study

During our initial period of co-teaching (1996–7) we met weekly to prepare and review. We discussed what we were doing – what was going well and what we needed to improve. As we began to grapple with questions of framing professional discourse with teachers, our meetings changed. We were not simply reviewing and adapting the content of our classes. We listened more to teachers, and we asked questions. Then a critical event happened:

> One day some of the teacher learners said to us "It's no use talking to us about group practice and collaboration ... we know it doesn't work ... teachers are too busy ... you can get things done quicker on your own ... besides, it's just something we have to do to please the administrators". It felt like our enthusiasm and energy were colliding with a thick wall of

indifference. After much anguish and soul-searching, we realized we were just another pair of enthusiasts in a long line of people telling teachers that we knew the answer, that we were the ones who could tell them what to do.

(Journal)

At the next class we gave each participant an almost blank sheet of paper; there was a circle on the paper divided into four quadrants with four questions and lots of space. We asked them to make an individual profile, and then get together in a group and create a group profile. This was the beginning of a new way of working, and a new understanding of self-study.[7] We found that when people consider the phenomena of group practice based on their experience, they are able to begin to take a fresh look at the topic and to rebuild their understandings in partnership with us. We had to change as much as they did. Over the next few years, with different groups, we continued the self-study and gradually developed the PWT instrument and process. All the principles and processes have been incorporated into our work together.

We used concept mapping and drawing to bring our reflection to life, and by doing so we managed to be critical of our work and develop our teaching. At that time, we were part of an international group of women educators in Oregon. We used this group to support our collaborative reflection-on-practice. In 1998, when Hafdís returned to Iceland, we extended our self-study through e-mail and phone conversations and travel (to conferences and visits; Mary to Iceland and Hafdís to Oregon).

Our goal is to improve our professional dialogue with teachers in ways that extend our capacity to critically reflect on, evaluate, and improve our practice. This is a process of dialogue and mutual growth for us and for the teachers in our classes. Our research has developed through three stages.

Stage 1: introduction of PWT instrument and process in teacher education classes

We used the PWT instrument in our courses and projects, and then discussed our experience and continued the development as we learned. We began by asking teachers to work on their PWTs as individuals, but we learned it is better to use a combination of individual reflection and dialogue with colleagues.

Stage 2: extension of the instrument to include critical, cultural, and socio-historical perspectives

Teachers found making connections between their personal experiences and what was happening in the school and broader community difficult. Based on our evaluation data and a related research project, we developed the process to support broader and more critical dialogue.

Stage 3: continued use of the PWT instrument and incorporation of new ideas

We extended the use of the PWT to different groups of teachers (including whole school communities), other professional groups, and research projects. In response to our research and to suggestions from teachers who had used the PWT for one year or more to support their professional growth, we added an introductory page so that teachers could begin with a more open-ended and visual concept map of their work before starting on the more analytical sections.

Research and evaluation data include:

1   evaluation data from classes and workshops,
2   document reviews (that is, teachers' documentation of their Professional Working Theory, and research proposals using the PWT),
3   the self-study of our use of the PWT framework for five-and-a-half years, and
4   two related research projects (Dalmau, 2001; Guðjónsdóttir, 2000).

The nature and purpose of self-study

Our efforts to frame the discourse for teachers led to two outcomes that are relevant to this discussion:

For the teachers

The framed and situated dialogue led the teachers to a rich analysis of their professional identity, which was articulated in terms of their practice and supported their work on their own self-studies.

The teachers located their professional identity in the consideration of the phenomena of their professional role as it was visible in their practice. Their felt experience was not sufficient to unlock this understanding for them. This occurred over time as they located the personal experience of their role in the shared experience of the teaching profession and used analytical frames of meaning to support connection-building between implicit and explicit (or formal) theory and between lived experience and socio-cultural/political influences and there was a stronger sense of personal professional identity in these groups of educators.

For us

The systematic framing of the dialogue quickly led us beyond the improvement of our teaching to questions about the nature of the processes we were using with teachers and the nature of the knowledge that was thus generated.

The self-study process not only provided us with information about "what worked" or "how we could improve our discourse with teachers", but also raised questions about the *processes* of learning, knowledge creation, and research.

These experiences led us to question the nature and purpose of self-study, and to identify three broad understandings of self-study in our work:

1   exploration of our professional identity (psychological or therapeutic focus),
2   systematic understanding and recreation of our practice (practice research and improvement focus), and
3   creation of new knowledge and contribution to educational discourse (conceptual and dialogic focus).

While each of these aspects is important, the "self" in the title sometimes seems to tip the balance in favor of personal exploration and a quest for self-understanding. However, in this experience, we found that if we and the teachers remained at this level, we were often trapped in stereotypic and unidentified tacit assumptions. Conversely, as we extended the research focus, a deeper level of personal and professional understanding was achieved.

Self-study and knowledge creation

In July 2000, we created for discussion a tentative map of the knowledge-creation process in practitioner research. In this schema we identified four possible processes that are more or less sequential, but may also be iterative and overlapping. For each process we have begun to identify actions, relationships, and questions related to meaning and knowledge creation.

Four research processes

Throughout the four processes, practitioner researchers remain focused on the "real world" of their work and important questions related to their practice. However, at each stage of the research they will also ground their study in broader contexts and discourse. The outcomes of practitioner research will be related to the quality of:

1   research partnerships,
2   critical and supportive contacts with "questioning others", and
3   support to go beyond unconscious local assumptions about the *status quo*.

The four processes support a dynamic and creative partnership in local and systemic knowledge creation.

Process 1: designing and beginning the research

Practitioner researchers are focused on questions about practice and the improvement of practice. They are interrogating their ideas, their questions, the research milieu, and the positive and negative implications of doing the research, and they are establishing research partnerships, with a particular focus on those who will be directly involved (for example, students, other faculty members).

Process 2: collecting and reviewing data – an iterative process of data collection, review, action, and continued collection

Researchers also review the impact of the research process on all participants, and begin to identify trends, contradictions, dilemmas, and questions emerging from the process.

Process 3: interpretation and testing of meaning in the local context

Researchers continue to work in collaboration with *close* others and research partners, students, other educators, administrators and support personnel, parents, and local, district or academic partners. They are engaged in the overall review of data and the process to date, generation of new questions, identification of early assumptions of meaning, and framed relational analysis.

Process 4: extension of meaning into broader contexts

Researchers continue to work in collaboration with close others and research partners, students, other educators, administrators and support personnel, parents, and local, district or academic partners. They begin to extend the discourse to other members of the educational community (with similar and

divergent perspectives in district, state, national, and international environments). They also relate their understandings to established educational
theory.

We are interested in the flow between the local, the practical, and reflexive
dialogue. Knowledge is tested at two levels, both the rigorous demands of practice and the questions from the broader field work together in a dialectical
process that keeps knowledge alive and growing rather than stagnant and repetitive. It is equally important that practitioner researchers and academic
researchers are contributing partners in the dialogue of knowledge creation.

The questions of knowledge creation and the extension of discourse beyond
the local are important for self-study and teacher researchers. We have incorporated the questions that emerged in this study and the dialogic approaches into
new research projects at the same time as we continue the self-study. This
chapter represents our attempt to explore the creation of meaning and the
extension of the dialogue within the self-study framework.

Extending the inquiry

This inquiry arose from a perceived issue in our practice as teacher educators.
Our improved theoretical dialogue with teachers opened up new vistas of
inquiry into the nature and scope of the role of "responsive professional educators". Our experience also raised questions for us about the nature of self-study.
What are the relationships between improved practice, knowledge creation,
and participation in non-local educational discourse?

Teachers' voices are marginalized in the knowledge-creation discourse. Self-
study provides an important opportunity for university and school researchers to
do their "separate work together" and frame a shared discourse. The seriousness
with which we value the unique knowledge and experience that teachers bring
to educational discourse will be a measure of the seriousness of our endeavors to
include them.

ATTACHMENT 1

Example of teacher's use of the Professional Working Theory (PWT) instrument

The example in the following pages is the work of Rebekka Jónsdóttir, a teacher in an Icelandic school (K-9), which was translated from the Icelandic by Hafdís. Rebekka has about ten years' teaching experience since she graduated as a teacher. It is typical for Icelandic teachers to remain with the one group of students for several years, and Rebekka has taught her Grade 6 students for three years. She is strongly interested in diversity and in developing learning that responds to the individual needs and abilities of all students. This may be due in some part to the presence in her school of children from Islamic families of migrant workers from Eastern Europe (a new experience for Icelandic teachers). Rebekka's PWT was created during a professional development program in her school. All teachers and the principal participated in this program, facilitated by Hafdís.

Using the PWT instrument and process

Within the context of the one-year program of professional development, Hafdís and the group worked through the following stages:

Introductory presentation

Hafdís introduced the idea of Professional Working Theory, how it is developed, and how and why the instrument could be used.

Working on PWT in small groups

The whole group was divided into groups of two to four that met three times over a semester. At each meeting they focused on one of the sections – they began with "Practice" – and (a) discussed the topic, (b) talked about the reflective questions provided in the instrument and created new questions, and (c) took notes that related to their PWT. Between meetings the teachers worked on the related sections of their individual PWT, and completed the first stage of the process with their personal statement.

Facilitation

They integrated the PWT into an ongoing process of professional learning and school improvement, and made connections between reflections on their individual professionalism, and discussions of curriculum, student welfare and relationships between the school and the local community.

Individual teachers gave Hafdís a copy of their PWT, which enabled her to ask questions that led to further reflection in particular areas. For example, Rebekka noted in the practice section that she collaborated with parents – Hafdís asked her to think about what attitudes and expectations in the local community would support collaboration with the teachers (and what might make it difficult), and then reviewed the three levels of reflective questions related to this issue.

Reflective dialogue

The PWT instrument does not stand alone: it is used to support reflection and dialogue. In our reflections on this project though, we realized that this group of teachers had more difficulty in extending their reflection and discussions through the three levels of analysis than we had seen in some other projects. We think this is because Hafdís was not so closely involved in the dialogue. In the Fall, Hafdís will record her own and her students' reflections as she supports the dialogue that accompanies the development of the PWT with a group of teacher education students.

Continuing inquiry

As the teachers worked together during the year, they did not regard their PWT as finished, but as a living document that they changed, updated, questioned, and discussed. At the end of the year, they asked to continue working on the PWT during the next school year as they form their shared school mission.

New ideas

One of the teachers in this group suggested that he would like to begin the process with an open-ended exercise that would give him the opportunity to visualize all the many aspects and relationships of his day-to-day professional life. This led to the idea of starting with a new page (see example below).

Student teachers

Rebekka and her colleagues used the PWT differently from beginning teachers in teacher education programs. We have found that the process has supported students of teacher education to make connections between the theory they are studying in their classes and their experience in schools (and as learners themselves), and encouraged them to ask probing questions.

The example

The following example includes:

- The cover page of the PWT instrument.
- A summary of the contents of the instrument.
- Rebekka's notes on the pages for "Practice", "Theory", and "Ethics", and her "Personal Statement".

It does not include:

- The introductory page with an overview of the PWT.
- The new second page that is headed "Picture your role as a teacher".
- The pages that contain the reflective questions for consideration in each section (see Table 8.1 for an example of this material).

Professional Working Theory

Contents of the (PWT) Instrument

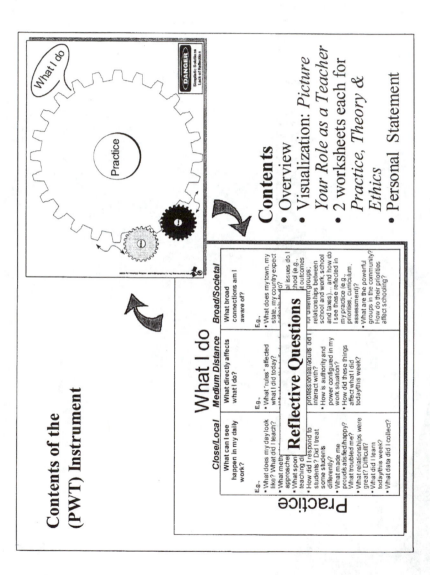

What I do

Practice

DANGER
Simplistic Solutions
Lack of Reflection

What I do

Close/Local	Medium Distance	Broad/Societal
What can I see happen in my daily work?	What directly affects what I do?	What broad connections am I aware of?
E.g.,	E.g.,	E.g.,
• What does my day look like? What did I teach?	• What "rules" affected what I did today?	• What does my town, my state, my country expect
• What meth... approache... teaching ol...		al issues do I nod (e.g., t outcomes
• What spon...		o?
• How did I respond to students? Did I treat some students differently?	professionals/adults did I interact with?	or unerent groups, relationships between school and work, school and work and taxes)... and how do I see these reflected in my practice (e.g., priorities, curriculum, assessment)?
• What made me proud/satisfied/happy? What troubled me?	• How is authority and power configured in my work situation?	
• What relationships were great? Difficult?	• How did these things affect what I did today/this week?	• What are the powerful groups in the community? How do their priorities affect schooling?
• What did I learn today/this week?		
• What data did I collect?		

Reflective Questions

Practice

Contents

• Overview
• Visualization: *Picture Your Role as a Teacher*
• 2 worksheets each for *Practice, Theory & Ethics*
• Personal Statement

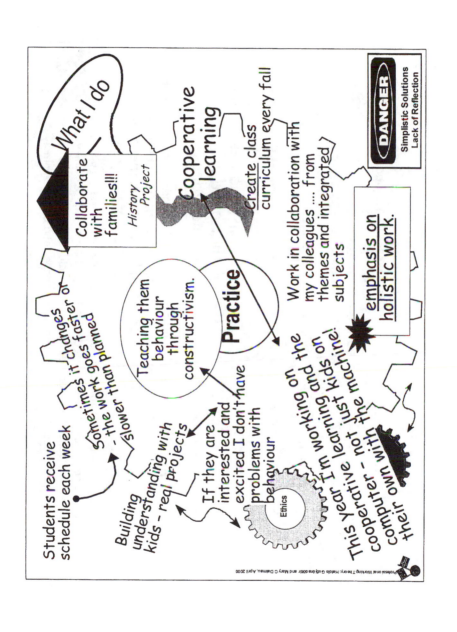

What I do

Collaborate with families!!!
History Project

Cooperative learning

Create class curriculum every fall

Work in collaboration with my colleagues .... from themes and integrated subjects

DANGER
Simplistic Solutions
Lack of Reflection

Practice

Teaching them behaviour through constructivism.

emphasis on holistic work.

Students receive schedule each week

Sometimes it changes or the work goes faster or slower than planned

Building understanding with kids – real projects

If they are interested and excited I don't have problems with behaviour

Ethics

This year I'm working on the cooperative – not just machine! computer with the kids on learning their own with

Professional Working Theory; Hafdís Guðjónsdóttir and Mary C Dalmau, April 2000

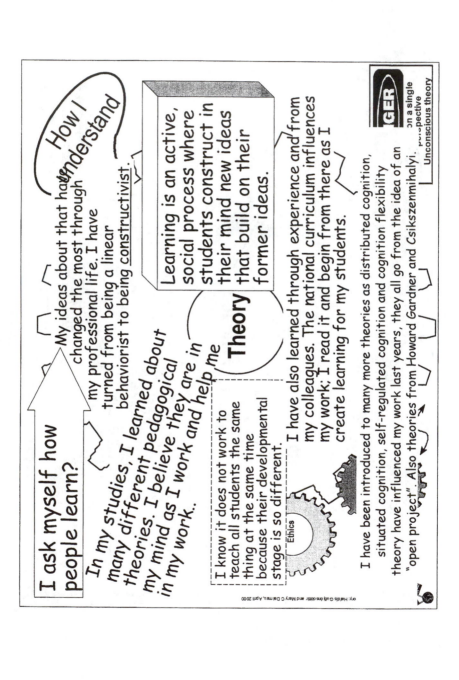

I ask myself how people learn?

How I understand

My ideas about that have changed the most through my professional life. I have turned from being a linear behaviorist to being constructivist.

In my studies, I learned about many different theories. I believe they are in my mind as I work and help me in my work.

I learned about different pedagogical theories. I believe they are in my mind as I work and help me in my work.

Learning is an active, social process where students construct in their mind new ideas that build on their former ideas.

Theory

I know it does not work to teach all students the same thing at the same time because their developmental stage is so different.

I have also learned through experience and from my colleagues. The national curriculum influences my work; I read it and begin from there as I create learning for my students.

Ethics

I have been introduced to many more theories as distributed cognition, situated cognition, self-regulated cognition and cognition flexibility theory have influenced my work last years, they all go from the idea of an "open project". Also theories from Howard Gardner and Csikszenmihalyi.

on a single perspective
Unconscious theory

GER

ory: Hafdís Guðjónsdóttir and Mary C Dalmau, April 2000

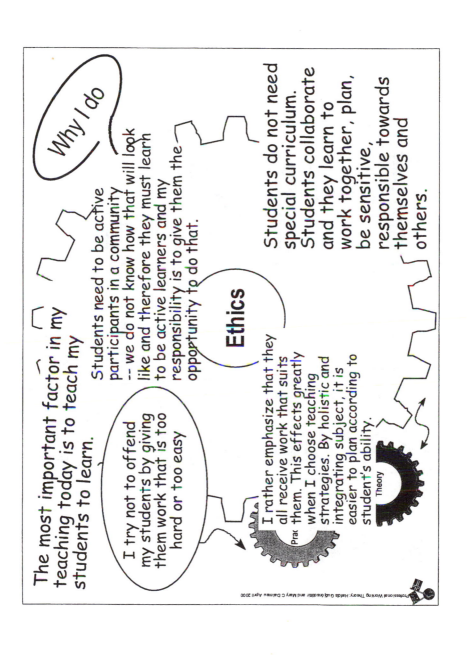

The most important factor in my teaching today is to teach my students to learn.

Why I do

I try not to offend my students by giving them work that is too hard or too easy

Students need to be active participants in a community -- we do not know how that will look like and therefore they must learn to be active learners and my responsibility is to give them the opportunity to do that.

Ethics

I rather emphasize that they all receive work that suits them. This effects greatly when I choose teaching strategies. By holistic and integrating subject, it is easier to plan according to student's ability.

Prac   Theory

Students do not need special curriculum. Students collaborate and they learn to work together, plan, be sensitive, responsible towards themselves and others.

Professional Working Theory

Personal Statement

I believe it is the most important is to prepare or support students to be independent, positive, believe in themselves and have the ability to work with others. If I manage that, I am satisfied.

My professional working theory is established from all kinds of ideas. It has developed through time. What influences it to change are ideas from others that I take notice of or I question. Sometimes I take them up again and other times I do not. I construct my P.W.T. myself; no one can do that for me because my P.W.T. is what I do or what I want to do as the teacher of my students. I try ideas with my students and they work.

Ideas come from all over, my colleagues, journals, from workshops, my mother, from the world news or from my subconsciousness that suddenly has set an old idea into context with even an older idea. In this whirlpool process, the sureness and the question are constantly exchanging but together they are the driving power in these constant speculations about human kind.

Professional Working Theory: Hardis Guoj dotitir and Mary C. Dalmau, April 2000

Notes

1   We would like to acknowledge the contribution made to this chapter by the many teachers who worked on PWT with us and taught us so much; our colleagues in the S-STEP SIG of AERA (see Note 7); the International Women's Group (Eugene, Oregon), in particular the participants at the third Herstmonceux S-STEP Conference (2000); Anne Freese, Melissa Heston, Clare Kosnik, Barbara Morgan-Fleming, Tom Russell and Anastasia Samaras who worked with us on the paper at the S-STEP Pre-conference in Seattle (2001); Françoise Bodone, Joyce Dean, Nitza Schwabsky, Jane Gathoni Njoora and Hafthor Guðjónson who reviewed the text for us; and, last but not least, John Loughran and Mary Lynn Hamilton for all their support.
2   Action, teacher, participatory, and self-study research.
3   See the second part of this chapter: "Five years of collaborative self-study".
4   We have published or presented earlier versions of this analysis in Dalmau (2000, 2001), Guðjónsdóttir (2000), Guðjónsdóttir and Dalmau (2000), Dalmau and Guðjónsdóttir (2001).
5   These roles have been further developed through Hafdís' research with Icelandic teachers (Guðjónsdóttir, 2000).
6   In addition to the citation referenced here, we found the following texts enriched our understanding of this perspective: Britzman (1991), Baird and Northfield (1992, 1993), Gitlin (1994), Gitlin and Russell (1994), Lamphere (1994), Loughran (1996), and Hamilton (1998).
7   At the same time we joined a new community of practice: the American Educational Research Association (AERA), Special Interest Group (SIG) Self-Study of Teacher Education Practices (S-STEP). We thus began to share the discourse of self-study research and teacher education – a process of immense learning and growth for both of us.

References and further reading

Ainscow, M. (1991) "Effective schools for all: An alternative approach to special needs in education", in M. Ainscow (ed.) *Effective Schools for All*, London: David Fulton Publishers, pp. 1–19.

Anderson, G.L., Herr, K. and Nihlen, A.S. (1994) *Studying Your Own School: An educator's guide to qualitative practitioner research*, Thousand Oaks, CA: Corwin Press.

Apple, M. (1995) "Cultural capital and official knowledge", in M. Berube and G. Nelson (eds) *Higher Education under Fire: Politics, economics, and the crisis of the humanities*, New York: Routledge, pp. 91–107.

Baird, J.R. and Northfield, J.R. (eds) (1992) *Learning from the PEEL Experience*, Melbourne: Monash University Printery.

—— (eds) (1993) *Improving the Quality of Learning and Teaching: An Australian case study – the PEEL Project*, 2nd edn, Melbourne: Monash University Printery.

Bertrand, Y. (1995) *Contemporary Theories and Practice in Education*, Madison, WI: Magna Publications.

Britzman, D. (1991) *Practice makes Practice: A critical study of learning to teach*, Albany, NY: State University of New York Press.

Chaiklin, S. and Lave, J. (eds) (1996) *Understanding Practice: Perspectives on activity and context*, Cambridge: Cambridge University Press.

Cochran-Smith, M. and Lytle, S.L. (1993) *Inside Outside: Teacher research and knowledge*, New York: Teachers College Press.

—— (1999) "The teacher research movement: A decade later", *Educational Researcher*, 28 (7): 15–25.

Dalmau, M.C. (2000) *Taking a fresh look at education: Asking powerful questions, seeking powerful answers (Invited Address)*, paper presented at the National Academy for Academic Research Symposium: Association for the Advancement of Educational Research, and National Academy for Educational Research (Joint Meeting), Sawgrass, FL, November.

—— (2001) *Will the mountains we face, be accessible from the roads we have traveled? Reconstructing learning and change with teachers*, unpublished Ph.D. thesis, University of Oregon, Eugene, OR.

Dalmau, M.C. and Guðjónsdóttir, H. (2001) *Framing professional discourse with teachers: Professional working theory*, paper presented at the AERA pre-conference meeting of the S-STEP SIG, Seattle, April.

Dalmau, M.C., Hatton, G. and Spurway, O. (1991) *ISI Program: Inclusive Schooling Integration*, Melbourne: Department of School Education, Victoria.

Darling-Hammond, L. (1997) "Reframing the school reform agenda: Developing capacity for school transformation", in E. Clinchy (ed.) *Transforming Public Education: A new course for America's future*, New York: Teachers College Press.

Day, C., Calderhead, J. and Denicolo, P. (eds) (1993) *Research on Teacher Thinking: Understanding professional development*, London: Falmer Press.

Duckworth, E. (1987) "Teaching as research", in M. Okazawa-Rey, J. Anderson and R. Traver (eds) *Teachers, Teaching and Teacher Education*, Cambridge, MA: Harvard Educational Review, pp. 261–75.

Elmore, R.F. (1996) "Getting to scale with good educational practice", *Harvard Educational Review*, 66 (1): 1–26.

Freire, P. (1993) *Pedagogy of the Oppressed*, trans. M. Bergman Ramos, New York: Continuum.

—— (1998) *Teachers as Cultural Workers: Letters to those who dare to teach*, trans. D. Macedo, D. Koike and A. Oliveira, Boulder, CO: Westview Press.

Gitlin, A. (ed.) (1994) *Power and Method: Political activism and educational research*, New York and London: Routledge.

Gitlin, A. and Russell, R. (1994) "Alternative methodologies and the research context", in A. Gitlin (ed.) *Power and method: Political activism and educational research*, New York and London: Routledge, pp. 181–202.

Guðjónsdóttir, H. (2000) *Responsive professional practice: Teachers analyze the theoretical and ethical dimensions of their work in diverse classrooms*, unpublished doctoral dissertation, Department of Special Education and Community Resources, University of Oregon, Eugene, OR.

Guðjónsdóttir, H. and Dalmau, M.C. (2000) *Professional working theory: Beginning (and extending) theoretical discussions with teachers*, paper presented at the meeting of the AERA, New Orleans, April.

Hamilton, M.L. (ed.) (1998) *Reconceptualizing Teaching Practice: Self-study in teacher education*, London: Falmer Press.

Handal, G. and Lauvås, P. (1982) *På egne vilkår: En strategi for veiledning med lærere*, Oslo: J.W. Cappelens forlag a.s.

—— (1987) *Promoting Reflective Teaching: Supervision in action*, London: Society for Research into Higher Education/Open University Press.

Hargreaves, A. and Goodson, I.F. (1996) "Teachers' professional lives: Aspirations and actualities", in I.F. Goodson and A. Hargreaves (eds) *Teachers' Professional Lives*, London: Falmer Press, pp. 1–27.

Hargreaves, A., Earl, L. and Ryan, J. (1996) *Schooling for Change: Reinventing education for early adolescents*, London: Falmer Press.

hooks, b. (1994) *Teaching to Transgress: Education as the practice of freedom*, New York: Routledge.

Jóhannesson, I.A. (1992) "Af vettvangi íslenskra menntaumbóta: Kennarafræði sem kapítal", *Uppeldi og menntun*, 1 (1): 147–64.

Kincheloe, J.L. (1991) *Teachers as Researchers: Qualitative inquiry as a path to empowerment*, London: Falmer Press.

Lamphere, L. (1994) "Expanding our notions of 'Critical Qualitative Methodology': Bringing race, class and gender into the discussion", in A. Gitlin (ed.) *Power and method: Political activism and educational research*, New York and London: Routledge, pp. 217–26.

Loughran, J.J. (1996) *Developing Reflective Practice: Learning about teaching and learning through modeling*, London: Falmer Press.

Loughran, J.J. and Northfield, J. (1996) *Opening the Classroom Door: Teacher, researcher, learner*, London: Falmer Press.

McLaughlin, M.W. and Talbert, J.E. (1993) "How the world of students and teachers challenges policy coherence", in S.H. Fuhrman (ed.) *Designing Coherent Education Policy: Improving the system*, San Francisco, CA: Jossey-Bass, pp. 220–49.

Northfield, J.R. and Loughran, J.J. (1996) *Learning through self-study: Exploring the development of knowledge*, paper presented at the first international conference on S-STEP, Herstmonceux Castle, East Sussex, August.

Rizvi, F. and Kemmis, S. (1987) *Dilemmas of Reform: The Participation and Equity Program in Victorian schools*, Geelong, VA: Deakin Institute for Studies in Education.

Ross, E.W., Cornett, J.W. and McCutcheon, G. (eds) (1992) *Teacher Personal Theorizing: Connecting curriculum practice, theory and research*, Albany, NY: State University of New York Press.

Slee, R., Weiner, G. and Tomlinson, S. (eds) (1998) *School Effectiveness for Whom? Challenges to the school effectiveness and school improvement movements*, London: Falmer Press.

Smyth, J. (1999) "Researching the cultural politics of teachers' learning", in J.J. Loughran (ed.) *Researching Teaching: Methodologies and practice for understanding pedagogy*, London: Falmer Press, pp. 67–82.

Sykes, G. (1990) "Fostering teacher professionalism in schools", in R.F. Elmore (ed.) *Restructuring Schools: The next generation of educational reform*, San Francisco, CA: Jossey-Bass, pp. 59–96.

Van Manen, M. (1991) *The Tact of Teaching: The meaning of pedagogical thoughtfulness*, Albany, NY: State University of New York Press.

Whitehead, J. (1993) *The Growth of Educational Knowledge: Creating your own living educational theories*, Bournemouth: Hyde Publications.

Zeichner, K.M. (1994) "Research on teacher thinking and different views of reflective practice in teaching and teacher education", in I. Carlgren, G. Handal and S. Waage (eds) *Teachers' Minds and Actions: Research on teachers' thinking and practice*, London: Falmer Press, pp. 9–27.

9 Can self-study challenge the belief that telling, showing, and guided practice constitute adequate teacher education?

Charles B. Myers

Introduction

As a teacher educator who has been engaged in inquiry into my own practice for a long time, I have been troubled by what I see as the apparent reluctance of many fellow teacher educators to use self-study to reform their work of educating teachers. For some, the stumbling block seems to be the very activity of serious and thorough self-study of their personal practice. They just do not look at what they do professionally in a probing and critical way. Others study their own work and themselves in that work well, but they do not take the next step of expanding that self-study beyond themselves to include their teacher education colleagues, and the programs in which they and their colleagues work. A result, at least as I view the situation, is that self-study is rarely used in significant ways to reform teacher education programs. Teacher educators appear to be ready to study the teacher education practices of others, but not their own or those of the programs in which they conduct their practice of educating teachers.

My discomfort with this phenomenon is rooted in my personal conceptualization of self-study. I see it as both a means of investigation and analysis that starts with one's self, and as a tool for professional improvement. I think of it as a conscious, conscientious, honest, organized probing into one's professional work. Its focus, for me, is on what I and my colleagues do, or should do, as teacher educators. Its guiding questions include: "What do I actually do as a teacher of teachers and as an investigator of teacher education?", "Why do I do what I do?", "How good is my practice?", "How can I improve?", "How can I inform others about teacher education?", "How can I, my colleagues, and those whom we inform make teacher education better?" In short, I see self-study as a form of self-analysis that leads to self-improvement for individuals, groups, and institutions.

From this perspective, the nature of and need for self-study does not change in form as it moves from a focus on an individual to a program, but it does become more complex and more difficult to initiate and sustain. This increase in complexity and difficulty occurs primarily because more individuals are involved, more cooperation and trust are required, and there are more opportunities to choose not to participate.

There are three primary reasons why I am concerned about this reluctance to use self-study to reform teacher education. First, there seems to be consensus that teacher education as it is now practiced is in need of reform, and that teacher educators as a whole are not willing to lead that reform. In fact, many would suggest that teacher educators are more a part of the problem than a part of the solution.

Second, the widely practiced approach to teacher education is an approach that stresses telling, showing, and guided practice, an approach that is in conflict with current ideas about how learning occurs and how teaching can best produce learning. This existing out-of-date approach assumes that learning to teach is a rather static process by which more experienced and better read teacher educators tell their teachers-in-training what good teaching is, show them how to do it, and guide them as they try to do it themselves. It presumes that the "stuff" of teaching is a rather stable, already known general set of principles and skills that are to be handed down from one generation of artisans to another. This view of teaching also conflicts with the thrust of Piagetian (Piaget, 1968, 1977) and Deweyan (Dewey, 1933) ideas about how learning occurs. It conflicts with what informed teacher educators "tell" their students about the nature of constructivist learning and teaching. There is, then, an ongoing contradiction between what we know about learning and teaching, and what we do as teachers of teachers. One wonders whether we see the contradiction or are simply reluctant to change.

Third, self-study, in my view, is an obvious way of critiquing our current practice and making it better – genuine reform. Self-study, then, should be an effective way for teacher educators to be informed about their practice so that they can practice what they preach. However, I have come to believe that many teacher educators do not engage in self-study for this purpose. My concerns have led me to ask the research question that is the focus of this chapter: *How can self-study, particularly the self-study that is pursued by the members of the American Educational Research Association Special Interest Group: Self-Study of Teacher Education Practices, reform in significant ways the telling, showing, and guided-practice manner in which most teachers are now educated?*

Research question

Because of my self-study orientation, this question developed over time from my personal and professional experiences as a teacher educator. My inquiry is therefore guided by experiences that include:

1   my teaching of prospective teachers and future teacher educators,
2   various strands of my own professional study of teacher education,
3   efforts by both myself and my colleagues at Vanderbilt University to promote reform in our own teacher education program, and
4   my efforts to promote reform in how teachers are educated beyond my own institution.

Through my reflection on the combination of these professional experiences in teacher education, I have developed perspectives on teacher education practices, the potential reform of teacher education, and the use of self-study as an investigative tool.

These experiences also include activity on two professional planes – at my own institution and at the national (US) level. Considering my own efforts, it seems reasonable to say that, beyond my own teaching, my efforts at reforming teacher education at my own institution – both my research and my push for programmatic reform beyond the telling, showing, guided-practice approach to teacher education – have had only limited success in improving the way my department's prospective teachers are educated. Ironically though, my activity and efforts in reform of teacher education at the national level have had some impact.

It is interesting as a member of the teacher education community for me to consider carefully this difference in impact. For example, although significant, well-recognized research on how school students learn is a hallmark of my institution's research efforts (see, for example, Thompson, 1996; Kinzer and Leu, 1997; Risko, Roskos and Vukelich, 1999; Cognition and Technology Group, 2000; Cobb, 2001; Cobb *et al.*, 2001; Kinzer, 2001; Risko and Bromley, 2001; Reith *et al.*, forthcoming), our teacher education program as a whole, as well as our graduate programs for teacher educators, seem mired in the past. Most of our faculty seem almost unwilling to engage in reform activity in *our* teaching-of-teachers' responsibilities. This apparent reluctance to study and improve our own teaching in teacher education then affects our entire program. Strangely enough, it happens even though our teacher education reputation places our programs at the top of national rankings.

At the national level, my efforts at formulating and implementing the National Council for the Social Studies (NCSS) national standards for the preparation of secondary- and middle-school social studies teachers have developed into models for the reform of the subject-matter components of teacher education programs, for national teacher accrediting and licensing policies, and for federal and state teacher licensing requirements. Because these efforts have been incorporated into the accreditation standards and procedures of the National Council for Accreditation of Teacher Education (NCATE), and a number of state standards and procedures for approving college and university teacher education programs, my national standards work is being used in a top-down fashion to force teacher educators to improve their practice.

This phenomenon, in effect, means that my work at teacher education reform nationally is having a greater impact on improving teacher education through the imposition of standards from outside of teacher education programs than through self-initiated self-study by individual teacher education faculties – especially the one of which I am a member! This situation makes me uncomfortable because I want to believe that self-study by teacher educators can be as good a means for teacher education reform as the imposition of requirements by outsiders. I want to see us as teacher educators being involved in self-study, and therefore taking on the responsibility of reforming ourselves.

Purpose

Because I think of self-study as profession-long investigations and analyses that center on self – what one does, who one is, and why – this chapter is not a report of research already completed. Instead, it is:

1 a reporting of my journey as I have engaged in and continue this inquiry,
2 a step in the inquiry process itself, with the listing of questions I have been addressing and tentative responses that I have been considering, and
3 an invitation to readers of this chapter to join the inquiry.

I have therefore organized this chapter by describing (briefly) my own professional experiences as an educator of teachers, as an educator of teacher educators, and as a teacher education reformer. I do this to explain how I think my own self-study has played a significant role in what I do professionally. Next I list and explain the questions that have occurred to me as specific probes into the general question I raised at the start of this chapter. I follow each question with attempts to provide some personal tentative responses. I then conclude the chapter by drawing parallels between my experiences and responses to the questions, and the professional experiences and ideas that I have heard other self-study-oriented teacher educators express over the years as they describe their professional work and their self-studies.

I have organized my approach to this chapter in the hope that, by considering my journey in this way, the questions I raise will further our thinking about how we can better use self-study to promote programmatic and institutional reform in teacher education.

My professional experiences

My teaching of prospective teachers and future teacher educators

I teach three courses each year: the multi-section, required, introductory course for all undergraduate teacher education students at my university (about 115 students each year), and two graduate-level seminars for experienced teachers who are preparing to become teacher educators (usually 10–15 students each). All three courses are constructivist in nature because of the manner in which they ask students to continuously assess their previous and current learning, trace their changing ideas and values, and relate what they think of themselves and their beliefs to their evolving conceptualizations of teaching and learning. My general intent for all three courses is to force the students to modify (in radical ways, I hope) their ideas about teaching, learning, and themselves. I try to create interpersonal exchanges and intellectual experiences for the students which make them realize that their ideas at the start of the courses, which I think emanate from what Dan Lortie (1975) called "the apprenticeship of observation", are both uninformed and inadequate for the professional careers they plan to pursue. I believe all three courses are far removed from the telling, showing, and guided-practice approach to teacher education.

All of the courses are demanding in terms of the amount of reading required, the questions that are probed, the amount and depth of student-to-student intellectual engagement expected, and the extent of personal reflection that evolves. The undergraduate course is also technologically intensive, and has been characterized by students as "too hard for an education course but essential if you think you want to be a teacher". The graduate-level seminars are intellectually intense, and center upon student-to-student joint and competitive assignments in which students consciously push each other to think deeply about teaching, learning, and their anticipated professional lives as teacher educators.

So, why is my teaching of these courses relevant to this chapter?

- My approach to all three courses is radically different from my teaching ten or so years ago, and my involvement in self-study is why I have changed.
- Much of what I am trying to do in all three courses comes from my belief that self-study is a central core of learning, especially the learning of teachers.
- My perception is that my faculty colleagues at Vanderbilt are primarily telling, showing, and guided-practice teacher educators who do not know what I attempt to do in the courses and show little interest in learning about it. But the graduate student course participants do understand, and often become converts even as they continue as teaching assistants in the telling, showing, guided-practice courses. This creates a dissonance that provides wonderful learning opportunities for the graduate students and for me.

My professional study of teacher education

My professional study of teacher education over the past two decades or more has engaged three somewhat parallel clusters of questions:

1   What would truly good pre-K-12 schools look like? How can we create them? How can current schools be re-created?
2   What are the essential characteristics and capabilities of good teachers for these good schools? How can we educate/develop them? How can current teacher education be reformed?
3   What are appropriate standards to be expected of pre-K-12 teachers, particularly in terms of teacher subject-matter knowledge and competence? My personal focus for this question has been secondary social studies.

My study of what constitutes good schools and how to create them has involved long-term efforts at forming and guiding local professional development schools, at studying other professional development schools and the professional development school movement in general, at conceptualizing images of what good schools might look like, and at initiating and guiding teacher-based school reform endeavors in local high schools. The effort at conceptualizing good schools resulted in a book with Douglas J. Simpson called *Re-creating schools* (Myers and Simpson, 1998). The teacher-based school reform project, Practice-based Professional Improvement Project, was a three-year endeavor that completed its third year in June 2000.

My search for essential characteristics and capabilities of good teachers, and how to develop them, rests primarily on my experimentation with the analyses of my own courses. This has led to a manuscript in development titled *Re-Creating teacher education* (my thinking has been influenced by, for example, Cochran-Smith, 1991, 2001; Eraut, 1994; Gardner, 1995; Russell and Korthagen, 1995; Darling-Hammond, 1996; Loughran, 1996; Loughran and Northfield, 1996; Loughran and Russell, 1997; Palmer, 1998; Korthagen *et al.*, 2001).

My standards development activity is focused on the formulation, adoption, and implementation of new national (US) standards for the preparation of middle- and high-school social studies teachers in the NCATE system of teacher education accreditation. I have chaired the NCSS task force that developed the standards, served as primary writer of the standards documents, chaired the Standards Assessment Criteria Project (which helps institutions assess their social studies teacher education programs), and served as lead author of the *Guidebook for colleges and universities preparing social studies teachers* (Myers *et al.*, 2000a, 2000b, 2000c; Wise and Leibband, 2001). Currently, I coordinate the national review of university programs that prepare new secondary- and middle-school social studies teachers; I serve on several national boards and committees associated with this standards development effort; I am conducting a six-university, three-state study of the processes universities follow as they attempt to meet the standards; and I consult with institutions for their standards-meeting self-studies and program reform endeavors.

My efforts at teacher education reform

In my roles of faculty member, department chairperson, associate dean of academic affairs, assistant to the dean for teacher education, and designer and director of experimental teacher education programs over more than thirty years at Vanderbilt University, I have tried to promote in our programs continuous improvement in, and experimental models for, teacher education. Some of these efforts have met with success, at least for a time, but I believe that, as the title and tone of this chapter imply, our current programs are more static and tell/show/guided-practice endeavors than they are constructivist, continuous-learning, and experimental. And this is the case even though, unlike many other colleges of teacher education, my institution has few external forces that inhibit experimentation or serious programmatic self-study and improvement.

In contrast, my work at reform beyond the university seems to have much more noticeable positive impact on how teachers teach and how students learn.

This is very troubling for me because, although my beyond-the-university endeavors incorporate self-study principles and practices, they also contain two elements that are not characteristic of my local attempts at reform: they are either theoretical studies with little by way of implementation-level changes in teacher education practice or they include serious top-down pressures to change.

Why self-study?

As I have journeyed through these three parallel paths of my professional career – teacher educator, investigator into teacher education practices, and teacher education reformer – I have become disgruntled and impatient with what I have seen. Thus, I have developed the following critical opinions:

- Teacher education across many institutions is not good. As a whole, teacher educators are more a part of the problem than part of the solution.
- Few teacher educators, including those who readily critique and criticize classroom teachers and other educators, make serious attempts to improve their personal practice or the programs in which they teach.

As I have drawn these conclusions, I have gradually eased into (rather arrogantly, I admit) a role of subtle rebel. I decided to "make a difference" in my part of my professional world. About that time, I began to learn about self-study among teacher educators. What I discovered seemed to be an appropriate tool to help me in my rebellion. It identified for me a place to concentrate my energies, and it put me in contact with other teacher educators who shared my concerns. I could start with my own practice and push out from that point. At a minimum I could affect what I do. I became a convert to the process and an advocate for its use.

Questions and possible responses

At this point in my journey, I am asking the questions and considering the tentative responses that follow.

1   *Why do so many teacher education programs continue to follow a telling, showing, guided-practice approach to instruction at a time when research and teacher educator opinion suggest that it is not an effective way to learn and teach in a rapidly changing, post-modern society?*

Because of my knowledge of my own institution's programs, the programs of professional colleagues at other institutions, and the many programs that I learn about through my national standards work, I firmly believe that the telling, showing, guided-practice approach to teacher education is dominant and well entrenched. I see it in the teacher education classes I observe and study, in the complaints of doctoral students who approach teacher education with an idealism that is dashed in the courses for which they assist, and in the disappointment of teacher education students who feel their courses are not engaging and less than scholarly. I see it also in the intellectually weak coursework that is described in the institutional reports submitted for review as part of my national (US) teacher education program accreditation responsibilities. But why is this the case? I suggest the following as possible reasons:

- Many teacher education faculty as individuals and as cohorts are simply dated in what they do and what they know about their field, and about the impact of their work. They were taught in a tell, show, guided-practice way, so they teach that way.
- Many of these faculty are too busy, or think they are too busy, to study and improve their practice at the same time that they teach and conduct their research. For them, self-study of their practice comes only after the more routine day-to-day demands of their professional work are satisfied; and their work in meeting those demands is rarely done.
- Many are not secure enough in what they do to risk self-study, especially study at the programmatic level with colleagues. Doing so exposes too many weaknesses – their own, their colleagues, and those of their program.

2   *Why do some teacher educators seriously study their own practice, continuously reflecting upon it, and experiment with their own hypotheses about reform, while others do not?*

I think my last point in the above response is also instrumental here. Study of one's own practice makes one vulnerable, and a willingness to allow oneself to be vulnerable requires both security and courage. Despite what we know about learning and teaching, many teacher educators are not secure and courageous enough to question what they do, to experiment. They choose to view teaching as doing what they do "the right way", rather than as a continuous process of experimentation, reflection, analysis, and learning from experience. They seem to think that teaching in ways that are not "the right way" is, in effect, poor teaching. They cannot risk being thought of as poor teachers. Teacher educators cannot be poor teachers.

3   *Why do some of the teacher educators who engage in individual personal self-reflection and professional experimentation with their own courses and students do so only privately and avoid engaging colleagues from their home institution in similar cooperative endeavors?*

This phenomenon is one that I find most challenging, because I face it so often in my work. I see it in colleagues who simply refuse to participate in joint self-study endeavors and in institutional accreditation reports that avoid serious critical descriptions of what they do. I think there are at least three reasons for this:

- Even teacher educators who have overcome the fear and threat of personal self-study are fearful of the exposure that comes with the more public self-study with colleagues and the possible loss of face, for themselves and their colleagues, when things get difficult.
- The colleagues of many, maybe most, individual teacher education faculty members who engage in personal self-study are simply not willing to participate in self-study with them.
- Programmatic and multiple-faculty self-study efforts are always more public, more risky, and more difficult than those at the personal level.

4   *Why are some of these self-studying teacher educators more willing to explore their efforts with their AERA S-STEP colleagues from other institutions than with their own home-institution colleagues?*

I think there are three primary reasons:

- S-STEP colleagues have chosen to be active self-studiers, so they have positive orientations toward self-study before and as they develop their S-STEP relationships.
- They do not see each other's day-to-day work up close, and can hide what they choose to hide.
- They can focus on their personal activity rather than on what they do programmatically.

5   *What are the circumstances and conditions that inhibit teacher educators who engage in personal self-study and individual professional experimentation from going public to the extent of effectively promoting self-study and reform throughout the programs and organizations with which they are affiliated?*

I see this phenomenon in the statements of teacher educators who complain in casual conversation about the programs in which they work, but avoid putting their statements into writing and speak more cautiously in settings in which they can be overheard (I admit I do this myself). I think that at the core, these inhibiting factors are associated with personal security, interpersonal relationships (especially status relationships) among colleagues, and the fact that self-study among colleagues is really different from – and much more public, complex, difficult, and threatening – than personal self-study.

6   *Does the phenomenon of "unappreciated local expert" play significantly in inhibiting the spread of personal self-study to self-study among program colleagues and program reform?*

My response to this question is based on my personal experience, and on conversations with S-STEP colleagues. For example, a major topic of discussion at all S-STEP meetings concerns the question: "How can we persuade our colleagues at home and in the broader profession that self-study is worthy research?" So I think self-studiers are unappreciated in significant ways for three central reasons:

- College and university faculty tend to lack appreciation for colleagues whose work is different from their own.
- Self-study is not widely understood. Consequently, this lack of understanding leads to a lack of respect for it as a type of either research or means for professional advancement.
- Most self-studying faculty engages in their self-study in isolation from their local colleagues.

7   *Is the "bottom-up" approach of spreading personal self-study, reflection, and experimentation among individual teacher educators to clusters of colleagues and then to program-wide faculty (such as I imply with the above six questions) possible, feasible or efficient?*

I would like to hear others' responses to this question, because my response is rather negative. In my own work, my "bottom-up" efforts meet primarily with either non-response or passive resistance, while the outside standards that I helped to develop and impose upon teacher education faculty produce improvement in those teacher educators' teacher education programs. However, I do not know how thorough or how long-lasting the changes that result from outside pressure will be. I think they may lack serious self-study, reflection, and thoughtful experimentation, and, therefore, can easily be only superficial.

8   *Is a standards-based, legislated, "from-the-top" push for reform in how teachers are educated more appropriate/expedient for change in teacher education than a "bottom-up" approach based on the self-study of thoughtful, experiment-oriented teacher educator professionals?*

My response here parallels my answer to Question 7, and it is similarly negative in terms of my self-study biases. I think "from-the-top" reform is expedient, but it is appropriate only to the extent that it results in program improvement, and I fear that this type of improvement is often very limited. In my national accreditation work, I see teacher educators respond quickly and substantively to legislative and accreditation association demands, but I also see them revert to "business as usual" as soon as the outside pressure and scrutiny fades.

On the other hand, I believe that approaches that are based on the self-study of thoughtful, experiment-oriented teacher education professionals are more thorough, more significant, and more likely to be continuous. I see this also in my personal studies of change, and in my own case studies of institutions and programs. In essence, I think efforts to conform to imposed standards are usually seen as one-time chores to be completed, rather than long-term challenges to be pursued, and that changes based on self-study are more often parts of continuous programmatic improvement.

9   *What do these questions and our responses to them say about the nature and status of teacher education, and about how teacher education is perceived by teacher educators, as well as by those outside the profession?*

I think that my raising of these questions and my responses to them imply a pessimistic outlook on my part about the current nature and status of teacher education in general. I believe that most teacher educators are willing to perpetuate the telling, showing, guided-practice approach to what they do, and that most are not willing, or prepared, to engage in serious self-study of their work. They do not view teacher education as an evolving, learning professional experience.

10   *What do these questions and our responses imply about the future of teacher education?*

In my view, teacher education will not improve nearly as much or as fast as it needs to improve in the years ahead. The improvement that does occur will be more as a result of externally imposed standards than as a result of self-initiated self-study. But self-studiers must continue to push on. At a minimum, they can continue to improve their own practice.

11   *What do these questions and our responses imply about teacher educators as learning professionals? Are most teacher educators learning professionals?*

I think that most teacher educators are not learning professionals to the extent that they should be. But those who are engaged in self-study are different from most other professionals. They are continuously learning teachers and teacher educators, and continuing to do self-study is a contribution that they can make, not only to their own practice, but also to the profession as a whole.

Parallel questions and experiences

I chose to raise the eleven questions in this chapter not only to report on my own inquiry journey, but also because, over the years, I have heard other self-study-oriented teacher educators ask similar questions and describe similar personal professional experiences. I think an open discussion around the questions might help me and many others continue to address my general question: *How can self-study reform in significant ways the telling, showing, guided-practice manner in which most teachers are now educated?*

That question is at the heart of my professional work, and I am looking for suggestions, insights, and more probing questions. I need help as I investigate my own practice as a teacher educator/learner, and I suspect other researchers of teacher education would benefit as well. More importantly, if we continue to journey together, we will be better able to reform teacher education, at home and in the profession at large.

So let us have continuing discussions about how self-study, including our own self-study, can contribute to how teachers are educated and how the profession of teaching can be improved, both locally and nationally. Let us continue our collaborative study of our own and each other's self-study. Let us push that self-study beyond our personal activity to teacher education *programs* – those in which we work and those that we study.

References

Cobb, P. (2001) "Supporting the improvement of learning and teaching in social and institutional context", in S. Carver and D. Klahr (eds) *Cognition and Instruction: Twenty-five years of progress*, Mahwah, NJ: Erlbaum, pp. 455–78.

Cobb, P., Stephan, M., McClain, K. and Gravemeijer, K. (2001) "Participating in classroom mathematical practices", *Journal of the Learning Sciences*, 10: 113–64.

Cochran-Smith, M. (1991) "Learning to teach against the grain", *Harvard Educational Review*, 61 (3): 279–310.

—— (2001) "Editorial: Higher standards for prospective teachers: What's missing from the discourse", *Journal of Teacher Education*, 52: 179–81.

Cognition and Technology Group (2000) "Adventures in anchored instruction: Lessons from beyond the ivory tower", in R. Glaser (ed.) *Advances in Instructional Psychology: Educational design and cognitive science*, Mawah, NJ: Erlbaum, pp. 35–99.

Darling-Hammond, L. (1996) "The quiet revolution: Rethinking teacher development", *Educational Leadership*, 53 (6): 4–10.

Dewey, J. (1933) *How we Think: A restatement of the relation of reflective thinking to the educative process*, Boston, MA: D.C. Heath & Co.

Eraut, M. (1994) *Developing Professional Knowledge and Competence*, London: Falmer.

Gardner, J.W. (1995) *Self-renewal: The individual and the innovative society*, revised edn, New York: Norton. (First published in 1981.)

Kinzer, C.K. (2001) *Analyzing anchored instruction: Four ways of "unpacking" literate acts*, paper presented at the annual meeting of the National Reading Conference, San Antonio, TX.

Kinzer, C.K. and Leu, D.J. (1997) "The challenge of change: Exploring literacy and learning in electronic environments", *Language Arts*, 74 (2): 126–36.

Korthagen, F. A.J. *et al.* (2001) *Linking Practice and Theory: The pedagogy of realistic teacher education*, Mahwah, NJ: Erlbaum.

Lortie, D. (1975) *Schoolteacher: A sociological study*, Chicago, IL: University of Chicago Press.

Loughran, J.J. (1996) *Developing Reflective Practice: Learning about teaching and learning through modeling*, London: Falmer.

Loughran, J.J. and Northfield, J. (1996) *Opening the Classroom Door: Teacher, researcher, learner*, London: Falmer.

Loughran, J.J. and Russell, T. (eds) (1997) *Teaching About Teaching: Purpose, passion and pedagogy in teacher education*, London: Falmer.

Myers, C.B. and Simpson, D.J. (1998) *Re-creating Schools: Places where everyone learns and likes it*, Thousand Oaks, CA: Corwin Press.

Myers, C.B. *et al.* (2000a) *National Standards for Social Studies Teachers*, Washington, D.C.: National Council for the Social Studies.

—— (2000b) *Program Standards for the Initial Preparation of Teachers of Social Studies*, Washington, D.C.: National Council for the Social Studies.

—— (2000c) *Guidebook for Colleges and Universities Preparing Social Studies Teachers*, Washington, D.C.: National Council for the Social Studies.

Palmer, P.J. (1998) *The Courage to Teach: Exploring the inner landscape of a teacher's life*, San Francisco, CA: Jossey-Bass.

Piaget, J. (1968) *Six Psychological Studies*, trans. A. Tenzer, New York: Random House, Vintage.

—— (1977) *Psychology and Epistemology: Toward a theory of knowledge*, trans. A. Rosin, New York: Penguin.

Reith, H.J. *et al.* (forthcoming) "An analysis of the impact of anchored instruction on teaching and learning activities in two ninth-grade language arts classes", *Journal of Special Education technology*.

Risko, V.J. and Bromley, K. (eds) (2001) *Collaboration for Diverse Learners*, Newark, DE: IRA.

Risko, V., Roskos, K. and Vukelich, C. (1999) "Making connections: Pre-service teachers' reflection processes and strategies", in T. Shanahan and F. Rodriguez-Brown (eds) *48th National Reading Conference Yearbook*, Chicago, IL: National Reading Conference, pp. 412–22.

Russell, T. and Korthagen, F. (eds) (1995) *Teachers who Teach Teachers: Reflections on teacher education*, London: Falmer.

Thompson, P.W. (1996) "Imagery and the development of mathematical reasoning", in L.P. Steffe, P. Nesher, P. Cobb, G. Goldin and B. Greer (eds) *Theories of Mathematical Learning*, Hillsdale, NJ: Erlbaum, pp. 267–83.

Wise, A.E. and Leibband, J.A. (2001) "Standards in the new millennium: Where we are, where we're headed", *Journal of Teacher Education*, 52: 244–54.

Part III

Fostering social justice in teaching about teaching

10 The (in)visibility of race in narrative constructions of the self

Enora R. Brown

Introduction

> The social distribution of what is considered legitimate knowledge is skewed in many nations. The social institutions directly concerned with the "transmission" of this knowledge ... are grounded in and structured by the class, gender, and race inequalities that organize the society in which people live.
>
> (Apple and Christian-Smith, 1991, p. 11)

> Teachers have a long history of mediating and transforming text material when they employ it in classrooms. Students bring their own classed, raced, gendered, and sexual biographies with them as well.
>
> (ibid., p. 14)

The teaching/learning process is construed by some as a neutral one that stands above the meanings of race and other social constructions that manifest dynamic relations of power in society. This view is embedded in Bloom's and Hirsch's hue and cry for a "return to the basics and classics", and in the lament of some educators that "more time is spent on race and multiculturalism than on education". The assumption underlying this perspective is that written and verbal texts constituting the educative process are raceless, unbiased syntheses of a "common culture", and that the beliefs and values embedded in teachers' and students' racial identities have no bearing on the knowledge that they mutually construct in the teaching/learning process. My experiences as an African American female professor, teaching predominantly European American students, countered this view. In accord with Apple and Christian-Smith's statements above, I became acutely aware of powerful racial and other socially constructed meanings that are embedded in curricular texts, and in the dynamic relations that are forged between educators and their students.

This chapter, then, is a self-study that examines *the significance of race in identity formation processes*, and the pedagogical implications of racial identity for the teaching/learning process. This focal issue grew out of my observation of the relative (in)significance of race in students' personal narratives and the concomitant "normalization of whiteness" in traditional textbooks. These observations spurred and framed major revisions that I made to a graduate course entitled *Human Development and Learning* for pre-service secondary teachers at DePaul University.

My concerns over the significance of racial identity are embodied in two specific questions that guide this self-study:

1   How did societal meanings embedded in my own racial identity as an African American woman and the racial identities of my European American students inform my course revision and my re-examination of my role as an educator.
2   How did the lived experience of this course revision become a pedagogical intervention that prompted students' re-examination of their racial identity – whiteness and privilege – and informed their pedagogical decisions and personal metaphors as prospective educators (Bullough, Knowles and Crow, 1991).

Through this inquiry, I challenge the notion that curricular materials and pedagogical practices are unfettered by societal relations of racial and class inequity, and are unrelated to identity formation processes. In essence, I challenge the "myth of racelessness".

Initial insights and questions

Verbal texts

During the first year that I taught *Human Development and Learning* for pre-service secondary teachers, I noticed a pattern among the European American pre-service teachers that baffled me and was the genesis of my self-study. As a regular assignment, I asked students to write an autobiographical essay as a self-reflective entrée to the study of the developmental and social challenges facing adolescent youth. Students' essays chronicled their experiences through childhood and youth, noting the importance of their families and important personal experiences. To my surprise, I found that *race was not an explicit issue* in their autobiographies, and that *if* students were conscious of its role in their development and learning, race was not worth mentioning as they examined their own lives. This observation ushered in the initial stage of my self-study, from which the burgeoning questions emerged: Why is race not addressed in the autobiographies of European American students? Why did I expect it to be?

In addition, as I presented race as an integral part of the study of human development in the course, some students viewed explicit discussions and texts on "race" in a human development course as a supplemental topic on multiculturalism. Their view was that discussions of race were not central to understanding processes of human growth and change, that such discussions "narrowed" the field rather than broadening our understanding of development and meaning-making across multiple contexts. This perspective coincided with the dominant view presented in traditional texts, that human development is unfettered by race and other socially constructed sources of social inequity that profoundly affect the lives of children, youth, and adults. It was in stark contrast to my own view that discussions of race and social class could only broaden and deepen our understanding of human development. This situation prompted me to ask: Why is race central for me in considering processes of human development?

Written texts

These initial observations during my first year spurred my closer examination of texts for the course to bring race and social class to the fore, and to unpack this "oversight"/silence around race. I became increasingly aware of the racial, social class and gendered meanings that were thematically embedded in traditional textbooks and dominant discourse on human development. As I searched for central texts for the course, I noticed striking patterns in the dominant literature. Eurocentric developmental goals and the experiences of white middle-class children anchored "universal" theories of development, guided positivist research on human growth and change, and defined "normative" milestones for children and youth. I was bothered by the ways in which the experiences and achievements of poor children and youth of color were often pathologized and essentialized as cultural deviations from the norms of the dominant culture in the Western world.

My reaction to the textbooks reminded me of the revelation that I had while studying statistics in graduate school – there was bias inherent in constructing a "normal curve" that "stood above" the social inequities that systematically create patterns of difference across racial groups and social classes, and position them at the center or margins of the curve. In other words, how could the curve be "normal" if sources of the differences were consistently and consciously omitted from the calculations and analysis? By doing so, the "differences" were implicitly attributable to inherent differences between whites and people of color, males and females, the middle-class and the poor. This insight had renewed meaning for me years later, as I read primary research for the course. I was struck by the ways in which this "normal curve" legitimated standardized tests and complex statistical formulas that served to reify the view that certain racial and social class patterns are deviations from optimal standards of growth and change.

As I considered traditional developmental theories for study in the course, I recognized that the individual-focused psychological theories of the Western world were *socio-culturally embedded*, as are all theories and goals of development (Rogoff, 1990), emanating from society's political, socio-cultural and economic history (Coll *et al.*, 1996). Grounded in modern capitalism and the concomitant focus on individualism and self-sufficiency, the theories revered the *primacy of the individual* and *independence as a universal developmental goal*. This orientation constituted the dominant paradigm in educational psychology, privileging male patterns of development (Stern, 1990) and those of white middle-class children, while viewing patterns or ways of meaning-making of *others* as deficiencies in the individual or culture (McLoyd and Randolph, 1985; Miller and Goodnow, 1995). The texts marginalized or omitted theories and research addressing the impact of *social relations* (that is, interpersonal relationships or hierarchical societal relations along race, class, and gender lines), on socio-emotional, physical, and intellectual development, and on school achievement and failure (Kincheloe, Steinberg and Villaverde, 1999).

My concerns and reframing initial questions

I was disturbed by the racial, class, and gender bias that conceptually and methodologically structured psychological inquiry, shrouded in the cloak of "objective science" and neutrality. Traditional texts for this course would promote the deficit-model, marginalize the issues of race, gender, and social class, and support existing social arrangements. I did not want to promote among my students this perspective or ideological formations that would support social inequity. The pervasiveness of the dominant ideology in the disciplinary texts, as well as in students' initial orientation to the study of their own lives and the field as a whole, was somewhat daunting. It contrasted sharply with my belief that discussions of race, social class, gender, and sexuality were an integral part of psychological and educational inquiry.

This juxtaposition promoted other questions, beyond those initially posed. I pondered not only the reason for but the source of the difference between the marginality of race for my students and its centrality for me, as well as the implications for my teaching: Was the difference rooted in social meanings forged through our unique *personal* life experiences and/or through the *social* experiences that were related to our own racial identities? Was it my role as an educator to bring these issues to the fore and problematize the study of human development? As I began to reframe the questions and the nature of the self-study, *I came to the conclusion that this course had to be substantially revised.* Having made this decision, my role as an educator took on greater significance.

I was excited and energized by the prospect of searching for new materials to juxtapose against the traditional texts, and forging new ways for pre-service teachers to think about themselves and their students. However, intuitively I understood that this would be no simple feat. I knew that I wanted these second-career graduate students to examine the assumptions underlying their views and the knowledge legitimated in the dominant discourse on development and learning. I wanted them to examine their own lives, and to use self-reflection as a means to understanding themselves and others (Schön, 1983). I wanted them to wrestle with the complexity of human development, and with the individual and socio-cultural dimensions of thinking and learning, and to examine the issues of race, social class, gender, and sexuality as they framed the discipline of human development and shaped their lives and those they would teach. Ultimately, I wanted my students to have supportive and challenging experiences in the course that would inform their pedagogical decisions as educators and their ethical decisions as citizens.

Thus, my self-study entailed not only *understanding* identificatory processes, but also *promoting change* – growth and development. Hence, further questions emerged: How would I revise this course theoretically and pedagogically with issues of race, social class, gender, and culture at its center? Would the course revision reveal insights about the students' identity formation processes? Would the course revision prompt students to examine the social and structural factors that contributed to their own identities and to those of youth?

Course revision and pedagogical intervention

Changes in the text and process

> Identity ... a subjective sense of an invigorating sameness and continuity ... a process "located" in the core of the individual and ... in the core of his communal culture.
>
> (Erikson, 1968, pp. 19, 20)

Traditionally, this course has provided an overview of theory and research on child and adolescent development, and on motivation and learning. The first step I took was to delete the textbook and to resituate the course theoretically, decentering the implicit but pervasive assumptions within the dominant culture that structures the textbooks. In addition, I could broaden and deepen the research base of inquiry, include ethnographies, biographies, and other sources of knowledge about the process of human development in social and cultural context. I could incorporate the marginalized voices and interrogate accepted "universal norms and goals" of human development in the Western world.

The second step was to restructure the course around the *construction of identity*, based on the understanding that identity formation is the primary developmental task for adolescents (Erikson, 1968), and that the identificatory processes of teachers and students are central to the learning process. I reconceptualized the course around theoretical issues that students could grapple with in light of their own lived experiences and prospective pedagogical practices as educators. I chose materials that addressed the socio-cultural and contextual nature of identity formation and other developmental/learning processes. Students read the psychoanalytic and post-modern theories of Erik Erikson and Stuart Hall, in order to examine different perspectives on identity formation. We examined processes of development and learning in the context of interpersonal relationships and societal relations of power, along the lines of race, class, gender, and sexuality, through inquiries by Ellen Brantlinger, Carol Gilligan, Jay MacLeod, Peggy McIntosh, James Sears, and Jacqueline Ward. I incorporated readings that examined the social and cultural construction of "normalcy" and "universality" in the Western world, and hierarchies of power that both privi-lege and legitimate particular forms of knowledge from particular groups of people within the broad disciplines of education and psychology.

Third, each student had to write a *personal narrative* (Rosenwald and Ochberg, 1992), a self-reflective, conceptual inquiry into their developmental and socio-cultural experiences as youth that contributed to their identity forma-tion. This assignment was pivotal in orienting students to the premises that dimensions of identity are constructed at the intersection of the Self and Other, and that an empathic understanding of the Self is linked to understanding the Other. Strategically, I assigned these narratives to be due during mid-quarter, after students had read and discussed course materials on race, class, gender, and sexuality. I sought to enhance students' reflections on, and critique of, course readings by incorporating weekly response papers that they shared and discussed with each other.

Prior to the completion of their personal narratives, students went on sched-uled visits to two schools in communities that varied significantly along social class and racial lines. Following their participatory observations with adoles-cents in these contexts, they were responsible for a critical comparative analysis, grounded in the readings. The school visits also complemented the course reading of *Ain't No Makin' It*, Jay MacLeod's longitudinal, ethnographic study of the aspirations of and life outcomes for European – and African-American – working-class male youth in a housing development.

Finally, students worked on group projects around selected articles and books for the course that provided a range of opportunities for them to consider, weigh, and exchange views on theory, research, and practice related to youth development and identity. Class discussions anchored the critical examination of readings and lived experiences related to the complex interrelationship between intrapsychic and socio-cultural processes in identity formation, and the confluence of physiological, social-emotional, and intellectual changes that occur during adolescence. Ultimately, through these changes in the texts, both written and verbal, and broadening of the experiences that constituted the educational process, I hoped that the students *could* wrestle with identity forma-tion in the context of interpersonal and societal/structural relationships, and *would* explore the meaning, significance, and complexity of identity construc-tion for themselves and for the youth they would eventually teach.

Fruits of the intervention

Students' identities and the place of race

> How individuals recount their histories – what they emphasize and omit, their stance as protagonists or victims … all shape what individuals can claim of their own lives. Personal stories are not merely a way of telling someone (or oneself) about one's life; they are the means by which identi-

ties may be fashioned. ... We believe that the self-formative power of personal narrative may be constrained or stunted ... . Individuals and communities may become aware of the political-cultural conditions that have led to the circumscription of discourse. ... Discourse mediates between the fate of the individual and the larger order of things.

(Rosenwald and Ochberg, 1992, pp. 1–2)

As a first step in coming to understand the relative significance of race for the European American students, I examined the narrative constructions of the pre-service teachers. Their personal narratives provided *clear insights into the significance of race as an identificatory dimension.* The constructs of personal identity (that is, self-valuative meanings created through proximal, familial relations) and group identity (that is, self-valuative meanings created through one's racial, gender, class, or other societal group membership) provided a conceptual framework for my analysis (Cross, 1985). Following my analysis of the narratives and identification of pivotal themes that emerged across students' narratives, I shared the analysis and thematic categories with the students, collaborating and authenticating with them through interviews on our "reading" of the excerpts from the text. This was an extremely important step in the self-study process. I involved students in the analysis by reading and discussing the text with them, soliciting their feedback, interpretations, and critique. Through this collaborative effort, the pre-service teachers were able to validate and alter interpretations presented, and re-examine their own words and meaning in print. By revisiting their narratives, the students noted continuities and changes in their views, and valued the opportunity for their words and their perspective to be presented.

The analysis revealed that students constructed narratives around themes of *personal identity* (that is, personal trauma, significant familial relationships, and personal characteristics) and/or themes of *group identity* (that is, ethnicity, gender, religion, social class, and sexuality). These overarching themes provided insight into the relative significance of race and other issues in identity construction, and the source of these differences across students.

Personal identity

Overwhelmingly, pre-service teachers developed themes of personal identity. Familial relations and personal trauma were pivotal in structuring their identities and individual characteristics.

Familial relationships

I was one of six children ... . As a result of a sleeping position and an age advantage, I assumed a leadership role in the family ... that gave me sway over two younger siblings ... . One might call it a power position ... . My minor role as the leader of the bed in a small apartment formed what I consider to be a major part of my identity. My position in the family has evolved into my position among my peers. It may be the position of big fish in a small pond.

Parental trauma

One month before high school graduation ... my father lost the business he had owned for twelve years ... . In one week, we lost our cars, our house, and any luxuries outside of necessities ... I had never worked a day in my life ... . So working became an automatic habit for me; I developed an incredible work ethic because of it, which is still a huge part of my identity today.

Group identity

For a few, group identity was central and emerged from students' efforts to negotiate disparaging societal meanings based on group membership. These experiences heightened awareness of their relative positionality/power as a group member in society.

Ethnicity

My father's parents emigrated to the US from Italy ... embraced the American Dream ... . My father's heritage said to me, the harder you work the greater your success ... . Anything worth having ... should be worth a struggle to achieve it ... . One must be able to rely solely on oneself ... . These are vestiges of the American Dream Ideal. These tenets ... no longer speak to a nation of immigrants but rather on a very personal level to their descendants. On the downside, I have learned a certain aloofness and isolation from him. While I am so busy proving to myself that I can achieve what I want on my own, I also believe that I don't need anyone. This gets me in trouble sometimes.

Social class

I was born into an upper middle class professional family ... . Growing up I just came to expect nice clothing, good food, and a future college education ... . I was bombarded with the message that those who were not cultured and educated were simply trash. I believe this instilled within me a real sense of class identity at an early age.

Gender identity

I was a tomboy. My parents despaired. I was not a normal child … . Boys could be interested in science. I was a girl. If I was a normal girl I would have outgrown science … . I wanted to be out in the jungles finding new things, looking in caves, flying to the moon. But only boys did that and I hated it … . I have always believed, even if I had difficulty believing *I* could do it, that a female can do anything she really wants to do, and should be allowed to try. My female identity is not very compliant and conventional.

Place of race

The very category of something called "whiteness" is revealed as a kind of collective neural toboggan run, encouraging good people to slide, to shush at high speed right on through the realm of reason.

(Williams, 1997, p. 52)

Race was not a central group identity theme in any personal narratives. Most European American pre-service teachers had not considered their racial identity until adulthood. They addressed their racial identity by *accepting or disavowing racial privilege,* or by *omitting it* from their narratives. Some students espoused "color-blindness" and were angered by attention to racial identity.

Disavowal of race

I am happy the way I am … . We should all be this way and not concern ourselves so much with people's outer appearances.

I think I belong to the *human* race. I don't want to think of myself as a color or part of a race … I just want to think of myself as me and think of you as you. I don't take someone else's race, ethnicity, or nationality into consideration when I meet them. I believe my identity is separate from what I look like on the outside or what countries my ancestors came from … . I am proud of my accomplishments and I don't feel I received them because of my skin color … . My race just classifies me into a group based on color, not based on who I am and not on my identity. Gender is a "puzzle" piece that I am very proud to have in my identity … . My gender … is one of the strongest, most priceless pieces … of my identity.

Race … I feel that people make more out of what is there than there is … . Whites are the standard that the other ethnic groups hold themselves to and

... because of whites, or society, they have negative images of themselves ... .
Other races might contribute to the negative images as well.

Others acknowledged, but were bothered by, their recent awareness of invisible privileges related to their racial identity, and wrestled to come to terms with the history of oppression.

Acknowledgment of race

In looking back, I believe that my family *unconsciously* assumed our privileged position regarding both race and class. Though my parents did not mention racism, my family lived in a very racist neighborhood ... . My father is a third generation white flighter. His mother and her parents both flew from neighborhoods being encroached upon by the increasing population of African Americans ... . This history was never spoken of while I was growing up ... . My whiteness was very much determined by "decisions" about whom to marry and date, where to live, where to go to school, what is taught, how to move about in one's community and surrounding area, where to shop, for whom to vote, and what occupation to pursue.

Race is something that I have never really had to "think" about before ... . While I have been struggling about my gender construction and upbringing, so many other people have been struggling so hard about their race ... . White privilege is described as an "invisible package of unearned assets" (McIntosh, 1995, p. 76). The idea of unearned assets struck me the most. For the white person, simply being white is the biggest asset of all. I am ashamed to admit that I have never really thought about my color as being an asset ... . Why have I gone so long without really looking at how color stands in relation to my identity? ... There are always two sides to everything, and as a future educator, I need to live my life that way, everyday.

New insights

Pre-service teachers were more likely to disavow or omit any mention of their racial identity if their personal narratives were structured around personal identity themes. Their focus on "the individual" and "human race" subverted attention to privilege. This pattern, at the individual level, mirrored racial meanings created in the broader culture: the normalization of whiteness equals racelessness, and the invisibility of whiteness renders salient the "difference" of "racialized others". Narratives omitting race poignantly reflected this societal meaning.

Pre-service teachers were more likely to acknowledge their racial identity and strive to integrate racial privilege into their self-constructions if their narratives were struc-

tured around a group identity theme. Having grappled with issues of difference and stigmatization in a dimension of their identity, they could make sense of the inequity, privilege, and attendant racial meanings that are embodied in their own and others' racial identity. This suggested that the differential relations of power embodied in one dimension of group identity (for example, gender) provided a conceptual link for them to consider race as another dimension of identity, influenced by inequitable societal relations.

The absence of race as a group identity theme in personal narratives mirrored the broader culture's normalization and, hence, invisibility of whiteness. As expressed in the students' own words, what might have appeared initially to be an oversight by some, actually reflected a worldview, lived experience, and social context that did not require students to think about themselves daily in racial terms. "Race" and "difference" was reserved for the "other" since they were normal. The illumination of this blindspot prompted some to re-examine their identities – who they are or are becoming – in the context of their families, educational experiences, and the larger social order.

Self-reflection and pedagogical implications

My racial identity

> Racism is an enormously subtle perceptual matter. Understanding its conventions involves figuring out how to insinuate one's way through all sorts of well-guarded social hierarchies …
>
> (Williams, 1997, p. 63)

In order to further address the two-fold question guiding this self-study, I reflected on my own history and identity formation process. There are aspects of my own personal and social history that contributed to my racial identity as an African American woman, and informed my decision to reorganize the course, repositioning race as an explicit identificatory dimension. Having grown up in a middle-class, integrated community, race consciousness was a daily reality. It was a social marker determining my rights, others' reactions to me, and the meanings attributed to my personhood, my experiences in school, church, and other public institutions, and the familial guidance that prepared me for life as an African American woman. I remember my puzzled disbelief while watching the hosing of black people on television as they sat-in against segregation in Selma, juxtaposed against the excitement on those rare occasions when a black performer was on The Ed Sullivan Show. I recall the complimentary and simultaneously disparaging conversational entrée from European Americans, "You're not like them", and the veiled communication of lowered expectations that came from teachers and school counselors. Through these and other experiences, I *had* to *consciously* negotiate the dominant society's racial meanings embedded in what it meant to be black.

The assassination of Dr Martin Luther King, Jr, in 1968 had a profound impact on me, and made this point abundantly clear. It dispelled any hopeful notions that "things were getting better" or race was insignificant in the United States. Rather, it confirmed the fact that the struggle for social equality and the meaning of race were linked to the physical survival of African Americans. At that time, I became keenly aware of the current social location of African Americans and the poor, despite *de jure* desegregation, as an outgrowth and continuation of particular structural, socio-historical relationships and societal institutions in the United States. My lived experiences and processing of these experiences made me conscious of race as an ever-present dimension of identity. My understanding of my own racial identity, and implicitly that of others, was further influenced by my growing knowledge of the social order here and abroad, by my progressive work in the 1960s, and by life in the climate of social retrenchment in 2001. Given this country's social history, as it framed my own personal history and experiences of racism, it was impossible for me *to be* without considering race. How then could I/one study human development without examining race, social class, and other constructs of social inequity that shape humans' lives and the discipline-based study of human life?

Having reached this point in my self-study, I had unearthed some of the societal meanings embedded in our respective/interdependent racial identities which contributed to the course revision and reflections on my role as an educator. This greater understanding, however, prompted declarative questions about the discipline and my role as an educator: How could *anyone* genuinely study human development or contribute to the disciplinary knowledge-base without examining race, social class, and other constructs of social inequity that personally and institutionally forge identities and attendant racial meanings – the normalcy of racial privilege and racial subjugation and the stations in societal life that are accordingly created and maintained? How could these factors stand outside of the process of human growth and change? In particular, how can we as educators understand the aspirations, life trajectories, and foreseeable outcomes for youth in different contexts without considering the racial and social class dimensions of identity formation processes?

Pedagogical implications

The revised course prompted many students to re-examine their racial identities and their role as educators, and posed new questions for me. The personal narratives facilitated students' reflective inquiries and spurred reconceptualizations of themselves, curricula, and their relationships with others in society. Some pondered why they had never considered their racial identity, and re-examined earlier experiences in schools and other institutions that were imbued with hierarchical societal relationships. They considered the implications of meanings that were embedded in their racial identities for their work as teachers and change agents. Some noted that adults often dismiss the challenges of adolescent development and identity formation, and stressed the importance of supporting all dimensions of youth identities. In forging new self-metaphors as educators, some envisioned themselves as honest, available teachers, that could continue to grow and create a safe forum for student exploration. Others identified curricular needs that would support their work as educators:

> We can no longer view school curriculum as white only.
>
> Care must be taken when reviewing curriculum to ensure it is fair and truthful about other cultures ... *history* is a subject teachers will need to be *especially* on guard when it comes to racial/ethnic stereotypes. Teachers need to review their materials and supplement them when necessary to ensure a more honest view of *all* races. Teachers *need* to work hard to eliminate stereotypes, and they are in a unique position to do so.

These and other comments by students provided valuable feedback about the impact of the course revision: both the written and verbal texts. Some had begun to rethink their notions of self, and began to attend to what was present and absent in their own narratives, as well as the narratives that constitute textbooks. Some students were not pleased with the attention given to race and other issues of difference, and were ideologically committed to focusing attention *solely* on their "inner selves" and the commonalities of the human species, while denying the presence of difference and its attendant meanings. While it is impossible to talk about human development without discussing the human species, it is also impossible to talk about what it means to be human by denying the presence and significance of difference in the social relationships through which development occurs. Ultimately, the course revision provided insights into the students' identity formation processes and prompted students to wrestle with the social and structural factors that contributed to their own identities and to those of youth they will teach. While the thought-provoking nature of the course created some tension and discomfort, it also energized students as they considered the possibilities before them, with an eye towards changes in who they were becoming as educators and citizens.

My role as an educator and the import of this work

This self-study illuminated the significance of:

1   my own and students' experiences of societal racism or privilege in constructing in/visible racial identities,
2   our respective, interdependent racial identities in fostering the course revision and its mutual impact on us,
3   problematizing the study of human development, and
4   the social roots of my identity, in affirming my commitment to social equality as an African American educator.

This inquiry reaffirmed the importance of examining the dialectical relationship between dimensions of my own identity, the identities of my students, the curricula, and the institutional practices that we employ. This work also reaffirms the importance of examining my educative practices as they interface with and contest dominant and other discourses. This inquiry also reaffirms my commitment to "look beyond the surface", to continue to encourage students to examine the assumptions underlying their views, beliefs, and practices, and to embrace the idea that their understanding of the complexities and ambiguities may create the freedom to knowingly participate within, and change the boundaries of, those views, beliefs, and practices. Hopefully, this self-study will validate the experiences of some educators, provide insights for others, and challenge still others to push the boundaries of their thinking and their practice.

Though I sought to debunk the "myth of racelessness", it is a social construction that becomes a "social reality" and takes on a life of its own, as institutional policies and practices reify the "truth" of racialized meanings and power relations. Through this self-study, I gained insight into the disjuncture between our lived experience of race, and the social construction of two interdependent myths: the "racelessness, neutrality" of whites and the "salient, bias" of people of color.

On the one hand, I could see that my students' narrative self-constructions centered around their individual experience as humans, neutralizing the explanatory function of race as a dimension of their social reality or internal self-representations. Their identities seemed untouched by whiteness as the "unearned knapsack of privilege" (McIntosh, 1995). Their lived experience seemed to mirror the historical pattern in the disciplinary texts on human development that *whiteness* is neither identified nor named explicitly. Constructed as the norm through the assumptions and design of empirical research, it is rendered *invisible and neutral*.

On the other hand, in accord with the normalization of whiteness, students attributed the *bias of race* to "others", whose difference stood out from the norm, whose presence in the texts and in social life was noticed and often exoticized as an interesting variation on life. In accord with this attribution, initially students felt that the discussions of "the racialized other" somehow deviated from the study of human development, and that talk about race would exacerbate bias and racial tension. Their view was that discussions of race in the context of human development *obscured/diminished* one's understanding of human growth and change, rather than deepened one's understanding of one's humanity in socio-historical context. Their view reflected the common assumption in research that the inclusion of the "others" skews the sample, rendering it *salient, biased, and non-generalizable*. The parallel between the structure of the discipline and the reflective lived experience of my students was striking. Conceptually, I could see the inextricable link between the mythical neutrality of whiteness and the representation of "others of color" as outliers.

The disciplinary construction of whiteness as the normative, "neutral center" of human experience, around which all others oscillate and with which all others can be compared, forges the following assumptions: *to be white is synony-mous with what it means to be "human", hence raceless.* Implicit is the idea undergirding sample validity and research design: *to be racial is to be inherently different from the norm.* The salience of race for my students as an identificatory dimension of "the other" mirrored its salience in the experience of myself and others whose humanity is forged within the disciplinary discourse and social context of racism as opposed to racial privilege.

My ongoing observations and study revealed that this disciplinary pattern of not-naming-whiteness was reified in the public sphere throughout visual and print media, magazines, books, formal and informal conversations, interviews, broader discourses in society. I noted that the representational neutralization of whiteness was a cross-disciplinary phenomenon. For example, there is History and then there is Native American History, Black History and so on. While these delineations may reflect areas of scholarly specialization, the study of "history" has become, both implicitly and explicitly, the *authentic, unbiased* story of past human experience. This mythical representation obscures the social reality that this particular version of history has traditionally been *of, by, and for whites (men, in particular)*, and reaffirms the *grand narrative and myth* of "'great men' of Western heritage overcoming 'wild lands and wild men' to plant the seeds of 'civilization'" (Morrison, 1997, p. 7). In fact, one could hardly tell the story of past human experience in this country, or the economic and political ascendence of the US, *honestly* without acknowledging, for example, the painful collective history of exploitation and oppression of Native Americans, African Americans, Mexican Americans. This cross-disciplinary pattern of not-naming-whiteness, thereby representationally – not actually – served to neutralize or *mythologize* its social meaning in the lived experiences of my students as reflected in their personal narratives.

The observations, self-reflections, and experiences in this self-study high-lighted the disjuncture between our initial views of what it means to be human and the place of our own racialized lives in that phylogenetic process. It was clear that the relative social location of one's racial group (social class, gender, and other forms of social inequity) in society may render it in/visible to preserve the social order. This suggests that while myths are not "true", they reflect a dynamic in the social fabric of society that we as educators may challenge through curricula to reinvent our own and others' identities, working towards personal transformation and social equity.

References and further reading

Apple, M. and Christian-Smith, L. (eds) (1991) "The politics of the textbook", in M. Apple and L. Christian-Smith (eds) *The Politics of the Textbook*, New York: Routledge, pp. 1–21.

Bullough, R., Knowles, J. and Crow, N. (1991) *Emerging as Teacher*, New York: Routledge.

Cochran-Smith, M. (1995) "Uncertain allies: Understanding the boundaries of race and teaching", *Harvard Educational Review*, 65 (4): 541–70.

Coll, C.G. *et al.* (1996) "An integrative model for the study of developmental competencies in minority children", *Child Development*, 67: 1, 891–914.

Cross, W. (1985) "Black identity: Rediscovering the distinction between personal identity and reference group orientation", in M.B. Spencer, G.K. Brookings and W.R. Allen (eds) *Beginnings: The social and affective development of black children*, Hillsdale, NJ: Erlbaum, pp. 155–72.

Erikson, E. (1968) *Identity, Youth and Crisis*, New York: W.W. Norton.

Kincheloe, J., Steinberg, S. and Villaverde, L. (1999) *Rethinking Intelligence: Confronting psychological assumptions about teaching and learning*, New York: Routledge.

McIntosh, P. (1995) "White privilege and male privilege: A personal account of coming to see correspondences through work in women's studies", in M. Andersen and P.H. Collins (eds) *Race, Class, and Gender: An anthology*, 2nd edn, Belmont, CA: Wadsworth.

McIntyre, A. (1997) *Making Meaning of Whiteness: Exploring racial identity with white teachers*, Albany, NY: State University of New York.

McLoyd, V. and Randolph, S. (1985) "Secular trends in the study of Afro-American children: A review of child development", in A.B. Smuts and J.W. Hagen (eds) *History and Research in Child Development: Monographs of the Society for Research in Child Development*, 50 (4–5, Serial no. 211).

Miller, P. and Goodnow, J. (1995) "Cultural practices: Toward an integration of culture and development", in J. Goodnow, P. Miller and F. Kessel (eds) *Cultural Practices as Contexts for Development*, San Francisco: Jossey-Bass, pp. 5–16.

Morrison, D. (1997) "In whose hands is the telling of the tale?", in D. Morrison (ed.) *American Indian Studies: An interdisciplinary approach to contemporary issues*, New York: Peter Lang.

Rogoff, B. (1990) *Apprenticeship in Thinking: Cognitive development in social context*, New York: Oxford University Press.

Rosenwald, G. and Ochberg, R. (eds) (1992) *Storied Lives: The cultural politics of self-understanding*, New Haven, CT: Yale University Press.

Schön, D. (1983) *The Reflective Practitioner: How professionals think in action*, New York: Basic Books.

Stern, L. (1990) "Conceptions of separation and connection in female adolescents", in C. Gilligan, N. Lyons and T. Hammer (eds) *Making Connections: the relational worlds of adolescent girls at Emma Willard School*, Cambridge, MA: Harvard University Press, pp. 73–87.

Williams, P.J. (1997) *Seeing a Color-Blind Future: The paradox of race*, New York: Noonday Press.

11 "Nothing grand"

Small tales and working for social justice

Morwenna Griffiths

Introduction

This chapter is a self-study of myself and some colleagues as we continue to work collaboratively towards social justice in education. It has three main strands: the main project, which is getting better at working collaboratively for social justice; the idea of "small tales" and the place they have in that project; and being critical and reflective about both.

Our project, which we call the Fairness Project, was intended to find ways of working for social justice in education. It was originally set up in 1995 with the help of funding from the Economic and Social Research Council. During that year, a group of eleven Deputy Headteachers and Education advisers met with the intention of working out "a theoretical framework for effective practice". I had been careful to choose a group that included a variety of perspectives. They included people working in primary and secondary schools; in the inner cities and in rural areas; in racially mixed and in predominantly white schools. They also included men and women; black and white; migrant, British-born and first generation British; gay and straight. Between us, we come from a number of concrete contexts, in which the various constituencies mentioned above play a part in the kinds of perspectives we hold. However, none of us speaks *for* any particular group and, equally, almost nobody is one of a kind among the above categories (see Griffiths, 1998, for more details).

But what is social justice – and how do we think we can get some? There is no simple answer to these questions, and part of the purpose of the project was to try and come to some better understanding of possible answers. My own working definition is: social justice is the good of the community which respects – depends on – the good of the individuals within it, and the various sectors of society to which they belong. It is never achieved once and for all, but requires us to exercise constant vigilance as we hold to the vision. Social justice is a contested concept. It is true that there is some general agreement about it: that fairness, inclusion, empowerment, and oppression are central issues. Equally there is some general agreement that these abstractions need to be understood in relation to race, social class, sexuality, gender, and disability, as well as in relation to particular individuals' power to act, whatever social, political, and physical constraints they face. Furthermore, there is widespread agreement that "working towards" is the main point about social justice. The slogan "social justice is a verb" encapsulates this emphasis on actions, on social transformation, on actually doing something.

The form of this chapter is linear. But part of its argument is that neither life nor thought are as tidy or as linear as they are when presented in this form, so popular in academic presentations. The endnotes to the chapter provide the rest of the story. The notes appear in two styles. I put notes *about self-study in italics* and about **small tales (examples of them, and also reflections on them) in bold**. I try to bring the *self-study* notes together in Note 14. The **small tales** notes are brought together in Note 15.

Aims: trying to be fair to everyone

This is me (in 1994) talking to a newish headteacher in a small primary school who was moving her school towards more gender equality. She had recently completed an MA module I taught – she appears as "Jacqui" in our book (Griffiths and Davies, 1995).

MORWENNA: One important thing about social justice for me is that there is no one right answer. Teachers need vision, principles – and some methods to try to realize them. The process is not just a means to an end. It is part of the end.

JACQUI: Yes! That is, I think, as near to what we are trying to do in our very small way as we could possibly get. Not that we're doing anything grand! Because we can't! But, it's like, just an ongoing attitude, and an engendering of attitudes, isn't it? That's just going on, all the time, in everything we try and do.

This chapter is part of a continuing effort of mine. I hope that my work can be described as working for social justice in education, in relationship with everyone in the educational community: learners, teachers, researchers, and policy-makers. Informally, I include myself in all of these to some extent; formally, I am a teacher and a researcher. Therefore I am keen to understand – to do self-study on – what it is to work for social justice, so we (me, you, me and you, me and they, you and they) can do more of it better.[1]

Context: trying to work out what to do for the best

> It remains to be said that the author of the report is a philosopher, not an expert. The latter knows what he knows and what he does not know: the former does not.
> (Lyotard, 1984, p. xxv)

The context of this particular bit of self-study is my revisiting members of the Fairness Project, the collaborative project that we had all carried out some years before. I wanted to see if we could take it forward. The group is roughly centered on Nottingham where I am, but its members live and work up to two hours' drive away. They (we) are also all very busy. So after a preliminary phone call I visited each of them individually to discuss the possibilities. As a result, I have begun to rethink what it might mean for an educator to have a personal, active commitment to social justice.[2]

The meetings were only intended to be a pragmatic way of seeing who, if anyone, wanted to be involved with moving forward with the project – and if we did, to work out what to do. That is, they were not undertaken in order to research "small tales". I realized that this work, like everything else, would have to fit into all the competing pressures in my job, and I risked losing the thread of the different conversations. I taped the conversations and transcribed them so as not to forget what we had said. In the end it took me from November 1998 to March 1999 to meet all eleven of my colleagues. Meanwhile I was turning over in my mind a paper I had heard in August 1998, which related Lyotard's phrase "little stories" to social justice (Smith, 1998). The meaning of "little stories" was not yet clear to me, except as a counterpoint to the "grand narrative" of modernist explanation, but the idea was resonant and exciting. In July 1998 I had just published a book based on the Fairness Project, so I thought I had just got clear my thinking about social justice. However, Richard Smith had got me re-thinking the whole thing again.

Method: trying to keep an open mind, trying to hear all the voices

Peripherality
I am a footnote to the world it seems
left out on scanning reading, seldom missed[3]
my silence gleams
extraneous to the central run of things
a bracketed aside[4]
sidling tangential to the main affair
I slip between the leaves of others' lives
smiling obliquely through uncertain lips
essential superfluity I dance
betwixt your present and my sideline glance[5]
(Carrie Paechter)

As I said, the taped conversations were only meant to help me remember the suggestions about practical ways forward. But as I transcribed the tapes I found them interesting for another reason. I was surprised by what everyone said; yet I might have said much the same, myself, in their places. This self-study began with that surprise, and with how I used it to structure an exploration of the transcripts. I found that I was using the idea of little stories (and grand narrative) to understand what was being said; though as I continue to think about it (with help from others) I realize I prefer to think of small tales and tall tales because, first, a tale need not be a spoken narrative and, second, this form of words alters the value relation between "little" and "grand".

This self-study research appeared almost by chance, it seemed. The issue of small/tall tales emerged between the lines, and developed a tangential life of its own. If I had not taped the chats, I would have gone away satisfied with the practical answers, and, probably, I would also have remembered how enjoyable it had been to meet again.[6] I had not expected to get more from these encounters. Indeed, I had not been looking forward to transcribing the taped interviews. But now I am glad that I did, because that laborious process gave me time to reflect on the details, and also on the overall patterns in each conversation. Both of these seemed to be describable as small tales. That is, the interviews seemed to be giving me an insight into the small tales my colleagues tell themselves about working for social justice in education and how they use them in that work. Moreover, I got some insight into how particular tales relate to some of the taller tales: those dealing with large-scale political/social structures. I could not help but think again about my own tales, too.

I said: "The issue of small/tall tales emerged between the lines ... ". It would be more accurate to say that I was taken aback by some of the answers, and the issue of small/tall tales crystallized as a result of thinking about that. In other words, puzzling over these answers seemed to me to be a case of puzzling over issues related to small tales. Thus the method of analysis could be represented as follows. I was interested in the influence of the research on my colleagues and on me, and thus about the best ways of influencing others. And I was surprised by the answers. I then investigated the roots of that surprise by looking again at the transcripts. It was in terms of small/tall tales that I could best understand the kinds of answers I got about what my colleagues had remembered, valued, acted on, or would want to do next. This made me think about small/tall tales and social justice in education.

Methodologically, then, my analysis was not the result of a systematic search for categories, themes, particular terminology or grammatical structures. It would have been inappropriate to carry out any such search, because the conversations evolved. I talked about what I had taken from earlier conversations with the people who happened to come later. And my preoccupations changed, anyway, as time went along, moving for instance from a preoccupation with *whether we wanted* to take the Fairness Project further, to *how we might* take the Fairness Project further. So my reflections are not the result of a recognized system of qualitative analysis. Rather they are representative of the effects of "the lovely ... intractability of the field" (Miles and Huberman, 1984, p. 38) on the kinds of interpretations I could make of our talks.[7]

Results: trying to make sense of it

I had expected my colleagues to be task oriented and to remember the original project only so as to guide the future (that is, that they would be working within a standard "act, reflect, plan" kind of action research cycle). But that did not happen. Many of them had valued the chance to articulate their values through telling me their professional life stories. I had not expected these thoughtful, articulate, and dynamic people (the group was chosen to be made up of such individuals) to tell me the same kinds of things as they had three years previously. But they did. And as a result I wondered, too, about my own responses to the questions I was asking them: here is the nub of this self-study.[8]

Task orientation

I had found during the original project that this group of people, like me, were task oriented. They wanted real practical outcomes from what they did. So I thought that action-planning would be our preferred mode. Instead I found that they had valued their involvement in the project at least as much for other features: the company, the processes, the chance to think aloud, the atmosphere. They had vivid memories of personal feelings about shared events: the pleasant room where we had met; eating strawberries; the other people and the ease of the meetings.[9] And, as I said before, I am very much part of this group and I also value such memories.[10] All of which meant we all wanted to be involved in order to enjoy meeting each other so as to do something practical. This is not about having a jolly for the sake of it.[11]

It's the same old story

I was interested in the influence of the project on us all, so I was disconcerted to find that some of my colleagues repeated what they had said three years previously. Sometimes they retold incidents and sometimes they repeated intentions about what they might do now. Most of them had the same kinds of concerns and focus of interest that they had had previously. Those who began by being most interested in race, gender, class, special needs, or sexuality remained focused on that. So, at the level of the personal (small tale) and at the level of the larger political structure (tall tale), had much changed? I thought I, myself, had changed my own mind as a result of the project. I could even think of examples.[12] And yet I can see plenty of instances where what I have done could equally be said to be "the same old story", even if with a new twist. It is not hard to trace the continuities in my preoccupations with justice from my anti-feminist views when I was a young woman to my post-modern kind of feminism now (Greene and Griffiths, 2001). Am I wiser as well as older? And, if so, how did the project influence that?

Discussion: trying to work out what I learnt ... what we learnt

> Never doubt that a small group of thoughtful, committed citizens can change the world. Indeed it's the only thing that ever does.
>
> (Margaret Mead)

Self-study

I am claiming that I have done an exercise in self-study. But is it? If it is, then the following four things must be taken into account in S-STEP (Self-Study in Teacher Education Practices). They relate to S-STEP; S-STEP; S-STEP and S-STEP. First, consider S-STEP – "self". My account depends on a notion of the self in relation. So self-study is not just about the study of individual human beings, nor even about the study of those individuals in context. It is about each of us in relation to others. To put it another way, it is about "we" and "us" rather than about "I" and "me" – even though I am part of more than one "we", and even though I am not always sure which "we" I am part of (Griffiths, 1995, p. 16).[13] Second, S-STEP – "study". My account assumes that at the heart of self-study is critical reflection and evaluation of purposes and their practical realizations in everyday life. So evidence has to be got on the run, and be given wide-awake, open-minded, critical attention. Methods need to reflect this. (I hope mine did.) Third, S-STEP – "teacher". This study is about the education of all teachers (including ourselves, including me). So while it may be about teachers in their initial phase of education, and it may be about teachers as students, it can also be about the education of teachers who are in no formal accredited program – which is why it includes me! Finally, S-STEP – "education practices". Education (not just learning) can happen through the practices of educational research, as well as through traditional pedagogic relationships of teachers and students.[14]

Small/tall tales

This self-study has helped me develop my understanding of both small and tall tales. It is easiest to begin with the latter, since that is the best understood term, at least in its guise as "grand narrative". Having tales about overarching political structures like race, gender, and social class is indispensable for any theory of social justice that goes beyond individual civility. One was provided by Karl Marx: the march of history as understood in terms of the class struggle. Another is the Liberal version of Enlightenment. I would add to these explanations another set of tall tales, less well worked out by political philosophers but grandly influential all the same: the power that myths and story forms have to structure our understanding in terms of heroic successes and failures, monsters and romance (Warner, 1994).

However, the tall tales are not enough. The telling of small tales is personal and expressive; it shows in silences and patterns of life, as well as in straight talk. They are not just narratives but also inclusive of other expressions of self: polemical outbursts, e-mail messages, poems, metaphors, critical incidents. In the case of our group, they include the shout of laughter with which Jacky told of her staff learning to Salsa, and they include the cold anger with which June told of the time when a young relative was assumed to be of the inner city because he was black. They include Carolyn's ways of holding to an equality agenda amid the flurries of her habitual speedy busy-ness, and Sue's sharp eye for hypocrisy and quiet tenacity in dealing with it. My own small tale is partly constituted in the form in which I chose to write this chapter.[15]

Educators working for social justice

As Jacqui pointed out in the quotation at the start of this chapter, we work with vision and do 'nothing grand' as best we can, in the context of our own work. This is what it is like. However, neither she nor I considered the nature of that "we": the possibility of overlapping visions and the individual small tales.

Conclusions: what now?

> "Self" grows out of "otherness" and "sameness" is gradually patterned from "difference" ... . The identity of a collective such as Europe can be theorized along the same lines as that of the collective that counts as "the self": in terms of a (temporary) patterning or propensity that emerges from an infinity of singularities under certain conditions. As such these identities are fluid and might be transformed – or dispersed or metamorphosed into new structures and propensities – as the configurations are subject to further historical change.
>
> (Battersby, 1998, p. 209)

I was more dismayed than surprised to find how wildly different and personal the answers were to "What now?"; and, come to that, how different and personal the answers were to "What might influence other teachers?" In one sense, the small tales interlocked with the tall tales of justice and oppression – and so to each other. On the other hand, such interlocking would be loose indeed if the tales were so contextualized that a sufficiently common purpose could not be found for something to be done. That would be very depressing, dooming us to work only with those with very similar experiences, unable to do much outside our particular interests, and fighting other groupings for attention, resources, and the moral high ground. I want us to move beyond that.

At two linked conferences in 2000–1, focused on "Approaches to social justice" (Dunkwu and Griffiths, 2001), a group of us, including some of the original members of the Fairness Project, agreed that little stories are a resource for

> organic (or public) intellectuals who work *with* and *as* rather than *on* or *for* the communities, teachers, students, pupils, as they encounter economic and social injustices concretely in their real lives.

They went on to emphasize that little stories are seen as:

> a way of representing real diversity, in which people are authorities of their own experience, and which readily include the emotional as well as the rational aspects of social justice. Stories can be told visually, and also in poems, imagery, movement (dance) etc. There are dangers that little stories

can be merged into stereotypes. There are also dangers of the merely anecdotal. It is important that the broader picture is linked. Indeed little stories
can push big stories and they can snowball into big stories.

I had hoped that we would interlock in the sense of interlocked gear wheels,
all moving to a common purpose. And after some of the interviews I feared we
might be grid-locked, as we all tried to pursue our own journeys and found
ourselves stuck in the small space currently available for social justice work in
educational institutions. However, what I hope we have achieved is a way of
interlocking arms – sometimes with one partner, sometimes with another.

Most recently I have been working with two colleagues from the Fairness
Project. In one case we have been trying to find evidence for the long-term
effects of a nursery set up by a community organization twenty-five years ago.
She was a member of the organization and also its first Head. Another has asked
me and some colleagues to act as critical friends evaluating the policies he has
been responsible for setting up for the Education Authority in a northern city
with a socially and ethnically diverse population. The form of the evaluation
resonates with the form of the framework we had constructed during the first
year of the project.

I think of this interlocking of partners as being like a dance. We can all help
each other (s)step out in the dance, sometimes swaying in one direction and
sometimes in another. And if one or two people need a breather for a bit, that's
all right too. As Syble said, "All of us were going to the same place, but taking
different routes".[16]

Notes

1   *Is this self-study?*
    I am interested in the e-mail conversation on self-study (S-STEP, 2000). Sometimes it looks
    as if the focus was only on those who were working with students, especially those in initial
    teacher education. But in my self-study I am not dealing with students, though I am dealing
    with teacher education (including my own!). Maybe this makes me more conscious than
    most that I am as concerned with my colleagues' influences on my learning as my influences
    on theirs. Or, to be more accurate, I am concerned with our influences on each other.

    Everyone who e-mailed seemed to talk about their concern with how their practice fitted
    with their underlying theories, values, politics, academic thinking, and/or "what matters".
    But I was left wondering if those abstract ideas themselves were as much the subject of
    investigation as the practice. I hope so, because in my self-studies I am just as much
    concerned with understanding my theories, values, politics, academic thinking and what
    matters to me, as I am concerned with seeing where it is realized in practice. I cannot sepa-
    rate the two. If one is in question, so is the other. I think of what I am doing as a kind of
    practical philosophy.

    What a complex set of ideas this is! But that is inevitable. If I am right, self-study is
    about each of us and what is important to us. This cannot be told in any simple, linear
    story. That is why I have written this chapter using a complex format.

2   *Is this self-study (2)?*
    Somebody who read an early version of this paper asked: Is this a self-study or a study of
    others? Therefore, an important question to be elaborated is: How does it affect your work?
       I found this thoughtful question difficult to respond to. I wanted to say "Yes, but … ".
    YES, I need to elaborate. BUT there is a real ambiguity in the English word "your". I take
    it as plural and I think you take it as singular. I say more about this in Note 8.

3   **though sometimes when the story's corkscrew twist**
    has finally uncurled
4   **I offer just**
    my toe-dip tasting of another stream
5   **and would you leave my rippling notes unread**
    without such glistenings, so dull, so dead?
                                    (© Carrie Paechter)

Carrie Paechter sent me this poem after she had heard me present an earlier
version of this paper.

6   The enjoyment I mention in passing is significant to all of us, as I point out in the
    section called "Task orientation". This is part of my own small tale, I think; a
    tale of what it is like to work with others in a group brought together specifically
    to work with a number of very different people to find ways of improving social
    justice in education. Our small tales are structured by our feelings about each
    other as people: guilt, apprehension, commitment, friendship.
       My own journal reflections show this. Here I am just after making contact
    again with my colleagues. I had been encouraged by my research cluster in the
    university to go ahead, in spite of my doubts, and just contact the group again.
    This entry was written very soon after I had contacted the first few by phone.

> It was so difficult actually starting to contact the co-researching group, that I
> didn't actually think through why in too much detail before I did! I'm sure
> this was right, because I could trade on good relationships to let me be vague,
> and it meant that I couldn't put it off indefinitely while I thought it through
> properly. Now of course I have to think it through, pretty damn quick … .
> *Why was it so hard?* After all I had really enjoyed working with them all.
> Well, there was the sheer *lapse of time*, for one. Why is this significant?
> Humanly: picking up, especially when it isn't an old, old friend (and even
> then). When I felt I might have done it earlier, and had said I would do it
> earlier. So I knew that they had probably given up on me. And that brings
> me to a second reason: the guilt I've just displayed. Which would be mixed
> up with guilt on their part as it was with Carolyn for instance, that she
> thought she hadn't actually done anything much … . A third reason: My
> own theoretical changes as a result of reflecting and writing on [principles of
> educational research for social justice] means that I have almost certainly
> thought about the nature of collaboration more … and am now viewing the
> whole thing a bit differently – and I need to convey that very quickly. As I
> found myself doing a couple of times.

And here I am after the first interview, "thinking aloud" in my journal on the train back home.

- [The interview] was not structured, nor ordered, nor was it intended to be.
- A pleasure seeing Syble again! It's a warm relationship, though professional, as I describe it in the [published] write-ups. This has to help the kinds of question I can ask, though it's not being an "insider" as usually framed.
- I was busking what kind of an "interview" it was. That is, I didn't want it to be [only] a conversation. Neither did I want a kind of re-run of the preliminary one [that is, a taped interview during Phase 1]. Why? Well, I wanted to hear what she had to say, so not to keep imposing my views. But (a) I didn't want to turn her into a subject, putting her views on the line, when mine weren't; (b) I wanted to re-affirm, re-assert, re-claim a we-ness for the research, if it looked as if it were there. Which I hoped it was, though I couldn't assume that from the start. (c) I wanted a human interaction, not a subject–object one: "research-with". I don't think this is quite the same as (a) or (b).
- Yesss!! Hurray! It was very cheering. She certainly felt a we-ness, even about the principles. Not to mention feeling she'd like to do more. And I was really struck by the similarity in what we had both taken away from the research.

And here are some of comments drawn from the transcripts I made of the interviews with my co-researchers, that show something of their feelings about being involved – that is, their small tales about this project. (Each one has seen and approved these extracts.)

BERYL: I think it's on both sides. You say, well you haven't made contact for a while. On the other hand, neither have we ... nor have I followed it through as much as I ought to have done.

DAVID: The principles: Yes, I remember some more than others. Now I read through them, I can see where we came from. It's those early ones that particularly speak to me.

MAX: ... being involved in this piece of research is part of a much more complex piece of personal and professional evolution ...

7   *I am trying to be explicit about what I did, as a good researcher should. But if you had asked me at the time, as my journal shows somebody did, I would have replied "Goodness me! To be honest, I transcribed while my brain was in gear". But I realized as I said it that this would not be a useful contribution to methods of self-study of practice. Or, then again, perhaps it would?*

8   *I am trying to do "research with ... " not "research on ... " or "for ... " (Griffiths, 1998). So this self-study is of the whole of the group in so far as we are working with each other. I, the individual Morwenna Griffiths, am part of that group. The study began by my looking at the transcripts of what other members of the group said, and it then continued with me*

questioning my own responses. The self, then, is not just me. It is also us. The individual self is relational; what I do and think depends on this group (and also other groups of which I am a part). Nada captures this well for herself in relation to the group:

> *[One of the main] things I remember … where discussions were supporting me in tracking where I'd come from, and perhaps why particular issues were important to me. I think that made quite an impact in terms of recognizing that, perhaps a bit more explicitly.*

When I am trying to do something "public", like act in relation to social justice in my workplace, I can only do that in relation with others. So it makes no sense to study myself as if I were detached from them. Nor is it productive even as a strategy. For instance, how could I have recognized patterns in my own responses to questions about the project if I had not noticed recurring patterns in some of my colleagues' responses? This project was not mine or theirs: it was ours. That is true, I think, even if any of them do not recognize their own part. In Note 6 my journal entry shows me worrying about the existence of such recognition. But even if Syble had not felt a "we-ness" about the principles, I could not truthfully claim them as mine. I could not have produced them on my own: they are ours. I say some more about this in Note 13.

9   Here are some excerpts from the transcripts:

> I remember sitting in the room at the University and really enjoying listening to what people … . Because everyone was coming from different directions. That was quite remarkable. It felt like a learning experience. I think everybody there was learning … I do remember a really nice lunch we had with strawberries … when we were talking about things, it was far more "Yes! Yes!" than "Ooh, I disagree about that." That was really something.
>
> (Sue)

> I remember coming to the university, and having a really good meal! (Laughter) … Although I was worried about being with all these intelligent people, clever people [the meal] made me feel comfortable … . It was a nice day … a lovely sunny day.
>
> (Carol)

> I can remember the university … discussing a curriculum set for social justice … . It's not a detailed memory. I can remember sitting and having the lunch. (Laughter) … What I do remember are the feelings and the emotions that were there, and the people who had their different, in a way, life stories about where they were at.
>
> (Prakash)

10 **When I was discussing the importance of conviviality with another colleague, Melanie Walker, who had found the same in a collaborative project of hers (Walker, 2001), she told me of a remark attributed to Paulo Freire: "First we eat, and then we do the work." The excerpts from the journal entries quoted in Notes 6 and 9 are also relevant. They show that one feature of a small tale – if I am right to describe these excerpts as small tales – is that it is on a human scale, unlike tall tales which smooth over particular bodies, specific episodes of conviviality and recognizable, typically messy, individual relationships. Tall tales talk of abstractions of humanity, of human needs in general, of wants, drives, and progress in the sweep of history.**

11 *It is easy to see that I like lovely surroundings, good food and good company. I am quite interested to see how those likes connect with my own characteristic task-orientation. My first contribution to the February e-mail discussion about self-study was:*

> *"Why self-study?" Because I love the people who come to the Castle conference: their engagement, their creativity, their intellectual liveliness, their openness, the buzz ... the humanity ... the energy. So I turn my intellectual interest in personal–professional reflection into what is termed by this group of people, self-study.*
>
> (S-STEP, 2000)

> *But I would not come just for a good time. I can get that at home! The feelings I have about the Castle conference mean that it is better for severely task-oriented reasons too: I learn more at such occasions.*

12 *Some evidence of a change in my views can be seen in my journal. In the excerpt quoted in Note 6, I remark on my changed views about collaboration. But the journal was not kept in order to track such change. It is hard to see how it could! It is logically difficult to guess where a change might occur, after all.*

13 *I say that I do not know which "we" I am a part of. Here is part of the argument as I expressed it in my book on the self:*

> *Language is developed in a community of participants and so their understanding is constrained by that community and the language it has developed. Therefore, however individual an experience is, it is understood through an understanding developed in a community: a "we". "We" is indeed a slippery word. Feminists have long noted how the "we" of male academic discourse slips from inclusion to exclusion and back again, with respect to women. Women are better placed to notice this than men. Black women have further noted how the "we" of white feminist discourse is just as dangerously ambiguous. I need others to work out with me when I am a "we" with them.*
>
> (Griffiths, 1995, pp. 16–17)

14 *This is a brief and assertive summary about self-study. Here I say some more in relation both to S-STEP (2000) and to Notes 1, 2, 7, 8, 11, 12, and 13:*

1   **S**-STEP – "*self*": *Self-study is about each of us in relation to others. To put it another way, it is about "we" and "us" rather than about "I" and "me". In Notes 2, 8 and 13, I set out some of the reasons why I say that. Yet in the e-mail conversation, I heard very little which supports this … . All the initial responses focused on the individual and separate self. I notice that even when the self-study is explicitly focused on collaborative research (as Allan's is) the emphasis is on the singular individual. Carl (the ninth e-mail, out of twenty) was the first, I think, to mention relations with others might also turn back on (include?) himself. A little later on, Terri says she gets more connected to her students as she lets them into her life. And I think Sarah was driving at the same kind of thing, in her focus on the multiplicity of self and the relationship between learners and teacher – and her implicit criticism of individualism. It is interesting that Sharon is the closest of anybody to my views of relationship, in what she said in the exchange – and she too is focused on race, class, gender, and hybridity.*

2   S-**S**TEP – "*study*": *My account assumes that at the heart of self-study is critical reflection and evaluation of purposes and their practical realizations in everyday life. As I said in Note 1. In Notes 10 and 11, I am actively puzzling over values and coming to a new appreciation of my own. Maybe it is something to do with the developing conversation, but none of the early e-mails really mentioned values and politics as a subject of inquiry. I think Lis's summary confirms this for me. On the other hand, neither did I mention them in my own e-mail! So I do not want to read too much into this. As the correspondence continued, discussion of values, and reflection on values, increased. I wonder why this is? The last e-mail in February, from Lis Bass again, focuses precisely on a study of how a transformative pedagogy was working – which must (mustn't it?) put the transformative pedagogy itself in question just as much as the methods by which it might be implemented.*

   "So evidence has to be got on the run, and be given wide-awake, open-minded, critical attention. Methods need to reflect this." In Notes 7 and 8 I say something about methods which can reflect this. My ad hoc use of found data was a practical example. In Note 8 I talk about methods of being wide-awake and open-minded: how research "with" keeps you on your toes. And also observations about other people help you adjust observations of yourself.

3   S-**S**TEP – "*teacher*": *"This study is about the education of all teachers (including ourselves, including me)." In Note 1 I said that I was not working with students, but nonetheless I was working with teachers. The difference in emphasis through the e-mail exchange about this is fascinating. To take two examples, Tom says he is researching his own living contradictions as a teacher himself, while Allan seems to imply (but I may be wrong) that university teachers require a different kind of study. (Is this because they also do research?) There is a balancing act to be performed, perhaps between (a) spending most of our time contemplating our own immediate (culture-bound) contexts while the wider world of education is ignored, and (b) looking out at the wider world and being in bad-faith with our own values and practices. I am sure we all have tales to tell of those who research and pontificate about matters where they themselves signally fail.*

4   *S-STEP – "education practices": "Education … can happen through the practices of educational research, as well as through traditional pedagogic relationships of teachers and students." I mention this in Note 1. I notice that virtually all the e-mails are about students and teachers-as-students, however. At the first Castle conference I wondered about this, because at that time I was one of the few contributors discussing colleagues rather than students. I wonder again how far out I am. But surely if educational research is to have value it should be educational to all concerned? Isn't it also an "education practice"?*

15 This is another brief and assertive summary, this time about small tales. This is an idea that is unfolding for me. The notes I have already included point to a developing understanding, but one that is not yet sharply expressed. For instance, I say at one point that small tales are not just anecdotes and critical incidents, and I say at another that these can be included as small tales. I think both of these statements are true! A small tale might be an anecdote, but it can only be under-stood *as* a small tale when it is seen in the context of its place in that the teller's view of, say, social justice. To take another example, a shout of laughter is not always a small tale. In the context of Jacky's understanding of her job it surely is, and I retell it as such. Similarly the remarks about conviviality and shared food are understood as small tales because of the way they appear and reappear in the responses by members of the group and can then be related to real collaboration, which itself is necessary for acting with social justice. Or so I would claim. I began to patch it in with tall tales by my allusion to theorists such as Battersby, Freire, and Lyotard.

16 Thank you to my colleagues in the Fairness Project: Beryl Bennett, Max Biddulph, Carolyn Goddard, June Hunter, David Martin, Syble Morgan, Carol Price, Prakash Ross, Jacky Smith, Nada Trikic, and Sue Wallace.

References

Battersby, C. (1998) *The Phenomenal Woman*, Cambridge: Polity.

Dunkwu, K. and Griffiths, M. (2001) "Social Justice in Education: Approaches and Processes", http://www.bera.ac.uk/.

Greene, M. and Griffiths, M. (2001) "Feminism, philosophy and education: Imagining public spaces", in N. Blake, P. Smeyers, R. Smith and P. Standish (eds) *The Blackwell Guide to the Philosophy of Education*, Oxford: Blackwell.

Griffiths, M. (1995) *Feminisms and the Self*, London: Routledge.

—— (1998) "The discourses of social justice in schools", *British Educational Research Journal*, 24 (3): 301–16.

Griffiths, M. and Davies, C. (1995) *In Fairness to Children*, London: Fulton.

Lyotard, J.-F. (1984) *The Postmodern Condition*, Manchester: Manchester University Press.

Miles, M.B. and Huberman, M. (1984) *Qualitative Data Analysis*, London: Sage.

Smith, R. (1998) "*The demand of language: The justice of the différend*", paper presented at World Congress of Philosophers, Boston, MA; repr. in M. Griffiths and M. Sardoc (eds) *Justice in/and Education*, special issue of *The School Field: International Journal of Theory and Research in Education*, XII (1/2, 2001): 43–54.

S-STEP (2000) "Why has self-study become important?", http://educ.queensu.ca/~ar/sstep3/feb2000.htm (accessed April 2001).

Walker, M. (ed.) (2001) *Reconstructing Professionalism in University Teaching: Teachers and Learners in Action 1998–2000*, Buckingham: Open University Press.

Warner, M. (1994) *Managing Monsters: Six Myths of our Time*, London: Vintage.

12 Change, social justice, and re-liability

Reflections of a secret (change) agent

Mary Lynn Hamilton

> None of us alone can save the nation or the world.
> But each of us can make a positive change if we commit ourselves to do so.
> (West, 1993, p. 159)

Some researchers suggest that change can be arduous (Fullan, 1991) while others consider change to be a thoughtful process, yet something that occurs all of the time (Richardson, 1994). Few, however, address the failure to change. As a teacher educator engaged in the reform process (change), I want to delve into my experiences as a change agent. In so doing, I will explore what my role was within the context of school reform, how I personally responded to change, and what my experiences, as self-study, contribute to our understanding of the change process.

This chapter explores one important facet of change agency – the failure to change – and raises issues about how people can engage in a change process without changing, and the way people's vested interests affect their understanding of events. The chapter also considers questions that arose for me, such as "Does a colleague viewed as unchanging have the same experience?" and "What is one's role in change?" On a personal level, as a leader asked to facilitate change, "Can change be brought about by force?" and "When does one's reliability shift to a *realization* of *liability?*"

In this chapter I explore the issue of change agency, using my institutional experience as a backdrop. To do this, I discuss the context of the study, describe the dilemma that launched my study, present how I framed and reframed the experience, offer evidence for my interpretations, and consider why the use of self-study contributes to a more meaningful understanding of the situation.

The context

The University of Kansas is a Carnegie Research I institution, and among the top thirty public research universities in this country, according to *US News and World Report*. As a part of the university, the School of Education (SOE) supports a first-rate student body of 400 elementary and secondary pre-service students with a strong grade point average (above a 3.4 on a four-point scale) who come from the surrounding bi-state area. The SOE also attempts to recognize its role within a diverse and changing world by initiating recruitment programs for students of color and asking questions about the relevance of its programs. Further, the SOE encourages faculty to work collaboratively with educators in the state and nation to improve education at all levels. As a leader within the state, the SOE strives to be at the forefront of providing the best education possible for its students. To support this intellectual growth, self-examination and change are constantly a part of its environment. Not surprisingly, then, in 1995 after the School of Education undertook its own self-study and our Board of Regents charged all State Regents' universities to "become examples of institutions willing to change to meet the needs of America and [the state] in an ever more competitive and complex world", discussions culminated in a decision to reorganize its structure and its teacher education program.

In response to the recommendations of our Board of Regents and our Provost, by July 1997 the SOE had implemented an energetic, new organizational infrastructure that realigned departments and created a new structure: the Teacher Education Division (TED). The initiation of the TED provided the opportunity for the SOE to respond more effectively to the changes in the state, the nation, and the world as it began to explore ways to best prepare its students for teaching. Over the past three years, the TED engaged in a committee-wide and school-wide continual self-study as it looked at ways to improve upon its already strong teacher education program, and discussed ways to respond to the pressures from the state and the federal governments regarding the reform of standards. These committees also considered issues of governance and curriculum in order to design the best teacher education program for our students.

First, a bit of history

Prior to our move toward reform, the University of Kansas had a five-year teacher education program. Students graduate with a bachelor's degree in education and then move into a fifth year that includes twenty-two weeks of teaching (eight weeks of student teaching in the Fall semester and fourteen weeks of internship in the Spring semester). The students are competitively accepted into the School of Education at the end of their sophomore year, and prepare for a rigorous two more years of coursework (they can only take three hours of education classes prior to their acceptance into the school). Once admitted into the SOE, our students identify subject-matter majors and/or minors, as well as a grade-level focus (elementary, elementary/middle, middle, middle/secondary, secondary). Many minors include at least thirty-two hours of coursework. For example, our elementary students must all take the multidisciplinary minor that includes fifteen hours of science, nine hours of humanities, twelve hours of social sciences, and fifteen to eighteen hours in English. In the fifth year, along with their student teaching, students take a series of graduate level courses focused on research, school law, and counseling. When the students complete their internship in the Spring, they have fifteen hours of graduate work and are certified to teach. As we moved toward reform, we asked ourselves "How can a School of Education address state policies, respond to changing standards, and design an effective teacher education program, while preparing its excellent students for a changing world?" and "What might a strong teacher education program look like?"

Literature that influenced our thinking (believe it or not!)

To answer those questions we visited the research literature, finding a range of ideas to consider. For example, not so long ago, Shulman (1986) noted that most teacher education programs defined successful graduates as those students with a high proportion of content-area knowledge, a familiarity with curricular and teaching models, and time to practice with both. It would seem, therefore, that teacher education programs then believed, and likely still do now, that theory about good teaching can easily be transposed into practice. Yet evidence suggests that these programs have been less than successful. In an extensive review of the literature on professional growth of pre-service teachers, Kagan found that most studies indicated that

> university courses fail to provide novices with adequate procedural knowl-
> edge of classrooms, adequate knowledge of pupils or the extended practica
> needed to acquire that knowledge, or a realistic view of teaching in its full
> classroom/school context.
>
> (Kagan, 1992, p. 162)

Prior to entering teacher preparation programs, pre-service teachers have experienced thousands of hours as students. During that time, they generate many untested notions about school and about teaching. These preconceived notions can interfere with their professional growth, particularly if they remained unexamined (Pajares, 1992). Some studies suggest that field experience fails to affect the deeply held beliefs of pre-service teachers. Often pre-service students do not realize that their beliefs have been developed from a pupil's perspective, and that learning to teach differs from previous school learning (Bird *et al.*, 1993; Johnston, 1994). Furthermore, pre-service teachers feel that their paths are predestined, and that they do not appreciate the complexities and unpredictable nature of teaching (Britzman, 1991). Consequently, pre-service teachers become disillusioned by their student teaching experience because it fails to live up to their expectations. To assuage these worries, gaps between preconceived theories and actions taken in the classroom must be bridged. Currently, the ghost of the teacher-proof curriculum haunts conversations about the ways to prepare teachers. Should schools of education encourage teachers to present a scripted curriculum? Or, instead, should teacher educators, utilizing the research on teacher thinking and reflective practice, develop tools to help their students understand and consider their beliefs and theories about teaching? Certainly some researchers assert that helping novice teachers elaborate on their theories about practice will help them recognize their teaching strengths, as well as their barriers to best practices.

According to Jordan-Irvine (2001), teachers leave the teaching profession because they cannot accomplish what they want – to be caring, competent teachers. Kozol (2001) concurs that we are not able to keep novice teachers in school because they are overwhelmed with lists and tests, and expected to teach scripted lessons that do not accommodate or encourage creativity. On the other hand, if novice teachers remain in the profession, they do so for the love of children (ibid.). There has been some work that suggests that strong teacher education programs can counteract these retention problems (Darling-Hammond, 2000), while other research (Wright, McKibbon and Walton, 1987) proposes that mentor programs sustain teachers in their profession.

The world of teacher education is quite conservative and resistant to change (Zeichner, 1993) but, despite this, some teacher education programs do make changes. Although there is little discussion in the literature about what occurs in teacher education programs (Zeichner and Gore, 1990), we can read about programs that de-emphasize the development of specific skills and emphasize reflection (Russell, 1997) and narrative (Clandinin and Connelly, 1995). Britzman (1991) encourages a move away from the skill-orientation of teaching, identifying the restrictive nature of that view. With a greater focus on practice comes an emphasis on reflection – a tool to help students reconceptualize their own public school experiences. New programs emphasize reflective teaching, action research, and journals. There has been a transition from the implementation of the more traditionally described formal knowledge to a recognition of practical knowledge. In fact, there appears to be a merging of theory and practice into praxis in more innovative programs.

Often in teacher education programs, prospective teachers consider their in-the-classroom experiences to be the most beneficial aspect of their program (Munby and Russell, 1995). They define their university work as overly theory-laden and unrelated to the lives they anticipate as teachers. In turn, this can develop into the research–theory–practice triad of resistance in future years. The reason why we have denied the value of experience may have more to do with knowledge ownership than reality. Experience may be a powerful teacher, but it reinforces or contradicts private, not public, theory. Further, students need guidance in the reflective process as they navigate their way through the information gathered from both experience and coursework.

Within teacher education programs that incorporate the aforementioned ideas, addressing issues of diversity are also important. In the United States, typical novice teachers are white females in their twenties from lower middle/middle income families (Darling-Hammond and Sclan, 1996) living in suburbia (Grant and Secada, 1990). While these teachers may encounter multi-ethnic students from lower income families living in an urban setting (Florio-Ruane, 1994), they are not their settings. Cultural mismatches become important because of the potential clash between the understandings of the dominant culture of pre-service teachers and the ethnic minority student population. This lack of congruity can cause difficulties between students and teachers, and can affect student success. Research indicates that these teachers have little background to share with their culturally diverse students, and may have strong beliefs that infringe their teaching and relationships with their students (see, for example, Chapter 10 in this book). With little or no knowledge of people from diverse groups and few shared cultural understandings, these novice teachers can be filled with stereotypic notions about difference and beliefs about how to behave in their classrooms.

Studies (see, for example, Cummins, 1986; McLaren, 1986; Ogbu, 1991) suggest that, although teachers may not deliberately promote white, middle-class values, they nonetheless have different styles of communication, different words of communication, and sometimes different ideas to communicate, distancing dominant culture teachers and ethnic minority students. One way to better understand teacher behaviors and explore embedded cultural understandings is to examine teacher beliefs (Fenstermacher, 1986). Ladson-Billings (1995) suggests that revealing beliefs can lead to the amelioration of this cultural mismatch.

It is this research literature that informed my colleagues and me as we prepared to redesign our teacher education program. We planned to adopt a programmatic approach that focused on a look at theory through practice. Our program contained a strong field component that would be guided by university and school faculty. At the heart of the program was the theme of social justice. We planned to place social justice at the center.

Prompts to write about change, social justice and re-liability

For eleven years I have studied my development as a teacher educator and a member of the academy. Using letters, journals, e-mail communiqués, interviews, field notes, and observations from a self-study stance, I have documented my development as a teacher educator and observed my definitions of teacher knowledge. With this text I took an analytic turn, moving from a classroom to a program focus as I studied my practice within the context of the SOE. In essence, then, in this particular self-study I move beyond the study of my classroom practice into a self-study of the teacher education program. As I stepped into a high-profile administrative role involving interactions with my departmental and School of Education colleagues, they responded to aspects of the most current wave of teacher education reform, most specifically adopting social justice as a central theme for a teacher education program. At this point I broadened my view of the self-study of teacher education practices to include my experiences beyond the classroom.

For three years, as the Director of the TED, I worked with committee members to redesign our TED program. Over that time we generated a mission statement, a conceptual framework, a program plan, and a curriculum framework. Every step of the way we virtually informed the faculty via e-mail and the internet (http://www.soe.ukans.edu/) and engaged them in real-time conversations at departmental meetings, school assemblies, brown bag presentations (lunchtime meetings), and school retreats. We relentlessly interacted with faculty because we knew that ownership in our program proposal made it more likely to succeed. By May 1999 we had a program plan that the school faculty approved as a working draft. At the heart of the document rested social justice. As a human being and as an educator, I was quite proud of the document because it represented issues that I hold most dear. Who, I asked myself, would ever say that they did not support social justice?

In September 1999 the Curriculum Committee (the workhorse committee in charge of the redesign) voted to table the consideration of social justice as the major theme for the program. This arose after a very high-spirited meeting at which no one could agree on the most important issues – or even why we might want to support this issue (social justice).

Dilemma

Prior to the emergence of this dilemma, the Curriculum Committee spent time discussing these issues, talking with our colleagues – within the school and beyond. So, when this dilemma emerged, I suffered disorientation. Close colleagues had advised me that something like this could *never* occur. The Curriculum Committee had all agreed to support social justice as a theme. Or so I thought! Then, in September 1999, this committee voted to table the consideration of social justice as the major theme.

For most intents and purposes, under Roberts' Rules, the tabling of an issue indicates its lack of support. When this occurred it precipitated a number of questions for me: "Was this as an act of racism?", "Was it undermining me as the Director?" or "Was this a careful response to recent state-level (right-wing) decisions to remove elements from our state-mandated curriculum?" As the Director of this redesign process and an advocate for a focus on social justice, I had a strong desire to unravel this experience and understand my colleagues' responses. As a scholar interested in the intricacies of the socio-political elements in the process, I believed that the unraveling of the threads of the tapestry may also be of help to others working through their own redesign processes.

Framing and reframing the situation

In this situation the unexpected occurred and it puzzled me. For me, the best interests of our students were not being addressed, and I did not understand how that could happen. However, my colleagues did not understand my quandary. They felt that the best interests of the students involved *not* addressing social justice. Again, I questioned and wondered "How could this happen?", "How could we table the issue of social justice?" We had all read the same literature.

We had listened to each other's views. "How did this disjoint occur?" "Were we not listening to each other?"

Evidence

In undertaking a self-study of my experience as a (secret) change agent, I was conscious of the need to avoid a narcissistic, self-indulgent exercise in vindi-cating my position. I could see the need for my work to be a strong, careful self-study that moved from individual experience to program involvement that incorporated a well-grounded exploration of the methods used. Hence my sources included personal journals, field notes, interviews, notes, formal memos, documents, meeting minutes, and informal interviews. All of these comprised my database. Dialogues with colleagues outside the study have also been impor-tant. They have served as critical friends, and provided comparative perspectives from other institutions and teaching experiences.

Threads that stitch this experience together

There are many possible ways to unravel this particular tapestry. Before I begin, however, let me present a few details about the tapestry. There were two meet-ings where discussions about social justice occurred. They occurred one week apart. The first meeting set the stage for the second meeting. The members of the Curriculum Committee represented the various aspects of the teacher education program – that is, elementary, secondary, special education, founda-tions, and so on – as well as participants in the program – that is, students and public schools. At the first meeting, I presented definitions of social justice along with definitions presented by other members of the Committee. While our program explicitly held social justice at the heart of it, worries among the group emerged. According to the meeting minutes, the definitions "worried some members of the group because of the political implications and ... that this might take the focus off of good teaching" (TED Minutes 9/14/99, p. 2). Members suggested that social justice might be "caught not taught" (TED Minutes 9/14/99, p. 2). While Committee members recognized that this issue reflected state expectations, they still worried about whether or not to address these issues directly.

My assignment from that meeting was to provide a summary of the discus-sion. Using the work of Ayers (1998), Hunt (1998), and Oakes and Lipton (1998), I wrote:

> At its core, the definition of social justice mirrors democratic principles depicting a just society where every one has the privilege of participating in its ongoing process. Within this system, individuals treat each other with dignity, humanity, and honesty. They promote sensitivity to and knowledge about oppression and diversity, as well as an elimination of the domination of, exploitation of, and discrimination against any person, group or class on

the basis of race, class, gender, ethnicity, national origin, color, etc. In a socially just world, people are committed to the nurturing of all children. Given these ideals, these individuals are committed to change. For them, there is a recognition of social wrongs and injustices as well as a belief that people can change the world. When teaching for social justice, those involved teach what they believe ought to be and display a willingness to take risks in concert with others in order to live in a democratic world ...

Elements of Social Justice

Upon graduation, a student would:

- Work with all children.
- Understand and be responsive to diversity.
- Develop a desire to improve students' lives.
- Advocate policy issues supportive of young people.
- Promote actions and programs that support young people.
- Change situations in schools for working with young people.
- Recognize and have an understanding of the labyrinth of community services.

(TED Notes, 9/20/99)

During the second meeting, the definitions were discussed. I presented them, my colleagues responded to them. One colleague began with a statement that we needed "to look at the precepts associated with social justice from a positive perspective" (TED Minutes, 9/21/99, p. 1). Other colleagues suggested that we avoid using the label "social justice" because it "could have a negative effect on the public and some legislators" (TED Minutes, 9/21/99, p. 1). Even though the SOE faculty had approved this theme the previous Fall, the Committee members were now worried. As the discussion advanced, colleagues pointed out that we lived in a suburban setting where social justice was not a major concern. They suggested that we might be overreacting to the "needs of a small portion of our population" (TED Minutes, 9/21/99, p. 1) rather than our entire school student body. They also suggested that we "might maintain the values of social justice, but not use the term ... " (TED Minutes, 9/21/99, p. 1). Going nowhere, becoming hostile, holding no hope for approval, the Committee voted to table the discussion of social justice until we "considered how well the [curriculum] framework [upon which we were working] represents both the social justice theme and the work to which we [were] committed" (TED Minutes, 9/21/99, p. 2). Such as it was, the tapestry was complete. Although the SOE faculty had supported the idea of social justice, the Committee members (designers of the actual program) thwarted attempts to overtly bring the theme of social justice to the program plan.

In the next few paragraphs I explore the initial questions that emerged for me as I sifted through the rubble of the meetings. "What did happen?" I asked.

"What evidence supported my views?" "What did my mound of evidence reveal?" To address these questions, I present threads from the tapestry.

Undermining the Director

One thread might be the desire to undermine the power of the Director. In any organization, elements of power and control affect meetings and relationships. As a woman leading a mostly male committee, I had to consider this possibility. I knew that Committee members wished that I had a different direction-style (they had shared that information with colleagues who, in turn, had shared this information with me). It seemed to me that they wanted to be told what to do rather than be invited to participate. Sometimes they described me (as I had described myself) as a Pollyanna – someone who always approaches ideas and actions with optimism. Further, I had a reputation in the SOE as an advocate for social justice issues. Since this was not only something that the SOE faculty supported, but something that I personally supported, I had to ask myself: Was the act of tabling the issue a blatant attempt to undermine my power?

To respond to the query from a self-study perspective, I looked for evidence. Did I have evidence to support that claim? I could say that during the meetings colleagues sometimes began their comments with "We applaud your commitment to social justice, but … " as they launched into a strong statement that did not support the inclusion of the social justice theme into our program. I could also say that colleagues appeared to personalize this issue as if I was the only member of the Committee that supported this theme. I was not.

As I considered these points, although I found myself wondering whether my Committee members wanted to weaken my position, I could not find the support for that perspective in my documentation, in my notes, or in the conversations with colleagues. From my reading of my evidence, I was a messenger, and a supporter, of the theme of social justice, but my leadership did not seem to be the focus of the Committee interactions. Given that, what about the state politics of the time? Were my colleagues responding to worries that the state might look upon our program in a negative fashion if we blatantly stated our support of social justice?

Response to external events

Within the state, our legislators had just voted to remove evolution from our state science curriculum. This vote had occurred between the time that the SOE faculty voted to support the theme of social justice and the meetings held by the Curriculum Committee. The responses of my colleagues could have been a careful response to recent state-level (right-wing) decisions to remove elements from our state-mandated curriculum. With the recent actions of our state school board that removed the discussion of evolution from the state-supported curriculum, many educators in higher education worried about which area might next be under attack. During our discussions, statements like "use of the term social justice could have a negative effect on the public and some legislators" could be heard, and would suggest that this worry was present. Privately, we knew that the state of Kansas was the brunt of jokes because of the actions of our legislature. Publicly, colleagues seemed to worry about the repercussions of any actions we might take that could venture beyond the legislators' realm of approval.

From a self-study perspective, I reviewed notes, documents, and conversations. I asked myself about the influence of state politics and the work of the Committee. I found that, although they did raise the issue during the meeting, this concern was more of a screen than a real issue. I found evidence that my colleagues sometimes took stands that might be considered controversial by state officials. In fact, several of them had been quite vocal in opposition to the most recent state decisions. In light of that evidence, it would seem that the concerns raised about the theme of social justice emerged from elsewhere. Were these concerns generated from politics within the SOE?

Internal politics of SOE

As I considered the threads that made up the tapestry, I had to consider the influence of internal politics. As the Arizona Group (1994, 1996, for example) has written about and discussed in the past, academic politics can be quite influential on the events that transpire within an institution. The University of Kansas was not immune to that. Unfortunately, attempting to discern evidence of this was difficult. It was the power beyond the word, the nonverbal along with the verbal, that might convey this influence. When I reviewed the minutes I found no evidence of this element. When I reviewed my notes, I could find speculation, but no concrete evidence. At that time, we had no overtly feuding parties involved. Consequently, while this may have been an influence on the decisions made at the meetings, there were no bits of evidence to support that supposition. Recognizing that, I was left with another consideration. Was this an act of racism?

A racist thread

Was the tabling of this issue an act of racism? One might think so, given some of the comments during the meeting. As the conversation heated up, statements like "We are not training teachers for urban Chicago" were made. On the surface, this statement may seem innocuous. It is true that we do live in suburban Lawrence, Kansas, and not in urban Chicago, Illinois. However, this statement suggests that urban areas are the only places where social justice might be an issue. This statement suggests that social justice is not a global issue, but local to where there are more people of color or greater economic distinctions. When one considers that the Committee membership was all white, the question becomes a bit more piercing. As white scholars, we must be watchful about our potentially racist views to thwart the perpetuation of biased views, and I wondered if we were acting in the best vigilant fashion.

When I returned to my notes and the meeting minutes, the concern about institutional racism emerged more strongly. Although in informal interviews colleagues asserted emphatically that this was not the case, the clarity of their statements during the meetings cannot be denied. Because we work with a mostly white population, we thought that our students did not need to worry about social justice. It would seem that we figured that our students would return to their suburban homes upon graduation to do their teaching. From the evidence I reviewed, we behaved in a socially unjust way as we engaged in a discussion of social justice.

Within my own written note text, my horror that colleagues could vote against social justice emerged as the strongest theme. From my perspective, white privilege was at work. As I talked to my colleagues in a gently prodding fashion, most responses started with "I don't want you to think that I don't support social justice ... " or " ... maybe if we just use other terms ... ". (In the aftermath of the September meetings, I contacted colleagues within the SOE. Some were shocked with the decision. None attempted to influence the decision.) To me, this suggested that race was clearly a factor.

Did my colleagues and I act in a malicious way? The answer would be negative. Rather, we acted in a dysconscious (King, 1991) fashion, using our rhetoric to disguise our behavior. Perhaps most telling is the recognition that from the day in September when the issue was tabled, it was never discussed again – not at meetings and not within small group discussions. Although the words were written in certain documents, the topic was never mentioned during any meeting. In May 2000, when the topic of social justice was placed on the agenda for discussion, the meeting ended early (without discussion) because of low attendance. (By May 2001 the program finally proposed to the SOE faculty – including social responsibility as an element – was tabled because of faculty derisiveness. By June 2001 the Teacher Education Division was dismantled. The teacher education program returned to its 1986 structure.) Labeling these actions as simply racist may not adequately identify all elements involved, but the evidence suggests it was a powerful component.

Impact of self-study on my practice

For me, self-study of teacher education practices extends beyond the work we do in our individual classrooms. As teachers we are role models. As scholars we must understand our whole academic environment. This includes employing self-study in a broader sense. I did that as I documented my experiences as the Director of the Teacher Education Division. Addressing my experience from a self-study perspective allowed me to express my feelings and my ideas about what occurred, while demanding that I maintain a rigorous approach to my expression. I also believe that other teacher educators have an interest in the ways that we grappled with the issues involved in the reform of teacher education. The impact of self-study on my practice included an understanding that my colleagues needed an opportunity to critically examine their views. To some degree they needed to express their resistance to change and my encouragement to keep their minds open.

As I grappled with this situation I discovered that there are many factors involved in the reform of a program that do not arise until you are in the middle of the process. Further, sometimes it can be difficult to make quick turns to correct for oversight. Yet these things happen. Importantly, these factors are not a simple list of *things to remember*. Instead, there are insights to be gleaned from the process. Attempting to reform a teacher education program can be both overwhelming and intimidating. These feelings can be amplified during the continuing reform process when presenting innovative ideas to a faculty. Often schools and colleges of education are unsure about where and how to start their reforms. Importantly, the students in our program have been denied the opportunity to study issues of social justice in the context of teacher education. As program planners, we have modeled unjust social behavior. If, as teacher educators, we cannot recognize and respond to this issue, we cannot expect our students as future teachers to be socially just.

From my perspective as a white woman in a position of authority, I believe that my work can contribute to the exposure of white privilege. White privilege is too often an unseen barrier to social justice that dams the progress that might be made. Also, the use of a story form of self-study reporting might help other white scholars recognize their (personally unseen) privilege, and the study itself might contribute to our understanding of the change process related to teacher education reform efforts.

Research studies by white scholars confronting the hegemonic, racist structures within the institution have only been in the literature within the past ten years. Much of this work, however, has been theoretical rather than from a more self-reflective perspective. As scholars, particularly white scholars – as many of us are – we must call attention to our role in confronting these structures as well as our failures to address the tenets of our unjust system. This includes the promotion of social justice. As visible change agents, white scholars must ask questions and *confront* issues that are too easily overlooked in a privileged environment. As a secret agent – when visibility creates more problems than opportunities – white scholars must ask questions to confront the issues. Consequently, it is the aim of this self-study to address change agency and its many roles in confronting injustice, and the methodological quandaries of reporting this experience.

References

Arizona Group (Guilfoyle, K., Hamilton, M.L., Pinnegar, S. and Placier, P.) (1994) "Letters from beginners: Negotiating the transition from graduate student to assistant professor", *The Journal*, 8 (2): 71–82.

—— (1996) "Negotiating balance between reforming teacher education and forming self as teacher educator", *Teacher Education Quarterly*, 23: 153–68.

Ayers, W. (1998) "Foreword: Popular education – teaching for social justice", in W. Ayers, J. Hunt and T. Quinn (eds) *Teaching for Social Justice*, New York: Teachers College Press, pp. xvii–xxv.

Bird, T., Anderson, L., Sullivan, B. and Swidler, S. (1993) "Pedagogical balancing act: Attempts to influence prospective teachers' beliefs", *Teaching and Teacher Education*, 9 (3): 253–68.

Britzman, D.P. (1991) *Practice makes Practice: A critical study of learning to teach*, Albany, NY: State University of New York Press.

Clandinin, J. and Connelly, M. (1995) *Teachers' Professional Knowledge Landscapes*, New York: Teachers College Press.

Cummins, J. (1986) "Empowering minority students: A framework for intervention", *Harvard Educational Review*, 56: 18–36.

Darling-Hammond, L. (2000) "How teacher education matters", *Journal of Teacher Education* 51 (3): 166–73.

Darling-Hammond, L. and Sclan, E.M. (1996) "Who teaches and why: Dilemmas of building a profession for 21st century schools", in J. Sikula, T. Buttery and E. Guyton (eds) *Handbook of Research on Teacher Education*, New York: Macmillan, pp. 67–101.

Fenstermacher, G. (1986) "Philosophy of research on teaching: Three aspects", in M. Wittrock (ed.) *Handbook of Research on Teaching*, 3rd edn, New York: Macmillan, pp. 37–49.

Florio-Ruane, S. (1994) "The Future Teachers' Autobiography Club: Preparing educators to support literacy learning in culturally diverse classrooms", *English Education*, 26 (1): 52–66.

Fullan M. (1991) *The New Meaning of Educational Change*, New York: Teachers College Press.

Grant, C. and Secada, W. (1990) "Preparing teachers for diversity", in R. Houston, M. Haberman and J. Sikula (eds) *Handbook of Research on Teacher Education*, New York: Macmillan, pp. 403–22.

Hunt, J.A. (1998) "Preface: Of stories, seeds, and the promises", in W. Ayers, J. Hunt and T. Quinn (eds) *Teaching for Social Justice*, New York: Teachers College Press, pp. xiii–xv.

Johnston, S. (1994) "Experience is the best teacher. Or is it?", *Journal of Teacher Education*, 45 (3): 199–208.

Jordan-Irvine, J. (2001) *Caring, competent teachers in complex classrooms*, paper presented at the annual meeting of the American Association of Colleges for Teacher Education, Dallas.

Kagan, D. (1992) "Professional growth among pre-service and beginning teachers", *Review of Educational Research* 62 (2): 129–70.

King, J. (1991) "Dysconscious racism: Ideology, identity, and the miseducation of teachers", *The Journal of Negro Education*, 60: 133–46.

Kozol, J. (2001) *Opening night lecture*, paper presented at the annual meeting of the American Association of Colleges for Teacher Education, Dallas.

Ladson-Billings, G. (1995) "Multicultural teacher education: Research, practice, and policy", in J. Banks and C. Banks (eds) *Handbook of Research on Multicultural Education*, New York: Macmillan, pp. 747–59.

McLaren, P. (1986) *Schooling as Ritual Performance*, London: Routledge & Kegan Paul.

Munby, H. and Russell, T. (1995) "Towards rigour with relevance: How can teachers and teacher educators claim to know?", in T. Russell and F. Korthagen (eds) *Teachers Who Teach Teachers*, London: Falmer Press, pp. 172–84.

Oakes, J. and Lipton, M. (1998) *Teaching to Change the World*, New York: McGraw-Hill.

Ogbu, J. (1991) "Low school performance as an adaptation", in M. Gibson and J. Ogbu (eds) *Minority Status and Schooling*, New York: Garland Press, pp. 249–85.

Pajares, M.F. (1992) "Teachers' beliefs and educational research: Cleaning up a messy construct", *Review of Educational Research*, 62 (3): 307–32.

Richardson, V. (1994) "Conducting research on practice", *Educational Researcher*, 23 (5): 5–10.

Russell, T.L. (1997) "How I teach IS the message", in J.J. Loughran and T. Russell (eds) *Teaching about Teaching: Purpose, Passion and Pedagogy in Teacher Education*, London: Falmer Press, pp. 32–47.

Shulman, L. (1986) "Paradigms and research programs in the study of teaching: A contemporary perspective", in M. Wittrock (ed.) *Handbook for Research on Teaching*, 3rd edn, New York: Macmillan, pp. 3–36.

TED Minutes (1999) http://www.soe.ukans.edu/.

TED Notes (1999) M.L. Hamilton's personal notes.

West, C. (1993) *Race Matters*, New York: Vintage Press.

Wright, D.P., McKibbon, M. and Walton, P. (1987) *The Effectiveness of the Teacher Trainee Program: An alternate route into teaching in California*, Sacramento, CA: California Commission on Teacher Credentialing.

Zeichner, K. (1993) *Reflections of a teacher educator working on social change*, paper presented at the annual meeting of the AERA, Atlanta.

Zeichner, K. and Gore, J. (1990) "Teacher socialization", in R. Houston (ed.) *Handbook of Research on Teacher Education*, New York: Macmillan, pp. 329–48.

Part IV

Exploring myths in teacher education

13 Myths about teaching and the university professor

The power of unexamined beliefs

Belinda Y. Louie, Richard W. Stackman, Denise Drevdahl and Jill M. Purdy

Introduction

As an interdisciplinary team of university faculty representing three disciplines (education, nursing, and business administration), we conducted a collaborative self-study project to examine our myth-based beliefs about teaching. For data collection purposes, we each wrote about our teaching successes and failures. These stories were then used to stimulate audiotaped group discussions about our teaching. The myths that emerged from the analysis of our writings and from the transcriptions of our team meetings fall into three categories: control of learning, preparation for teaching, and approach to teaching. Two examples illustrate how we have changed our teaching practices as a result of identifying and analyzing these myths. This self-study project has shown us both the power of unexamined beliefs to constrain teaching practices and the role of examining beliefs in changing teaching practices.

Myths about teaching and the university professor

Few university faculty members have received formal teacher training for their work in the classroom. Even if formal training is available on campus, it is rarely a viable option because of time constraints and faculty preference to be autonomous in their professional growth. A transformative and self-directed approach in instructional development may better serve faculty than formal workshops and seminars (Cranton, 1994). Because instructional practices are informed by professors' personal beliefs and cultural norms (Johnston, 1996; Oda, 1998), efforts directed at encouraging professors to examine and change their teaching must similarly be directed at both personal and contextual levels. In order to transform teaching beliefs and improve practice, critical reflection is necessary to reach a state of self-realization that enables professors to visualize the influence of past assumptions on their current teaching behaviors (Mezirow, 1991; Kember and McKay, 1996).

Faculty expertise is based on subject area knowledge, and a faculty member's knowledge of teaching is usually limited to insights gleaned from practice rather than from a study of the discipline (Cranton, 1994). A professor enters a classroom armed with years of experience as a student, and most professors have constructed assumptions about teaching based on role models, other people's comments, and their own teaching and learning experiences (Boice, 1996). This autobiography tells a beginning professor how to think and act like a university instructor, and provides a foundation that perpetuates specific assumptions and actions related to teaching. Imbedded in this foundation are images of the professor, "mythic images which tend to sustain and cloak the very structure that produces them" (Britzman, 1986, p. 448). These myths also contribute to professors' "taken-for-granted views of power, authority, and knowledge" in the classroom (ibid., p. 448), providing ideal images, definitions, motivations, and justifications for teaching activities.

Myths are beliefs given uncritical acceptance by the members of a group (for example, university professors) that support existing or traditional practices and institutions (*Webster's Unabridged Dictionary*, 1986). Thus, in the university setting, teaching myths can be construed as beliefs that faculty members have accepted uncritically and then use to justify their current actions (Rosenholtz, 1984; Britzman, 1986; Kleinsasser, 1991; Briscoe, 1993; Kugelmass, 2000). Though the resulting myths are neither entirely true nor entirely false, myths are developed with less than adequate evidence, resulting in the possible accumulation of distorted assumptions about teaching. Barthes discerned the function of a myth: "it points out and it notifies, it makes us understand something and it imposes it on us" (Barthes, 1985, p. 117). As a result, myths – since they are treated as if they are true – continue to influence faculty's instructional behaviors and easily become self-validating (Thomas and Harri-Augstein, 1983).

Like values, which are "global beliefs (about desirable end states or modes of behavior) that underlie attitudinal processes" (Connor and Becker, 1994, p. 68), myths serve as antecedents to attitudes and, ultimately, behavior. Myths can impose constraints on individuals "to act in a manner consistent with the associated taboos and customs generated from the myths" (Briscoe, 1993, p. 972). For example, the myth that the world was flat constrained the actions of many individuals because they "knew" that any exploration too far out onto the ocean would result in the ship falling off the edge of the earth (Campbell, 1972). We concur with Campbell that myths serve a purpose in our daily lives; however, at issue and central to this chapter is the perpetuation and "uncritical acceptance" of teaching myths by university professors that may hamper the development, growth, and exploration of their teaching.

Kugelmass (2000) emphasizes the necessity of engaging "the unconscious and the non-rational processes" in teachers' professional development. Examining one's myths is similar to the hero's odyssey in Joseph Campbell's *The Hero with a Thousand Faces*:

The passage of the mythological hero may be overground, incidentally; fundamentally it is inward – into depths where obscure resistances are overcome, and long lost, forgotten powers are revivified, to be made available for the transfiguration of the world.

(Campbell, 1949, p. 29)

Through the study of myths, we can learn to know and come to terms with the greater horizon of our own deeper and wiser inward self (ibid.). Scientific discoveries have been instrumental in the evolution, re-creation and disappearance of myths, resulting in the release of human potential (Campbell, 1972). Likewise, critical inquiry is fundamental to confronting faculty members' teaching myths, leading to transformative professional development (Sokol and Cranton, 1998).

By way of example, we propose the following myth: *Being knowledgeable in one's field is the sole requirement for being a university professor.* This myth implies that to improve their teaching, professors need only develop their intellectual acuity and knowledge bases. However, recent research indicates that intelligence is affective as well as cognitive. The growing literature on emotional intelligence suggests that individuals differ in the skills with which they process affective information (Salovey and Mayer, 1990). Emotionally intelligent people are believed to be better communicators and problem solvers; they understand and manage people more effectively (ibid.). Thus, to improve their teaching, professors should examine not only their intellectual responses to events they face in the classrooms, but their affective responses as well (Goleman, 1998). Through critical evaluation of the myth stated above, professors may recognize the role that emotional intelligence plays in teaching, and then work to enhance their ability to express, regulate, and interpret emotions in themselves and others.

Critical analysis of teaching myths presents a constructive way of understanding and transforming faculty members' teaching experiences and methods. Myths are rarely explicit, and faculty members seldom engage in reflection on those of their assumptions that may be faulty. Through self-reflection and critical discourse about teaching assumptions, teachers are able to revise those assumptions (Mezirow, 1991). In a similar manner, Posner, Strike, Hewson and Gertzog (1982) suggest that lasting conceptual change involves a process of articulating which of one's beliefs do not satisfactorily explain one's experience. The next step is to reduce inconsistencies between existing beliefs and reality by constructing alternative reasoning schema that seem more intelligible and plausible. To this end, we designed this research to examine our own myths about good and bad teaching through activities of individual writings (reflection) and group discussion (critical discourse) of our teaching successes and failures.

Method of study

Our interdisciplinary research team is comprised of four tenure-track faculty members in three disciplines: education, business administration, and nursing.

At the beginning of our two-year study, each faculty member had at least four years of teaching experience as a full-time university instructor in the United States. All four members attended US or Canadian universities for both their baccalaureate and graduate degrees, and these experiences contributed to our teaching beliefs and behaviors.

We were purposeful in taking a systematic approach to our collaborative self-inquiry so that the results of our work could go beyond self-enhancement to advance the scholarship of teaching (Pereira, 1999; Shulman, 1999; Greene, 2000). To examine our teaching myths, we used a collaborative self-study approach. Many researchers have documented that collaboration in self-study facilitates analysis (Hassler and Collins, 1993; Dana and Floyd, 1994; Boice, 1996; Maltbie *et al.*, 1996; Loughran and Northfield, 1998). Furthermore, in a collaborative self-study, participants can take advantage of multiple perspectives, creating a broad context for the interpretation of one's beliefs and practices. The social support also is useful in and important to the research effort.

Data were gathered in two phases. In the first phase, we each wrote about incidents representing our personal teaching successes and failures. Each faculty member wrote multiple success and failure stories that spanned early to recent teaching experiences. In the second phase of data collection, we met to discuss and analyze these stories. We held six monthly meetings of one to two hours each, discussing our beliefs, concerns, and current situations with respect to our teaching. All meetings were audiotaped, and the tapes were transcribed. Before each meeting, team members received the transcript of the previous meeting so that they could review, reflect, and respond to emerging ideas, thus allowing continuity in the conversations. Each discussion had a focused topic suggested by members, yet there was sufficient freedom to encourage exploration of meaningful tangents.

As we moved from data collection to data analysis, our data sources consisted of twenty-four pieces of focused writing on successful and unsatisfactory teaching experiences, and six transcripts from the group discussion sessions. We used a grounded theory approach to identify and analyze patterns related to each member's teaching, as well as patterns across the team. Following Miles and Huberman (1984), we used a conceptually clustered matrix to categorize and analyze information taken from the writings and the meeting transcripts for each faculty member according to its myth content.

Myths of teaching

One immediately apparent result of our analysis was that we did not share identical teaching myths, even within our small group. Each of us had different beliefs and assumptions that we derived from our personal experiences as teachers, leading us to create highly personalized myths; thus not all our myths were shared universally across all four faculty members. Our finding that myths were highly personal and context-based was supported by the title of an article published in a business education journal: "Never wear your pink shirt in the forum" (Brass and Gioia, 1985). The title refers to the authors' belief that teaching evaluations are negatively influenced by a professor's attire when teaching in a very large lecture classroom.

Despite the highly personal nature of our myths, our collective analysis revealed that the myths could be grouped into three categories: myths about the *control of learning*, myths about *preparation for teaching*, and myths about *how to approach teaching*. We believe these shared categories reflect the common elements of our experiences at research-oriented US universities. University professors usually receive extensive education in their content area and in research, but learn little about learning theories and instructional strategies (Edgerton, 1990; Ballantyne, Bain and Packer, 1999). This leads many to teach as they were taught, perpetuating traditional approaches without reflecting on the assumptions or the effectiveness of such methods (Wentzel, 1987; Weimer, 1990). As a result, professors perpetuate misbeliefs about teaching, such as "if you know it, you can teach it" (Boice, 1996, p. 94).

In the following sections, we describe each of the three myth categories that emerged from our analysis. In addition to providing specific examples of myth-based beliefs from our data, we offer relevant examples from existing research that illustrate how many myths are rooted in and derived from the culture and practice of university professors.

Control of learning

Some professors have the illusion that we can control everything, and especially the learning, that occurs in the classroom. In reality, regardless of one's academic discipline, often all an instructor can do is structure the course to support those who are motivated and ready to learn. Positive serendipitous teaching and learning moments occur too; students learn in circumstances that are beyond the best planning of any of us. However, at times, a negative classroom atmosphere prevails when students are tired and unmotivated to learn. Moreover, students may not learn at the rate we expect. We experience feelings of failure when students and the learning environment react in ways that we cannot control. Still, many of us share a teaching myth that good teachers can control everything.

Myths of control may have a significant impact on teaching attitudes and behaviors. Most professors expect to lead and anticipate that the students will follow (Petersen-Perlman *et al.*, 1999). Many avoid student-centered instruction because of concerns about losing control of the class (Felder and Brent, 1996). In general, faculty may not be enthusiastic about the spontaneous and egalitarian modes of teaching and learning that allow students to interact freely with the instructors and their peers in the classroom. Some faculty are skeptical of dynamic professors with high student involvement in class, perceiving that it is a way to cover one's lack of a solid knowledge base (Petersen-Perlman *et al.*, 1999).

Professors may worry that releasing control of the knowledge transmission process will dilute academic rigor. Academics usually hold strong disciplinary loyalties (Johnston, 1996). In fact, a love of one's discipline and the desire to share it with students are hallmarks of exemplary instructors (Ballantyne, Bain and Packer, 1999). In an analysis of the teaching evaluation instrument widely used on campus, Kolitch and Dean (1999) discovered that it operates within a knowledge-transmission paradigm of instruction, supporting the assumptions that the professor is the center of the classroom, the holder of knowledge, and the sole authority with respect to curriculum and instruction. This type of instrument further supports a teaching climate that encourages instructors to control various aspects of their teaching to ensure serious academic under-taking.

For us, the myth that professors must control both teaching and learning manifested itself in several ways. First, faculty members attempted to control the learning environment by, as one member stated, "creat[ing] an environment ... [in which] students connect with each other". Another member noted in a group discussion:

> To me, a wonderful instructor is a person standing in front of the class with good information and wonderful visual aids. After the person delivers the lesson, students will say, "Aha, the information is great. We learn from you."

Another element of controlling the learning environment is controlling what students learn. As one of us stated with respect to professors' responsibility for the content and structure of the classroom:

> It is not my job to make them learn, but it is my job to try to facilitate learning ... whether they choose to learn is their choice. But I need to know I have done everything I can do [to] try to establish a structure in which they can learn.

Our research indicated that faculty members struggle with conflicting ideas about what constitutes the right level of control. One faculty member acknowl-edged a fundamental conflict between her beliefs about control and the reality of the classroom in this way:

> It's difficult for me to take control. I mean learning happened and I didn't really plan it to happen that way ... it was really [accidental].

Further evidence of this conflict came from a faculty member's written "failure" story. In it, she noted that she expected to help each person in class to learn a specific skill, even though some of the students did not care about the topic and would never use the information. When this expectation was discussed during a group meeting, the response of another member was:

> If I connect with five or six students and I make a difference for them, then that has been successful for me … . We can't be all things to all people.

Beyond controlling class content and structure, faculty members also attempt to control when students learn. For some of us, the expectation was that learning occurs within the same time frame as the course, as the following "failure" journal entry reveals:

> Each of them [students] finished a major project at the end of the quarter. However, according to the course evaluation, none of them believed that they learned much in terms of knowledge. They were not my advisees. Later, their adviser informed me that their work in my course became the foundation of their master's projects. But, in my memory, this course was a failure in my teaching history.

Others of us thought that learning happened in the class, but it could also be delayed, as indicated by these comments from discussions:

> Now sometimes there are a few students in a class that in talking to them we know they have gotten it. But a lot of what we do is time delayed. If we can follow up on them five years later [we could better gauge whether learning occurred after the actual class]. We are like a cold tablet almost. Instead of a twelve-hour delay, we are on a twelve-year delay. Things are released over time.
>
> What I run up against, is that they won't understand my comments in week one until they have lived it and then they go "I see what you mean by that!"

These excerpts from our data paint a picture in which the teacher is in charge of the classroom and of any learning that students attain. Furthermore, they reinforce earlier research on the attitudes and behaviors of university professors, which reveal a widespread and institutionalized myth of control in university settings. Although each of us discovered from our experience somewhat different myths about control, we all found control myths that affected our perceptions and behaviors in the classroom.

Preparation to teach

The second category of myths that emerged from our data focused on teacher preparation. The widespread, institutionalized myth in this category is the notion that one cannot teach well unless one is fully ready. Our analysis suggests that myths about preparation were often related to the myths about control, as a good teacher should be prepared to control everything that may happen during the class time.

The skilled teacher is always ready for everything; otherwise "we [are] not doing our job". Furthermore, being prepared includes having the skill to bring real life and current examples into the classroom, what one faculty member called the "perception of utility". Although many members saw the need to relate course information to a broader context, one faculty member pointed out that the utility perception may be:

> an artifact of being in professional schools ... I do an awful lot of sense-making with the students about "so what" and "why does this matter?" ... I spend a lot of time [telling students] about how what I teach [them] matters to the enjoyment of [their lives]. It's not a careerist perspective or professional perspective where you have to pass the boards. It's kind of "learn because it will make your life better".

A major myth of preparation calls for instructors to demonstrate their role as the knowledge-holder. The image of a good, prepared teacher is one in which the teacher is the primary, if not sole, expert in the classroom. One member noted in a journal entry:

> Realizing that I needed to cover a lot of basic information in ten sessions, I organized the instruction really well. I started the class with a graphic overview to explain the direction of the course and the relationship among the topics. For each individual session, I had course handouts with outlines to facilitate students' note taking. I planned so well that when the students walked into the classroom, I could account for every minute that they spent in my class. This course was strongly aligned with my research; therefore, I felt very confident teaching it.

To this faculty member's dismay, students in this course were upset because the instructor "packed the class time so well that they could not relax and think". A well-prepared class session, leaving no room for serendipity, appeared to satisfy only the instructor. In contrast, another member articulated a belief in the importance of serendipity in students' learning experiences:

> What I see is a lot of evidence for each of our successes, something almost like surprise pedagogy. It's breaking the frame, jolting people out of their schema of what learning and education is, and introducing a new tool: whether it is course design, whether it's a game ... and that is where the engagement and teaching come in and there is almost an element of shock to it in some way.

Many faculty nourish a deep-seated belief that teaching is about knowledge transmission (Kember and McKay, 1996) that depends almost exclusively on the faculty member's quantity of knowledge. When professors over-prepare, they are following old university customs that are hard to change (Boice, 1996). The need to present a façade of omniscience can be emotionally charged for faculty members as many professors over-prepare, fearing that they may lose face if they present "embarrassingly imperfect materials" (ibid., p. 70). Faculty are sensitive to the possibility of being vulnerable when students discover that they are not masters of their domains (Petersen-Perlman *et al.*, 1999). Even senior faculty members may feel insecure about their knowledge in today's explosion of information (ibid.). Over-preparation offers a shield of protection to those faculty members who try to uphold the myth that professors must know everything in their fields.

Approach to teaching

The third category emerging from our self-study involves the myth that the excellent teacher employs certain approaches or techniques. It is a common belief that the good teacher ought to master multiple functions related to teaching, and various styles to cope with any situation (Bess, 1998). Professors organize information in accessible forms for students, deliver information in an engaging manner, enhance their teaching with active and relevant research, and monitor student learning with constructive feedback. Bess wonders how many faculty members "are so broadly talented or psychologically disposed" as to perform all these functions (ibid., p. 9). Rather than laboring at methods that hardly match their personality and temperament, Chambliss (1999) recommends that professors utilize tactics at which they are competent and feel comfortable. The master-of-all teaching myth sets up unrealistic expectations for faculty members, and often ends in frustration and discouragement.

Our myths about approach and technique include the idea that one best approach exists for all teachers and the elements of that approach should encompass a wide repertoire of teaching techniques. This best approach always includes a teacher who is enthusiastic and energetic. "Because it goes back to the myth that we are responsible for conveying the enthusiasm ... we have to jack up the students' interest, to motivate them to learn," one of us commented in a discussion session.

Conflicting myths emerged around the extensive use of lectures to convey information. For some of us, good teaching means avoiding presenting material through lecturing. After discussing the successful experience of helping students learn a large amount of information using a gameshow format, one team member wrote: "It was so much more meaningful, we thought, than a lecture approach to the material (which is how it's been handled in the past)." However, for others, lecturing is a necessary behavior because of its relationship to myths about control and preparation. A lecture-based pedagogy allows faculty members to feel confident in their content knowledge and offers them maximum control in the classroom.

The final myth in this category is that the good teacher acts on all student feedback. Each of us believed that good teachers incorporate student input in course delivery. However, upon further reflection, the validity of this statement faltered. From a journal:

This experience reinforced the fact that there are always a few "whiners" in every class who will refuse to understand or accept the benefits of a given assignment. Though I need to listen carefully to their complaints, I must trust my instincts. Students complained about the creation of a career port-folio at the time of the assignment. One came back three months later to report how the portfolio impressed the interviewer in a job interview.

Students do not always provide constructive feedback, especially when they try to pester the professor for a better grade (Placier, 1995). A member suggested that we could use students to counterbalance students' self-interest when evalu-ating a course or a professor by having them confront each other:

There were about 13–14 people there, and I interviewed them as a group. They got into debates with each other and disagreed with each other and I, as the observer, was able to reflect multiple opinions and multiple perspectives on things. You never get the ability to look at the whole picture from the yellow sheets, the student evaluations. All you get is conflicting information: use more of this, use less of that, etc.

In the category of approach, many professors embrace the knowledge-transmis-sion paradigm in which the act of teaching is seen as imparting information and learning is "taking in" or absorbing that information (Hendry and King, 1994). Dewey's *pouring in*, Freire's *banking* and Bruner's *deficit-filling* (Shor, 1996) are metaphors that capture the idea of the direct transfer of knowledge from teacher to student. In this model, acquisition of knowledge is more important than the construction of knowledge, which takes into account students' lives and experi-ences (Kolitch and Dean, 1999).

Teachers who dominate classrooms by doing all the talking not only work harder than they need to; they also deny students sufficient involvement in the classrooms.

(Boice, 1996, p. 86)

In fact, effective teaching requires two-way communication, not one-way *broad-casting* (Ballantyne, Bain and Packer, 1999). Students need opportunities to negotiate understanding during discussion, and to adjust to teaching and assess-ments; otherwise, learning is not occurring as it should.

Two examples of how examining myths influences practice

An essential component of this research was a self-reflexive one in which the uncovering of personal myths was translated into changes in our daily teaching endeavors. It is important to note that simply identifying one's myths about control, preparation, and approach does not eliminate the beliefs and experi-ences that precede them. However, the impact of many of our myths has been curbed in subtle and visible ways. Our awareness has led to changes in how we think about teaching and how we behave as teachers.

In the following sections we offer two examples of how the critical evaluation of professors' teaching myths has affected their practice as teachers. The first case documents a fundamental change in approach; the second describes the recognition of a core teaching value in relation to the myths we identified. Each example is presented in the first person, reflecting the perceptions of the author-professor.

Example 1: Belinda's experience

It is difficult for me to accept the fact that I consider lecturing to be the hallmark of an excellent professor. As an education faculty member, I have read much research and I acknowledge the benefits of cooperative learning. I also realize the power of a constructivist approach to teaching, which challenges students to integrate new information with what they already know. Deep inside of me, however, I have the notion that a professor-scholar is the knowledge-holder who is obligated to enlighten students with his or her mind. Being a Chinese-American, I have been socialized into believing that a professor is the authority in the teaching and learning environment. When I allow my cognition to guide my teaching, I put students in small groups to explore the topic at hand. Their subsequent reports to the whole class further enhance their understanding of the issue. As a result, students enjoy the experience and appreciate the knowledge gained. However, such an exercise provides me with little satisfaction, despite high student ratings, because I feel that I have cheated my students by not fulfilling my duty as a teacher.

During the collaborative study with my colleagues, I gradually became aware of my belief that lecturing was the essential element of good teaching. When we openly discussed this belief, I realized the discrepancy between my cognitive sense of good teaching strategies and my emotional tie to lecturing. With my knowledge in curriculum and instruction, I could hardly justify lecturing as a superior mode of teaching. Such an explanation has enabled me to adjust my teaching belief, aligning it more with my practice. I do not want to do the reverse (that is, adjust practice to belief) because of my acceptance that students learn just as well when they work in groups. Recently, I designed my courses with student group work without the usual guilt associated with feelings of laziness and incompetence. I still find it difficult not to lecture; however, I do not feel so bad when students learn as a community with me functioning as the facilitator. It has been, and remains, difficult for me to break the myth of approach with respect to lecturing; fortunately, the process has begun and continues.

Example 2: Richard's experience

Serendipity was the word that jumped out at me when I read our individual pieces of writing and our discussion transcripts. It was also the word that I kept reintroducing into our conversations. Since those conversations, I have come to recognize how much I value (and expect) serendipitous moments (or surprise pedagogy) when I teach. I rarely envision how a class will unfold. Instead, I have always walked into the classroom with an outline (or notes), with clarity about the learning objective(s) for the day, and with the hope that unexpected moments of learning will occur.

During our self-study discussions, I argued against many commonly held myths. I was adamant that one could not prepare for serendipity, that one could not exert control over the students' learning. And, of course, there could not be one approach that leads to serendipity, but there were many approaches that killed serendipity (namely, non-stop lecturing). This brings me to my *mea culpa*, and what I have learned from our self-study of teaching myths. I appreciate myths now. Myths no longer run counter to my beliefs about what should occur in a classroom, nor do they sabotage my self-esteem. Yes, the myths are seemingly ever-present, and yes, they create doubt. Have I prepared enough? Are my students learning? Could I have done better or taught differently? It took me time to realize that myths provide guidance in a very subtle way. By recognizing their existence and becoming aware of how best to apply them, I become clearer about how I wish to act as a teacher.

Only the finest of lines separate the appropriate level of control, the proper amount of preparation, and the correct application of an approach with respect to any resulting serendipitous learning moments. For serendipitous moments to occur, the learning environment cannot be completely devoid of control, preparedness, and approach. Consequently, serendipity has a very tenuous yet vital relationship to the myths identified in this chapter. The best analogy that I can think of to illustrate this point is the description of how best to grip a golf club. One is to grip a club as though holding a bird. You hold on just tight enough so that the bird does not fly away, but not so tightly as to squash or kill the bird. The grip comes with practice, and it is the foundation for the entire swing. A faulty swing results in a faulty golf shot. The application of pressure is the key, and so it is with the myths of control, preparation, and approach, and their proper application in my teaching.

Conclusions and implications for teaching process

Encouraging university faculty to identify myths that they use to make sense of teaching is an important first step in beginning the process of change. Recognizing their internalized beliefs about teaching and learning provides the foundation for teaching improvement (Candy, 1991). Our own experience illustrates that many of the attitudes and behaviors that are central to teaching in higher education are based on taken-for-granted assumptions learned from our experiences as students. Until coming together as a research team, we, like so many university professors, failed to use our skills of critical analysis for the purpose of improving teaching and learning. Only now can we acknowledge that our failure to examine our teaching beliefs has resulted in distorted assumptions about teaching. Furthermore, we can only guess at how these distorted assumptions have possibly impeded our professional growth and ability to be effective teachers.

Initially, this self-study was not motivated by our desire to change fundamentally how we approached teaching. Rather, the analysis of our meeting transcripts and critical incidents focused on isolating myths about teaching. Tangible change, however, as reflected in the two examples, was a welcome result of this analysis. We believe that the change that did transpire would not have come about without the collaborative environment we used to uncover our teaching myths. Our discussions were simultaneously humorous, blunt, supportive, and confrontational, as well as educational and motivating. Although we are an interdisciplinary team, what distinguishes us, and our ongoing work, is our respect for one another's approach to teaching, given how our own personal histories have profoundly influenced who we are as teachers.

Finally, our study provides only anecdotal evidence as to how our distorted assumptions – and the subsequent recognition of them – have affected the teaching of our students. Although we now wish we had examined our unexamined beliefs earlier, the learning that has taken place motivates us to continue to examine and uncover any additional myths. Through this ongoing examination, we fully expect to be transformed as teachers once again.

References

Ballantyne, R., Bain, J.D. and Packer, J. (1999) "Researching university teaching in Australia: Themes and issues in academics' reflections", *Studies in Higher Education*, 24 (2): 237–57.

Barthes, R. (1985) *Mythologies*, New York: Hill & Wang.

Bess, J.L. (1998) "Teaching well: Do you have to be schizophrenic?", *The Review of Higher Education*, 22 (1): 1–15.

Boice, R. (1996) *First-order Principles for College Teachers*, Bolton, MA: Anker.

Brass, D. and Gioia, D.A. (1985) "Never wear your pink shirt in the forum: Student evaluations of teaching the large course", *Organizational Behavior Teaching Journal*, 9: 100–2.

Briscoe, C. (1993) "Using cognitive referents in making sense of teaching: A chemistry teacher's struggle to change assessment practices", *Journal of Research in Science Teaching*, 30 (8): 971–87.

Britzman, D.P. (1986) "Cultural myths in the making of a teacher: Biography and social structure in teacher education", *Harvard Educational Review*, 56 (4): 442–56.

Campbell, J. (1949) *The Hero with a Thousand Faces*, New York: Pantheon Books.

—— (1972) *Myths to Live By: How we re-create ancient legends in our daily lives to release human potential*, New York: Penguin.

Candy, P.C. (1991) *Self-direction for Lifelong Learning: A comprehensive guide to theory and practice*, San Francisco, CA: Jossey-Bass.

Chambliss, D.F. (1999) "Doing what works: On the mundanity of excellence in teaching", in B.A. Pescosolido and R. Aminzade (eds) *The Social Worlds of Higher Education: Handbook for teaching in a new century*, Thousand Oaks, CA: Pine Forge, pp. 422–46.

Connor, P.E. and Becker, B.W. (1994) "Personal values and management: What do we know and why don't we know more?", *Journal of Management Inquiry*, 3 (1): 67–73.

Cranton, P. (1994) "Self-directed and transformative instructional development", *Journal of Higher Education*, 65 (6): 726–44.

Dana, N.F. and Floyd, D.M. (1994) *When teacher educators collaboratively reflect on their practices: A case study on teaching cases*, paper presented at the Annual Meeting of the Association of Teacher Educators, Atlanta, February.

Edgerton, R. (1990) *The making of a professor*, paper presented at the National Conference of the American Association for Higher Education, San Francisco, April.

Felder, R.M. and Brent, R. (1996) "Navigating the bumpy road to student-centered instruction", *College Teaching*, 44 (2): 43–7.

Goleman, D. (1998) *Working with Emotional Intelligence*, New York: Bantam.

Greene, E. (2000) "Scholars share findings on innovations in teaching [17 paragraphs]", *The Chronicle of Higher Education: Today's News*, on-line serial, 3 April.

Hassler, S.S. and Collins, A.M. (1993) *Using collaborative reflection to support changes in classroom practice*, paper presented at the Annual Meeting of the American Educational Research Association, Atlanta, March.

Hendry, G. and King, R. (1994) "On theory of learning and knowledge: Educational implications of advances in neuroscience", *Science Education*, 78: 223–53.

Johnston, S. (1996) "What can we learn about teaching from our best university teachers?", *Teaching in Higher Education*, 1 (2): 213–25.

Kember, D. and McKay, J. (1996) "Action research into the quality of student learning: A paradigm for faculty development", *Journal of Higher Education*, 67 (5): 528–54.

Kleinsasser, A.M. (1991) *Perpetuating teaching myths or debunking them? An analysis of the debunkings between a student teacher and a cooperating teacher*, paper presented at the Annual Meeting of the American Educational Research Association at Chicago, April.

Kolitch, E. and Dean, A.V. (1999) "Student ratings of instruction in the USA: Hidden assumptions and missing conceptions about 'good' teaching", *Studies in Higher Education*, 24 (1): 27–42.

Kugelmass, J.W. (2000) "Subjective experience and the preparation of activist teachers: Confronting the mean old snapping turtle and the giant big bear", *Teaching and Teacher Education*, 16 (2): 179–94.

Loughran, J.J. and Northfield, J. (1998) "A framework for the development of self-study practice", in M.L. Hamilton, S. Pinnegar, T. Russell, J.J. Loughran and V. LaBoskey (eds) *Reconceptualizing Teaching Practice: Self-study in teacher education*, London: Falmer Press, pp. 7–18.

Maltbie, C.V., Sapona, R.H., Kmitta, D. and Soled, S.W. (1996) "Working together: Creating collaborative context for team communication", in J. Richards and T. Russell (eds) *Proceedings of the First International Conference on Self-Study of Teacher Education Practices*, Kingston, Ont.: S-STEP Special Interest Group of AERA, pp. 124–7.

Mezirow, J. (1991) *Transformative Dimensions of Adult Learning*, San Francisco, CA: Jossey-Bass.

Miles, M.B. and Huberman, A.M. (1984) *Qualitative Data Analysis: A sourcebook of new methods*, Newbury Park, CA: Sage.

Oda, L.K. (1998) "Harmony, conflict and respect: An Asian-American educator's self-study", in M.L. Hamilton, S. Pinnegar, T. Russell, J.J. Loughran and V. LaBrosky (eds) *Reconceptualizing Teaching Practice: Self-study in teacher education*, London: Falmer Press, pp. 113–23.

Pereira, M.A. (1999) "My reflective practice as research", *Teaching in Higher Education*, 4 (3): 339–54.

Petersen-Perlman, D., O'Brien, M., Carlson, H. and Hilsen, L. (1999) "Choreographing partnerships: Modelling the improvement of teaching and learning", *Teaching in Higher Education*, 4 (2): 253–65.

Placier, M. (1995) "'But I have to have an A': Probing the cultural meanings and ethical dilemmas of grades in teacher education", *Teacher Education Quarterly*, 22 (3): 45–63.

Posner, G.J., Strike, K.A., Hewson, P.W. and Gertzog, W.A. (1982) "Accommodation of a scientific conception: Toward a theory of conceptual change", *Science Education*, 66: 211–27.

Rosenholtz, S.J. (1984) *Myths: Political myths about reforming teaching*, Denver, CO: Education Commission of the States.

Salovey, P. and Mayer, J.D. (1990) "Emotional intelligence", *Imagination, Cognition, and Personality*, 9: 185–211.

Shor, I. (1996) *When Students Have Power: Negotiating authority in a critical pedagogy*, Chicago, IL: University of Chicago Press.

Shulman, L.S. (1999) *Introduction: Advancing the scholarship of teaching*, paper presented at the annual meeting of AERA, Montreal, April.

Sokol, A.V. and Cranton, P. (1998) "Transforming, not training", *Adult Learning*, 9 (3): 14–16.

Thomas, L.F. and Harri-Augstein, E.S. (1983) "The self-organised learner and computer-aided learning systems: An exploratory study with the air intercept control skills trainer", final report of project no. 2066/020, Admiralty Marine Technology Establishment, Applied Psychology Unit, Uxbridge: Centre for the Study of Human Learning, Brunel University.

Webster's Unabridged Dictionary (1986) Springfield, MA: Merriam-Webster.

Weimer, M. (1990) *Improving College Teaching: Strategies for developing instructional effectiveness*, San Francisco, CA: Jossey-Bass.

Wentzel, H.K. (1987) "Seminars in college teaching: An approach to faculty development", *College Teaching*, 35: 70–1.

14 What gets "mythed" in the student evaluations of their teacher education professors?

Linda May Fitzgerald, Joan E. Farstad and Deborah Deemer

Introduction

The three women co-authors of this self-study are employed by the University of Northern Iowa and contribute to teaching courses within the professional teacher education sequence. UNI, a former state teachers' college and now one of three state regents universities, primarily serves residents of this agricultural state in the upper Midwest of the United States. UNI's motto is "Great teaching makes the difference". Each of us joined UNI at the same time, and while we have remained friends and colleagues, we each navigated our partnerships with UNI in different ways. Linda is an associate professor within the Department of Curriculum and Instruction. Joan is an adjunct faculty member in a service department (Educational Psychology and Foundations) teaching human development courses for pre-service teachers. Debbie is an associate professor in the same department, and provides courses for students in teacher education. We are all engaged in diverse forms of self-study (Boody *et al.*, 1998; Deemer *et al.*, 1998; Heston, East and Fitzgerald, 1998; Hill *et al.*, 1998; East, Farstad and Heston, 2000; Heston *et al.*, 2001).

The initiative for this particular reflection on our practice emerged within a shared press for accountability and a distrust of evidence from the institutional survey of student perspectives. Linda and Debbie were both preparing for tenure appointments. Joan is the only non-doctoral faculty member in our group. As an adjunct professor, Joan serves the institution on a semester-to-semester basis at the request of the department head, and has to be accountable for each semester of service. While Linda and Debbie have now attained whatever security is provided by tenure, new mandates related to the college's decision to seek NCATE accreditation, and pressure from the state for performance-based assessment in teacher licensure, keep accountability well within our sights. We all use a dynamic model of teaching where students interact with, and are engaged in, the course content and classroom context. Therefore, we all are at a disadvantage when students respond to an instrument developed for linear teaching ("teaching as telling") but are participating in classrooms developed for interactive teaching.

In the first year of our employment, Dr Roger Sell, Director of the Center for the Enhancement of Teaching at UNI, set up study groups for new faculty members and began a series of conversations about teaching and learning. All three of us participated. The next semester, Joan initiated conversations among faculty members who taught the same development course. Some of these members joined a parallel group in which Linda was participating (Boody *et al.*, 1998). The content for both groups was good teaching and learning, and the conversation has continued. The focus of these conversations has changed somewhat, from what makes good teaching and what does learning look like, to what does my teaching look like and does it in fact enhance learning and how could we measure that learning? Most certainly, the evaluation form given to our students at the end of the semester does not reflect this framework. Sadly, a collection of those student evaluations is used to measure teacher effectiveness. The disparity between what faculty were doing in their classrooms and what was transmitted as evidence of that "doing" made us rather defensive. We coalesced around a joint desire to make the accountability process work for us in some way.

This writing is motivated by a desire to reposition our stance from a felt need to defensively provide justification of our competence, to engagement in self-study by, and for, mutually respectful colleagues concerned with the improvement of our practice.

In this chapter we describe a movement from individualistic conceptions of teaching and assessment toward recognition of the intersubjective aspects of our practice. We critique checklist ratings of teacher performance, particularly when framed around teaching-as-telling aspects of pedagogy (which disconcertingly emerge as normative data for validating teacher performance in the tenure process). We offer two examples of self-study that explode the myth underlying the focus on isolated, individual educators. Alternative evidence of teacher performance is offered. More specifically, learning circles are evaluated using information from the perspectives of students and faculty colleagues. A co-taught course is evaluated using ethnographic methods.

Learning circles: an alternative to teacher-as-teller models of pedagogy

Joan writes:

As a young teacher, I thought and practiced teaching-as-telling. My methodology and the linear model of teaching were a match. I was passionate about my content matter and went to great lengths to present material in an engaging manner. I prepared outlines on overhead materials, slides to augment the highlights of the content, partially completed handouts for students to fill in, topographical maps to give shape to the geography, vignettes for all occasions. I was very engaged with the material, and as a result I had a wonderful time in class. I was having exciting new insights into my discipline and I was very energized. The problem was that I was the only one who was energized; my students weren't energized. They might ask questions about some content or a particular context, but I was the one who was excited about searching out the answers. I was showering them with my excitement, but I wasn't teaching them how to become excited, how to engage in the search for answers. Further, I actually thought that because I said something in class, it would be heard. Not only would what I said be heard, but also students would "take it in" and it would become formative. Now, some thirty years later, I believe that if I said something in class, I said it in class. Teaching-as-telling wasn't working and the questions that provoked my first attempts at self-study were questions about how I could get my students as engaged in the material as I was.

Eliciting pre-service beliefs: what doesn't work

As an instructor of pre-service and practicing educators, I have the good fortune of being in the company of thoughtful practitioners who engage in frequent formal and informal conversations supportive of good teaching and learning. As we engage in the classroom with pre-service and practicing educators, it is their deeply held beliefs about teaching and learning that we want to elicit and examine. Deeply held beliefs drive practice (Combs, 1982), and it is the practice of pre-service teachers that is of concern to us. If we are unable to bring those beliefs and attitudes to the surface, we will have little influence on practice.

In the past, we have tried to elicit these beliefs through journaling activities, direct inquiry, writing exercises, and other classroom strategies with very little success. In these forms of reflection, student comments remained private and what was submitted to the instructor was a set of platitudes that the student thought the instructor wanted to hear. As a result, statements of beliefs about children, about teaching, and about learning went unheard and unchallenged by student colleagues as writing assignments were completed privately and turned in to instructors for their eyes only.

Eliciting pre-service beliefs: a kind of self-study

Based on this experience, it seemed that our task was to provide opportunities for our students to become self-observers of their own metacognition regarding teaching and learning, and then to provide opportunities for our students to self-reflect on their metacognitive development. In essence, we were teaching our students to participate in self-study. Focusing on structuring and studying learning environments, the professors' self-study resulted in supporting and encouraging students in both the elicitation and examination of deeply held beliefs about teaching and learning (East, Farstad and Heston, 2000).

This self-study group really helped provide the formative conversation for these insights. We had been reading Bullough and Gitlin's *Becoming a Student of Teaching: Methodologies for Exploring Self and School Context* (1995). This text not only refuses to prescribe classroom practice, but also embraces an examination of the teacher's self as well as the classroom context. And it was this embrace of context that freed us up enough to think about the students' context. Here they were, students in a teacher education program, taking the first course in their professional sequence, involved in their first formal classroom field experience, impatiently wishing they could skip the rest of their coursework and just get their own classroom. What did they believe about teaching? About learning? About the children they would be teaching? The one thing we were sure of was that whatever they believed would be the driving force in their practice. How could we help them elicit and examine those beliefs?

In particular, we used Socratic-based learning circles (Metzger, 1998). These learning circles elicit student beliefs that we find more powerful than the carefully scripted written assignments submitted for teacher approval. For example, in student journaling we heard things such as "children have different learning styles" or "learning must be hands-on" or "learning must be fun". In learning circles, however, we hear "impoverished children can't learn" or "first graders will weasel their way out of doing work, you have to watch them" or "you can't trust those kids to be honest" or "what do you do when you don't like a student in your class?".

When a student brings to the surface a deeply held belief, such as "impoverished children can't learn", conversants immediately become ego-invested and proceed to challenge or defend the perspective. Voices may be raised, fingers may be pointed: notice is taken. In the former model (journaling) it wouldn't even have come up. No one would have known what a student thought save the instructor. If the instructor did not take it upon herself to engage in a dialogue, perhaps some comments would have been made on the student's paper, but no intersubjective dialogue would have taken place with student colleagues. As a result, there would have been no conversation to inform student practice.

Learning circle technique

The power of learning circles is that they revolve around focused, non-competitive discussion centered on a prompt. In preparation for a circle, students are asked to write three "annotations".

- Response 1 is the student's immediate take on the prompt. Using a dictionary, they are to look up words or word phrases they are not familiar with; they are to use a thesaurus, and see whether a switch of vocabulary will provide insight on a word or phrase.
- Response 2 is to involve the students in a little more rigor in their preparation and they are asked to use Meier's (1995) "habits of mind" as a framework. The framework employed by Meier includes concepts such as: What is the evidence for what you are saying? Whose viewpoint are you taking? What are your assumptions about this idea?
- Response 3 is supposed to reflect the work undertaken in Responses 1 and 2. Students are to rewrite the prompt and prepare for discussion using these

results. These responses are written out by the student (each response in a different color ink) and are submitted to the instructor.

So what takes place, prior to the circle, is that thirty-five students read, study, examine, and reflect on the prompt prior to the discussion. In addition, they have articulated their thinking in writing. Now they are "free to talk about" the topic at hand. This "freedom" allows their deeply held beliefs to surface and be vocalized and examined by student colleagues.

To form the learning circle, students count off by twos. Both groups form a circle with the ones becoming an "inner circle" and the twos forming an "outer circle". Both circles face "inward". The learning circle begins with the ones as conversants and the twos as observers. The observer function is critical for debriefing the circle. The observers record several elements of the conversation: What helped the group facilitate conversation? What impeded conversation? What private theory was brought to light during the circle? What public theory came to light? Did body language play a part in the conversation? When the circle is concluded, the class debriefs the circle using the insights gained from the observers. This is when the deeply held beliefs of student participants are examined. Beliefs are elicited during the circle itself and then examined during the debriefing.

Self-study data from the learning circles includes paper-and-pencil evaluations requesting feedback from the students on the circles in general and specifically on the prompts. In addition, individual conversations have been held with over 100 student participants. These data are persuasive in describing learning circles as excellent vehicles for eliciting deeply held beliefs about teaching and learning on the part of our students. The emotional engagement and intimacy feels significant in these conversations about beliefs and questions that are meaningful ("Are we really describing student learning, here, or are we describing *feelgood* teaching?") and at times troubling ("Black students take advantage of teachers by threatening them with their 'blackness'"). Additional evidence that something meaningful was occurring is that students took the initiative to request a learning circle, and developed the prompt for its occurrence, during the latter weeks of the class when no learning circle had been assigned.

Parker Palmer writes: "you don't think your way into a new kind of living but you live your way into a new kind of thinking" (Palmer, 1980, p. 11). Learning circles provide an opportunity for students to "live their way into a new kind of thinking" by unearthing deeply held beliefs, voicing them, hearing them perhaps for the first time, reflecting on them in a collegial setting, and making necessary changes to accommodate the dissonance aroused. In this exercise, deeply held beliefs can be influenced and practice may change as a result.

Colleagues convinced by self-study data

Other colleagues who teach on the Development Team also felt student practice could change as a result of eliciting and examining deeply held beliefs, and asked us to share our learning circle process. Seven or eight faculty members teach "The Dynamics of Human Development" each semester. As head of the Development Team, Debbie had become discouraged by what she experienced as faculty apathy with regard to calls for the creation of a more coherent curriculum and accountability measures. Neither actively resistant, nor engaged, most faculty merely failed to attend to these issues. Eventually she simply stopped calling meetings unless prompted by some external force. A positive shift occurred when a colleague, who had heard about our work with learning circles during a study group, asked if we would meet with other faculty to discuss our experiences. Faculty members were excited by the public reflection learning circles evoked, and particularly by the focus on socially constructed knowledge. Asking students to reflect on who is speaking, to whom, in what context, and for what purpose, resonated with others in the team as good practice.

As an outgrowth of this conversation the team is now talking about how to engage pre-service teachers in developmentally appropriate practice. Text-making (asking students to record what they are thinking for future consultation) is also taking hold. We have found the learning circle strategy to be challenging both for students, in terms of eliciting deeply held beliefs, and for teachers, in terms of time constraints and the intended examination of those beliefs. The challenge, to which our work contributes by providing the positive energy of self-study, is for the team to engage in and sustain a more intersubjective practice. Just as learning circles help students to "live their way into a new kind of thinking", so too do self-study groups help teacher education faculty live their way into new kinds of life in the classroom, to change current practice by challenging the beliefs on which it is based. "Selves"-study can be a professorial version of learning circles.

Problems with the student assessment of instructor instrument

Debbie writes:

I value student perspectives in thinking about my practice. However, the institutional instrument designed to assess student perspectives focuses on a form of practice that ill fits my own values. Each semester students have been asked to rate the course and instructor on a nineteen-item rating scale. Many of the items are consistent with a teacher-directed pedagogy and linear information-processing model of learning (for example, Objectives are Clear, The Instructor Enhanced Knowledge of Subject, Organized Class Sessions Well, Demonstrates Knowledge of Subject).

When I first came to UNI, I was intimidated by these student evaluations because I believed them to be overly focused on clear objectives and a class structure predicated on teacher control of the classroom. These survey items do not adequately capture what I hope to accomplish in the classroom, and I correctly anticipated receiving mixed reviews on this measure. Students may desire and need clearly presented knowledge, attained in a highly structured teacher-directed context (Grow, 1991; Kegan, 1994). But educational opportunities are impoverished if this is the only form of pedagogy provided. A rather monovocal assessment tool inscribes a particular vision of education, and fails to provide useful feedback to educators who teach in alternative ways. This narrow representation of education limits our vision of what "good" education might be, and privileges a particular mode of learning.

While I believe I have grown in placing student learning and development rather than end-of-the-year reviews at the center of my attention and thinking, in the early years of my practice these assessments created a rather hostile environment for reflecting on my practice. While members of my promotion and tenure committee were supportive, rarely did they fail to point out the poor ratings by students on some items of the student evaluation survey. Uncertain if my interpretation of the ratings would be convincing, I dreaded seeing the numbers come in, and became anxious about their presence. At the same time, I resisted changing my practice in ways that might lead to higher scores on items which presume teacher dominance in the classroom.

As I increasingly embrace feminist and qualitative forms of inquiry, I continue to struggle with lingering, dominant views of what it means to provide evidence of one's competence. If we accept Shepel's (1995) view that the context of learning and development is culturally, historically, and socially determined, in what way does it make sense to attend to the potential and performance of individual members of the faculty? Would it not make more sense to focus our attention on the ways in which students, faculty, and others within the institution together weave a context for development, thinking together about where these social and institutional arrangements may potentially take us, and what modifications to these sets of arrangements seem warranted? My commitment, to strive for both responsibility and accountability in my practice as an educator, provides only partial answers to the desired responses sought by both local and external audiences interested in accountability.

Concerns about the viability of self-study

Feedback on an early draft of our proposal for the Castle conference (a biennial conference sponsored by AERA's S-STEP SIG, held at Queen's University Herstmonceux Castle, East Sussex, UK) provided a liberating shift of perspective, encouraging us to focus on alternative evidence from self-study, rather than belabor the problems with traditional, institutional assessment procedures. Encouraged to move beyond institutional pencil-and-paper measures of accountability, toward self-study documentation, new questions arose regarding the validity and credibility of such practices. Calls to gather and articulate evidence of good practice have surfaced during the scripting of this chapter, both in the classroom with students, and in conference presentations related to this and similar self-study projects. In this section I take up personal concerns regarding the viability of cooperating in self-study projects with colleagues. I also address shifting grounds for establishing credibility, as the profession recovers from a long-term romance with empiricist illusions, and moves toward finding a way to live within the uncertainty of qualitative and constructivist leanings.

Concerns about connections

Work on the Castle conference presentation, and this related chapter, has provided a context by which to renew my commitment to collaborative engagement with colleagues. As part of this commitment I began to reflect on problems with my leadership style, and to seek improvement. One aspect of this effort has been to interview Joan, to draw on her expertise in leading study groups, and to take advantage of her perspective as an adjunct faculty. To begin the conversation, I asked Joan how she had successfully garnered commitment to study groups in her own practice. We also talked about whether it was realistic for me to attempt to replicate the experience she has had with colleagues in our college engaged in self-study.

In our conversation, I expressed concern over a felt responsibility to create a context in which faculty collaboration across the Development Team might occur. One of the most important insights for me arose as Joan told a story about assuming a care-taking role within her family. Feeling both responsible and overwhelmed when the need arose for her to care for her aging parents, Joan had taken counsel with her brother. He assured her that this was very doable, if she just remembered to be interested in them. I left that meeting pondering what I might do to demonstrate interest. Soon after, in a meeting with Linda and Joan, I expressed a desire to solidify my connections with them, and they have responded with increased efforts to help me feel included and cared for.

At the same time, in reflecting on how best to assume leadership in nurturing a self-study group among faculty on the Development Team, I am not convinced that Linda's and Joan's success with self-study can be "replicated" in some algorithmic fashion. Each new group must feel its own way forward. What complicates the process further is that some faculty in this anticipated self-study may be unwilling participants, given its association with accreditation demands. As Joan clarifies, self-study does not offer a series of strategies to be generalized. Our outstanding question, in terms of work with a broader set of colleagues, is "How do we get at our beliefs?" With no pat answers to this question, we are simply approaching the formation of the new self-study group with optimism, rooted in no small part in the success of learning circles among our students.

Faith in self-study as a form of professional development

As I begin to enjoy the seeds of active collaboration with faculty in the Development Team, more external challenges to the viability of self-study have emerged. Questions about the credibility of self-study parallel concerns and responses voiced at the 2001 AERA conference in Seattle. Much of the meeting of the Qualitative Research Special Interest Group was devoted to a presentation and follow-up discussion centered on the question of how to bolster qualitative inquiry's perceived rigor and credibility with external audiences (such as dissertation committees, granting agencies, and publication outlets). In paper sessions, methodological issues and the groping for grounds on which to stand within the "ruins of certainty" were popular themes (see Qualitative Research Special Interest Group, 2001).

While some speakers repackaged positivist strategies – such as Vincent Anfara and Kathleen Brown's (2001) call for audit trails, protocols, code mapping, triangulation, public inspection, and critique – others put forth criteria and strategies from within the qualitative paradigm. A particularly resonant voice for me was that of Peggy Gill (2001) who spoke of the "method of the possible" which builds on stories. She noted that while telling stories works to build relationships, it doesn't stop there, as desires emerge to respond to needs brought forth in these stories. Yvonna Lincoln (2001) similarly spoke of a move beyond rapport, toward empathy and solidarity with inquiry participants. Again the belief was expressed that we don't just tell stories. We listen to understand the meaning of stories, to make connections, which lead to activism. Finally, Linda Alcoff's question for inquirer reflection, "Where does your research go, and what does it do there?" (cited in Wolcott, 2001), strikes me as a profound focus when thinking about how to establish the credibility of one's work in self-study.

Beyond the self: "selves"-study using ethnography

Linda writes:

As the voices of Joan and Debbie reflect, many educators begin with the presumption that teaching is telling, and institutional assessment typically focuses on the individual as unit of analysis. The assumption of individual professor ownership of course construction and delivery is problematic. As Palmer (1998) notes in discussing standardized questionnaires given to students for rating their instructors toward the end of a course:

> Teachers have every right to be demoralized by such a simplistic approach – the nuances of teaching cannot possibly be captured this way. No uniform set of questions will apply with equal force to the many varieties in which good teaching comes … . There is only one honest way to evaluate the many varieties of good teaching with the subtlety required: it is called being there. We must observe each other teach, at least occasionally – and we must spend more time talking to each other about teaching.
>
> (Palmer, 1998, p. 143)

The individualistic "myth" of learning is that it occurs in individual student skulls as the result of an individual professor employing the set of practices that are operationalized in the "mythodology" of the Student Assessment of Instructor. A challenge to the myth, not to mention to the assessment instrument, is a course with two teachers working together.

Self-study data used to improve pre-service teaching

One of the most intensive self-studies that Linda was involved in was for a curriculum course co-taught with Rebecca Edmiaston, a colleague on loan from a research position. In the class that we co-taught, doctoral student Christie Sales carried out an ethnographic evaluation as a participant observer. This course seriously violated the assumption of individual class ownership that underlies the Student Assessment of Instructor instrument. Neither instructor could use data from that instrument, not to demonstrate teaching effectiveness to tenure and promotion committees, nor to figure out how to change teaching practices. Each of us had a distinctive teaching style, so that some responses about "the" instructor seemed to be about one or the other of us, while other responses seemed to be about the both of us together. "Ownership" of the quantitative ratings could not be determined reliably. In addition no valid attempt could be made to lump these ratings together with quantitative ratings from courses each of us taught individually, so as to give our evaluators the "score" for each of us as an instructor that they could then easily judge.

Data from the ethnographic evaluation, however, led to changes not only in each instructor's teaching of undergraduates in individual classes, but also in working with practicing teachers. One example of changing undergraduate instruction is the investigation we undertook when student group work showed problems, such as equitable turn-taking in discussions and staying on topic. We used multiple data sources: the doctoral student's informal interviews with students, written reflections from the students, and the co-teaching professors' processing of our observations after class. We discovered that, in spite of much use of group discussion in other classes, few students had received explicit training in group work. So we invited a local consultant in for a class session on effective group work techniques and noticed immediate improvements in our class – and learned a thing or two ourselves.

Interviews with students by the evaluator provided much more depth and context than the Student Assessment of Instructor instrument, leading to a change in the presentation and use of the alternative assessment system for the class in order to provoke less anxiety in the students.

Much of what was learned in this "selves"-study has been applied to make team teaching more successful at many levels – for example, for teacher educators and for partners teaching young children in their roles as classroom teachers. Other data sources that we used included joint planning sessions for the next class; debriefing immediately after class, with the assistance of the doctoral student; beginning to plan the next class to incorporate what was learned that day. When her employer withdrew support for Edmiaston to be in every class, much less for these debriefings, the quality of the teaming and of the class suffered, and was commented on by students, primarily to the doctoral student evaluator.

Self-study data used for accountability

In addition, Linda came up with assessment data for her own large binder of evidence of her teaching to submit to the tenure and promotion committee. The introduction to that binder stated:

> In the self-study of teacher education practice in which I have been engaged with my colleagues continuously since my first days on campus, I use a variety of data to inform my practice. In rough order of the value of the kind of data to changing my practice, the following techniques are represented in this binder:
>
> - Self-reflective writing after class.
> - Audiotapes after a site visit to a student teacher.
> - Practical argument technique with colleagues about a specific practice.
> - Critical reflection together after classes that are co-taught.
> - Colleagues observing classes annually.
> - Ethnographic evaluation of class.
> - Videotape of teaching with collegial comments.
> - Videotapes of classroom practice.
> - Student reflections on their learning – solicited.
> - Student reflections on their learning – unsolicited.
> - Graduates' unsolicited communications after getting jobs.
> - Student Assessment of Instructor – rating scale.
> - Student Assessment of Instructor – written comments.
> - "Repeat customers" – signing up to take a second or third class.
>
> (Fitzgerald, 1999)

Over time, some of the items at the top of the list have shifted in priority, with less time for reflective writing after night classes that end at 10 PM and much more benefit from "selves"-study undertaken with a variety of colleagues. As "repeat customers" voice their reasons for wanting to work with me again, and continue to seek me out after securing classrooms of their own, that form of data has become more valuable. Data from Student Assessment of Instructor drop to the bottom of the list.

In the same teaching binder, I went on to detail how I had been working against what I called "the tyranny of the student evaluation process" and for the heavier weighting of more self-study-friendly evidence of teaching effectiveness. Risking this reframing of criteria for tenure and promotion evidently was worth it. Not only was I awarded tenure, but also junior faculty have been encouraged by my evaluators to use my documentation as a model in presenting their own case for tenure.

Self-study data used to improve in-service teaching

Two other outcomes of the ethnographic "selves"-study involve practicing teachers with whom our pre-service teachers do field experiences. Teachers at Grant Early Childhood Center have been working hard to change their practice for a number of years, providing a model for and mentoring pre-service teachers at various stages. In a series of year-long study groups with these teachers, Linda and her partner in the ethnographic self-study, Rebecca Edmiaston, have been able to use their own experience together to support the teachers in their struggles to build collaborative relationships (Edmiaston and Fitzgerald, 2000). Rather than being University Experts with the Answer, we have been fellow-seekers, all learning from each other as we confront similar dilemmas in our various teaching partnerships.

Linda also has applied lessons learned in the ethnographic self-study to a subsequent co-teaching relationship with another professor, with whom she teaches a course and supervises a practicum in which pre-service teachers are placed with practicing teachers for most of the semester. Regular meetings between the professors to reflect together on what is working and what needs to be changed, and regular meetings with the practicing teachers who supervise the practicum experiences help to avoid the problems that occurred when Edmiaston could no longer meet regularly with Fitzgerald in the class on which the ethnography was done. Linda and her co-teacher also share their collaborative practice with their students to serve as explicit examples of the kinds of reflection they will need to do in their own practice as they join the teaching profession.

Conclusion

Reflecting on each of the above examples, we realized a tension and movement between thinking and working as an individual self while simultaneously being engaged in an intersubjective practice. In the last example, Linda and her collaborators were consciously aware of the intersubjectivity of their work, in stark contrast to the anxiety of the individual professor up against the wall of the Student Assessment of Instructor. Until the institutional structure gets transformed, we are cycling through these tensions for accountability (tenure file, student assessments, grading) as individuals. When we can stand outside that individual tension (for instance, after Debbie and Linda received their tenure letters), we can see ourselves as more intersubjective.

As we look toward the future and a continued proactive engagement in self-study, it seems important to keep our dynamic practice, and the student learning which moves our practice, at the center of our attention. Within the institutional press to document the outcomes of our practice for the purpose of accountability, we must nurture the space we have created for meaningful self-study. As reflective colleagues, participating in a mutually respectful, ongoing dialogue about our practice, we know that no one thinks and acts in isolation. We believe that surfacing the realization of our interdependence, and explicitly committing ourselves to fostering intersubjective understandings, will enhance the quality of our work.

As we, and like-minded colleagues, begin to take on the decision-making roles of senior faculty, including mentoring and evaluating our junior colleagues, we can attempt to change the institutional structure from the inside (while using "selves"-study group processes to keep ourselves from forgetting where we came from). Indeed, the fact that junior faculty in both of our departments are using Linda and Debbie's tenure file documentation as models (with Linda and Debbie now sitting on tenure and promotion committees as well) is some evidence that this can be done. And since we wrote our original proposal for the Castle conference, the university has acknowledged some of the worst features of the Student Assessment of Instructor instrument and has begun to use a modified version (whose worth remains to be tested). The university also encourages faculty to use the Small Group Instructional Diagnosis technique supported by Dr Sell's Center for the Enhancement of Teaching as a way to obtain student feedback in the middle of a course, to serve a formative, rather than purely summative, evaluation function that is more in keeping with the spirit of self-study.

To keep our eyes on the prize, we remind ourselves frequently that our self-study is not for self-justification to keep our places and paychecks in the university. For us, the end-user is the student in the classroom who will be taught by graduates of our program. We work to improve teacher education in order, ultimately, to improve the education our graduates will provide. Just as self-study led Joan to use learning circles in her classroom, the outcomes of that process have informed our own self-study, as we bring to the surface and challenge our own beliefs, leading to further changes in the way we teach. We try to practice what we preach, to serve as models of reflective practice and lifelong learning. We recognize that in order to help classroom teachers change their practice, we have to start by changing our own practices in teacher education. Joining together in self-study, including in our discussions of such colleagues-in-print as Bullough and Gitlin (1995) and Palmer (1998), we not only support each other to risk changing our pre-service teaching practice, but also try to change institutional assessment practices to make it easier for others to change their teaching practice as well.

References

Anfara, V.A. and Brown, K.M. (2001) *Qualitative analysis on stage: making the process more public*, paper presented at the annual meeting of AERA, Seattle, April.

Boody, R., East, K., Fitzgerald, L.M., Heston, M. and Iverson, A. (1998) "Talking, teaching and learning: Using practical argument to make reflective thinking audible", *Action in Teacher Education*, 19 (4): 88–101.

Bullough, R.V., Jr and Gitlin, A. (1995) *Becoming a Student of Teaching: Methodologies for exploring self and school context*, New York: Garland.

Combs, A.W. (1982) *A Personal Approach to Teaching: Beliefs that make a difference*, Boston, MA: Allyn & Bacon.

Deemer, D. *et al.* (1998) *Strengthening undergraduate education at UNI*, presentation at the Conference on the Qualities of an Educated Person, University of Northern Iowa, Cedar Falls.

East, K., Farstad, J.E. and Heston, M.L. (2000) *Examining the beliefs of educators: Preliminary experiences with learning circles*, paper presented at the annual meeting of AERA, New Orleans, April.

Edmiaston, R.E. and Fitzgerald, L.M. (2000) "How Reggio Emilia encourages inclusion", *Educational Leadership*, 58 (1): 66–9.

Fitzgerald, L.M. (1999) *Tenure and promotion application file: Teaching binder*, unpublished manuscript, University of Northern Iowa, Cedar Falls.

Gill, P.B. (2001) *Nonfictional narrative story: An inquiry guided method*, paper presented at the annual meeting of AERA, Seattle, April.

Grow, G.O. (1991) "Teaching learners to be self-directed", *Adult Education Quarterly*, 41 (3): 125–49.

Heston, M., East, K. and Fitzgerald, L.M. (1998) "Using practical argument to create communities of conversation", in A. Cole and S. Finley (eds) *Conversations in Community: Proceedings of the Second International Conference of the Self-Study of Teacher Education Practices* (August), Canada: Queen's University, pp. 195–8.

Heston, M., East, K., Miller, C. and Fitzgerald, L. (2001) *Visions of self in the act of teaching*, paper presented at the annual meeting of AERA, Seattle, April.

Hill, S., Fitzgerald, L.M., Haack, J. and Clayton, S. (1998) "Transgressions: Teaching according to bell hooks", *Thought and Action*, 14 (2): 41–8.

Kegan, R. (1994) *In Over Our Heads: The mental demands of modern life*, Cambridge, MA: Harvard University Press.

Lincoln, Y.S. (2001) *Interviewing as postmodern inquiry practice*, paper presented at the annual meeting of AERA, Seattle, April.

Meier, D. (1995) *The Power of Their Ideas: Lessons for America from a small school in Harlem*, Boston, MA: Beacon.

Metzger, M. (1998) "Teaching reading: Beyond the plot", *Phi Delta Kappan*, 80 (3): 240–6, 256.

Palmer, P.J. (1980) *The Promise of Paradox*, Notre Dame, IN: Ave Maria Press.

—— (1998) *The Courage to Teach: Exploring the Inner Landscape of a Teacher's Life*, San Francisco, CA: Jossey-Bass.

Qualitative Research Special Interest Group (2001) *Preparing knowledge workers in an information saturated world: Methodological bricolage in qualitative research*, business meeting at the annual meeting of AERA, Seattle, April.

Shepel, E.N.L. (1995) "Teacher self-identification in culture from Vygotsky's developmental perspective", *Anthropology and Education Quarterly*, 26 (4): 425–42.

Wolcott, H. (2001) *How do we know what we know? Because they said so: Charting the changes in contemporary educational interviewing*, symposium at the annual meeting of AERA, Seattle, April.

15 Research as a way of knowing and seeing

Advocacy for the other

Jeffrey J. Kuzmic

Introduction

> Engaged pedagogy not only compels me to be constantly creative in the classroom, it also sanctions involvement with students beyond that setting. I journey with students as they progress in their lives beyond our classroom experience. In many ways, I continue to teach them, even as they become more capable of teaching me.
>
> (hooks, 1994, p. 205)

This chapter represents a temporary end-point of a continuing journey, unknowingly started as an individual, probably back in high school, because my collaboration with teachers along the way has challenged me to rethink, reformulate and re-examine the ways in which I have come to understand research. Within the last ten years, the area of teacher research has seen a rebirth and emergence as a burgeoning area in teacher education scholarship and practice. A wealth of new books describe the methodological foundations of teacher research, address epistemological and ethical issues, and provide numerous examples of teacher research (Hopkins, 1985; Goswami and Stillman, 1986; Altrichter, Posch and Somekh, 1993; Cochran-Smith and Lytle, 1993; Anderson, Herr and Nihlen, 1994; Hollingsworth, 1994; Noffke and Stevenson, 1994; Burnaford, Fischer and Hobson, 1996; Atweh, Kemmis and Weeks, 1998; Freedman *et al.*, 1999; Arhar, Holly and Kasten, 2001). Perhaps this, in itself, provides some recognition of both its merit as a form of research and the absence of teachers' voices within the educational research community. Shulman has called this absence the "missing paradigm", which he described as referring to:

> the blind spot with respect to the content that now characterizes most research on teaching and, as a consequence, most of our state-level program of teacher evaluation and teacher certification.
>
> (Shulman, 1986, p. 8)

What Shulman suggests is that in much of the research on teaching it is clear that central questions remain unasked, in part because teachers remain outside the research community. He argues that there is a great deal of emphasis on what teachers do – how they manage their classrooms, organize activities, allocate time and turns, ascribe praise and blame, formulate levels of their questions, plan lessons and judge students' general understanding – but little with regard to why teachers do the things they do; that is, the knowledge-base that teachers themselves use as a means for informing and justifying their practice.

Defining the problem

Shulman's missing paradigm is still missing, and teacher research remains on the margins of educational research. This, I believe, is a direct result of the fissure between most academic researchers and teachers themselves. Drawing on Cochran-Smith and Lytle (1993), I am particularly interested in exploring the following myth that is very real for myself and the teachers with whom I work: *Knowledge about teaching is generated by those outside the classroom (that is, academic researchers), and the professional responsibility of teachers is to utilize this knowledge to improve their practice.* As with every myth, there is a need to recognize both the truth and fiction in this statement, as well as the historical, social, political, and, in this case, epistemological context in which it is embedded and which gives it meaning. For both myself and the teachers with whom I work, this myth is real and complicated, something we both embrace and reject.

Embedded in this myth (and the relationship of this myth to teacher research) are assumptions about the relationship between theory and practice (Anderson and Herr, 1999), the role and relationship of teachers to the knowledge-base about teaching (Cochran-Smith and Lytle, 1993), relations of power (Kincheloe, 1991; Cochran-Smith and Lytle, 1993; Freedman et al., 1999), and understandings about the meaning of professionalism (Kincheloe, 1991). It is precisely the ideological character of this myth and its power in shaping our understanding of research as a way (ways) of knowing that have become clearer to me as a teacher educator through the teachers with whom I work.

Research as a way of knowing: an autobiography

I recall being introduced to research through the scientific method back in high school. Throughout my undergraduate coursework I neither embraced nor challenged this paradigm; it just was. The use of the scientific method and experimentation were equated with (R)esearch and the validity of (K)nowledge. During my graduate coursework in comparative education and curriculum inquiry, I first became aware of Kuhn's (1962) notion of scientific revolution, quantitative/positivist and qualitative/post-positivist paradigms, and the epistemological debates surrounding research in education. I took a course with Egon Guba that convinced me not of the superiority but of the merit and value of naturalistic inquiry as a means for investigating educational phenomena (Lincoln and Guba, 1985). My introduction to critical, post-modern, and feminist theoretical discourses resulted in a doctoral research project that I framed as a critical ethnography (Thomas, 1993) closely linking qualitative research within a democratic and emancipatory theoretical project.

My own socialization as a scholar, teacher, and researcher provided me with a set of epistemological relationships: the need to explore the lived experiences and perspectives of teachers and students within a larger, social, political, and economic context (the relationship between theory and research); the value of honoring, even including in a collaborative sense, "the researched" in the research process (the relationship between research and practice); and the importance and power of the researcher, and because of this, the need to examine, articulate, and critique my role in the research process (the relationships between theory, research, and practice). These in turn have influenced the purpose, process, and product of not only my own research but also my understanding of research as (R)esearch and of (R)esearch as a way of knowing.

Teaching theory, research, and practice: a methodological context of sorts

Like many teachers, I wanted practical answers to practical questions. My own experiences as a middle and high school teacher left me with a wealth of questions, a dearth of answers, and frustration with not knowing where to begin to seek answers. As a graduate student, my experiences with the power of theories generated an epiphany of sorts. While this may not have provided practical answers to my questions, it helped me understand the questions themselves while contextualizing them at a personal and political level. I took comfort in this understanding and sought to incorporate it into my work as a teacher educator. Regardless of the course I am teaching (for example, *Introduction to Secondary Education, Teaching History and Social Sciences in Secondary Schools, Teaching as Research*), I always seek to contextualize our work, readings, and discussions of teaching within a wider social, political, cultural, historical, and theoretical context. For me and, I argue, for my students as future teachers, these frame, shape, and give meaning to our understandings of teaching, education, and their relation to the workings of wider society.

As a teacher educator I am guilty of looking at, and perhaps even privileging, a particular perspective on the nature of the relationship between theory and practice. My course evaluations (regardless of course type) consistently call for less *theoretical* and more *practical* knowledge. It is too easy to label such comments as indicative of an atheoretical focus that privileges practice over theory, an unwillingness to struggle with the difficulty of theory and implications for practice, or, at best, the inability of theory to speak to those concerned with practice. For a long time, I tried to live with these contradictions or tensions, justifying my approach to courses by convincing myself that, like me, the teachers with whom I worked would come to appreciate theory through practice, appreciate practice in light of theory, or develop more complex understandings of the interplay between theory and practice. This, after all, was my job, and for many students this ultimately seemed effective.

Only when I started teaching the course *Teaching as Research*, and began working collaboratively with a group of beginning teachers undertaking research in their classrooms, did I begin to more fully problematize these tensions. I came to see the power of research in thinking about the dialectical relationships embedded in our attempts to understand theory through practice and practice in light of theory. *Teaching as Research* is one of three induction-year courses in DePaul University's *Teaching and Learning* program – a first certificate master's program for students seeking to teach (often after a number of years in a another occupation). The induction-year courses are designed to be taken after certification and during one's beginning years as a teacher.

> The TandL 610/611, 612, 613 sequence is designed to help you explore the process and practice of becoming a teacher while developing the habit of critical reflection as a means of understanding and enhancing one's teaching and emerging conceptions of "self" as teacher … . This course [TandL 612], as part of that sequence, seeks to promote the types of reflection and dialogue begun in TandL 610/611 within a framework designed to explore how critical reflection can provide the foundation for understanding one's teaching/life-as-a-teacher as a form of research.
>
> (Syllabus, Spring 2001)

Another significant factor – actually an ongoing set of experiences – that helped reshape my understanding of research revolves around my collaboration with a group of six beginning teachers in their efforts to explore their practice through practitioner research and collaboration. This project emerged, in part, through my previous efforts in teaching *Teaching as Research* and the relationships I developed with these teachers in the pre-service component of the *Teaching and Learning* program. It has emerged from a nexus of factors and relationships surrounding the interaction of a university-based teacher educator and students enrolled in a first certificate master's program. Our relationship, initiated in several courses within this program, has developed over time and serves as the basis for what we refer to as a collaborative research project that has a dual focus. First, it seeks to examine the practice of teachers doing classroom-based research. Second, it seeks to promote the collaboration of a teacher educator and a group of educators seeking to understand the nature, practice, and issues involved in practitioner research while supporting individual group members in their efforts to conduct research. This project, now in its fourth year, has had a significant impact on my teaching and ways of seeing and thinking about research as a way of knowing. It is within the context of these interrelated experiences that this chapter has developed.

Learning with teachers

In what follows, I explore some of the key understandings that have emerged from my work with teachers and how these have helped me in moving from "blaming the victim" to a perspective that argues for the need to challenge what Anderson and Herr (1999) have called the "othering" of teachers by academics. That teacher research has been challenged as a way of knowing by those in the academic research community (Kincheloe, 1991; Cochran-Smith and Lytle, 1993; Anderson and Herr, 1999) and differentiated from research on teaching (done by academics), reflects not only a perspective on what counts as research, but also a perspective about teacher as "other". Through my own learning with teachers I have come to see this perspective as methodological and ideological, situated around the dynamics of power and the control of knowledge in re-search.

Originally I anticipated drawing on data collected within the collaborative project and the teaching of *Teaching as Research*. This mass of data proved unwieldy and effectively took my voice out of the narrative. I have chosen, instead, to build on two statements by one teacher (Allison), taken at different points as she began her career as a teacher and progressed through our program. I have drawn on these two statements for a particular reason: they continue to haunt me. Gordon (1997), in her book *Ghostly Matters: Haunting and the Sociological Imagination*, uses "hauntings" as a metaphor for talking about those issues, questions, and experiences of our research that are disturbing, unsettling, or problematic, and therefore need attention. I have found Gordon's notion of "hauntings" compelling as a mechanism for thinking about self-study. It is, indeed, those issues, questions, and experiences with teachers or students that continue to haunt me that I see as deserving of both reflection and self-study. Allison, a high school social studies teacher, has taken two courses with me: *Teaching, History, and Social Science in Middle and High School* just prior to her student teaching and *Teaching as Research* during her first year of teaching. She is also one of the six teachers involved in the collaborative research project. I use her statements as a point of departure for my analysis, and as an illustration of how teachers have helped me rethink my understanding of research in light of their own struggles.

Teaching as research: validating teaching, not invalidating research

Just as I did prior to graduate school, teachers often see (R)esearch as something that exists outside of them and as something done to them. In the first several weeks of TandL 612, the students and I examine our assumptions about the nature and conduct of research, trying to tease out what makes research into Research. Assumptions about objectivity, the need to prove something, and the validity of quantitative analysis are examined as we read about teacher research and research done by teachers.

What I have come to understand about this process is the ontological character and struggle of this process, one that is not so easily addressed in one course or even through study of one's own teaching or research more generally. While thinking about and doing research (and teacher research in particular) is epistemological in character, the ontological aspect of such work has been more clearly reified as I have worked with teachers.

> In addition to my desire to engage and inspire students to think and look at the world critically, I also want to continually examine the extent to which my actual practice jibes with my theories and philosophies of teaching ... . My hope is that my research would provide some structure and rigor to my reflections and my work ... . I also hope that my action research, as well as the growing field of action research in general, will provide useful insights to other practitioners and pre-service teachers. Many teachers yearn to see stories of teachers and read of lessons learned, being able to relate to many factors present in a classroom and teaching. This seems to be what is desired, as opposed to what some teachers see as reading another rendition of perceived irrelevant, impractical theory espoused by removed academics who never make the leap into the classroom. Thus critical issues and questions are ignored or brushed aside, sometimes being considered too mundane. Importantly, it is hoped that the sharing of teacher research will promote dialogue among teachers as well as bring teachers' voices into the present discourse in educational literature.
>
> (Allison, TandL 612 research proposal, Spring 1998)

For Allison, then, examining and doing teacher research amounts to redefining oneself on a personal and professional level that resituates oneself in relation to one's work and one's profession. In this sense, doing teacher research becomes less a project that serves to validate research in general (that is, to see its professional efficacy), and more a project that serves to validate one's role as a teacher and one's teaching.

While it would be easy to brush aside Allison's (haunting) comments about academics and the research they do (research from the outside rather than from the inside), I have come to appreciate this not so much as a critique but as a call for action. Rather than dismissing Allison's comments – and the echoes of them in similar comments by teacher education students and teachers – as being a form of resistance to educational scholarship and research, I argue that her comments represent an ontological perspective that teacher educators need to listen to and act on. In this sense, it is much more about how one views oneself than it is about how one views the other. For Allison, and for many of the teachers with whom I work, this is about rediscovering the relationship between theory, practice, and research in a way that is more connected to, and reflective of, one's professional life. I have come to realize that it is precisely this ontological relationship embedded in the epistemological foundations of teacher research that shapes its methodological character. For practitioners, then, it is

the very real relationship between research and practice that shapes its methodological stance, one that is oftentimes criticized by academic researchers. As I
have worked with teachers doing research, I have come to both experience and
better understand these differences with respect to my own ontological relationship to the research and the research process.

Increasingly, I see myself arguing for academics to take responsibility for
understanding teacher research as a form of research, rather than expecting
teacher research to mirror research done by academics. In this sense, teachers
themselves have forced me to examine the epistemological, methodological,
and ontological assumptions embedded in my understanding of what counts as
research. Thus I am more willing to try to understand how teacher research, as
research, appears through teachers' eyes, not my own. As a way of knowing,
teacher research needs to be acknowledged and understood in light of the
unique contextual, professional, and phenomenological realities that define
teachers' understanding of and efforts to engage in research.

Here I see the benefits of self-study in teacher education. On one level, self-study
enables me to better engage in my work as a teacher educator through critical
reflection on my practice and work as a teacher. At another level, more closely
related to this chapter, I think my own efforts at self-study (ontologically akin
to those of teacher researchers) have better positioned me to hear and understand how my students understand, make use of, and do educational research.
Finally, self-study provides teacher educators with a professional forum for
further examining, collectively, the pedagogical and scholarly merits of these
individual efforts.

Toward this end, I have sought to find and create mechanisms in class to
explore, deconstruct, and reconstruct our understandings of research through
teacher research. For example, for the second week of class in TandL 612, I ask
students to bring an example of a research article on teaching. We use these
articles as a basis for beginning to discuss definitions of research, typologies of
research, and the epistemological foundations of different forms of research.
The majority of students bring quantitative research articles, a few bring qualitative studies, but no one has ever brought an example of teacher research.
While not surprising, this affords us the opportunity to discuss not only their
understanding of research, but also their relationship to research. Increasingly, I
rely on teachers themselves (those in my classes and those doing teacher
research) to work through epistemological and methodological understandings
of teacher research. While my initial attempts at teaching TandL 612 were
designed to assist teachers in *doing* teacher research, my efforts more recently
have also sought to engage teachers in *understanding* teacher research as a form
of research.

Thus I face a pedagogical issue, and I have struggled to explore my own
understanding of research as a way of knowing and the implications of that
understanding for my teaching. I have found Fine's notion of "working the
hyphen" (Fine, 1994, p. 72) useful in rethinking my teaching and role as a
teacher educator more generally. For me, working the hyphen means constant

attention to unpacking the relationships that we often take for granted in thinking about teaching and research. For example, through a series of readings, assignments, and informal journal writings, the students in *Teaching as Research* join me in taking up the issues of what is research, who does research, and what are the consequences of our understandings. Inevitably, my voice as the instructor, an academic, and a researcher is a voice that students often take to be authoritative. Pedagogically, I have struggled with this, because it makes it more difficult to develop a shared understanding of research as we struggle with these issues. Each of the students in the class undertakes a teacher research project over the course of the quarter, and so, when I last taught the course in Spring 2001, I joined the students and did a teacher research project using our class as my research site, focusing on their changing perceptions of themselves as teachers in relation to research. Working the hyphen in this case enabled me to resituate my voice in the classroom in a way that reduced but did not eliminate its authoritative tone.

This has forced me to recognize how teacher research challenges the epistemological and methodological assumptions I bring to the table. What I have described above as the ontological situatedness of teachers' relationship to research has challenged me to more consciously explore the methodology of teacher research within a context that recognizes its epistemological, political, and ideological dimensions. It has also forced me, as a teacher educator, to acknowledge and engage teachers' voices, perspectives, and understandings in ways not previously envisioned. Because I feel it is my responsibility (and that of the university community more generally) to understand teachers' ways of knowing, how these may be similar to or different from my own, and how these may be challenged and reconstructed when thinking about the space between teacher research, teacher researcher, and teacher knowledge, the teachers' experiences and voices have become more central to my pedagogy.

Finding one's voice, discovering one's marginalization

Emerging directly from my collaborative relationship with a group of beginning teachers is a second understanding that has greatly influenced how I think about teacher research and how I approach the teaching of TandL 612. In initially discussing and designing the research project, I hoped it would accomplish two fundamentally different goals. The first goal was to conceptualize the project as a means of developing a collaborative thesis research project (which would require special permission) as a means of fulfilling the requirements for the Master of Arts in Education degree within their program of study. The second goal was to develop a manuscript that embodied our individual efforts in doing teacher research, as well as our efforts to accomplish these within a collaborative and supportive context designed to explore what it means to conceptualize teaching as a form of research.

Towards this latter goal, we envisioned a manuscript that would contribute to the growing body of literature on teacher research, while also validating the voices of teachers within the research community. In light of the first of these goals we had to select a group of three faculty members (two in addition to myself) to serve as the thesis committee and have a proposal defense meeting. After developing a proposal that reflected the individual projects to be undertaken by group members and the overall focus on collaboration, we scheduled that meeting. While the meeting was typical of proposal defense meetings, with committee members asking questions and offering suggestions, I was somewhat taken aback by the response of group members directly following the meeting and at our next scheduled research group meeting. Several of the group members were genuinely offended by what they perceived as the efforts of the thesis committee members to frame our project in particular ways that did not honor or understand teacher research. As Allison suggested, "I feel like they're trying to force a square peg in a round hole". In her second haunting statement, she went on to say:

> To be honest I've had this really sick feeling about the entire thing. I'd almost rather do another option for the Masters, and do this project as we really want to do it. I don't want to do someone else's agenda at all. I guess I have to be blunt if I want to make any sense at all; I don't really care about their agenda and their interests in my research and what I want to do. I really wanted to do this project. I feel like once it becomes somebody else's idea of what it should be, like a Masters committee, I really have no investment in it. I'm having a hard enough time struggling with my project as it is. I've just had a bad feeling ever since then. Like when Samuel [an adjunct faculty member and full-time practitioner for over ten years] brought up the idea about researching what it means to make curriculum within the structure. I just don't have any interest in that … . It's like they were saying just because it's an interesting question to you, or a story about your teaching, doesn't make it research, doesn't make it adequate for a Masters.
>
> (Allison, research group meeting, November 1998)

This conversation resulted in a decision by the group not to do the MA thesis (which several were invested in because of its perceived status) but to do the M.Ed. papers instead. In spite of the fact that they understood what they were doing to be research, and therefore in line with the distinction between an MA and the M.Ed., they chose to do the M.Ed. to avoid having their work framed by others' definitions of research. My own reading of this defining incident has shown me the silencing and marginalization of teachers' voices by researchers, the resistance of teachers to this marginalization, and my own and other university researchers' complicity in this.

Allison's comments were made in reference to one committee member's suggestion that, for each of the individual projects, there would need to be a more clearly articulated research focus and literature review that sought to "situate and validate their research questions in light of educational scholarship and research". Interestingly, I have used this argument with students myself. Allison's comments finally made me realize the privileging of academics' voices over those of teachers. Knowing Allison, it was not the reference to doing a literature review that she found so upsetting: she was knowledgeable, well read, and quite willing and capable of doing this. It was the requirement to validate her research through another discourse, thereby silencing and marginalizing her voice, that prompted her reaction (and that of the group as a whole) to our meeting with the thesis committee. It is one thing to discount or dismiss educational research because it does not speak to you. It is another thing altogether to find one's voice, only to discover it to be marginalized.

Increasingly, as I think about my teaching and my role as a teacher educator, I have come to see advocacy for the Other as a central part of both. I have come to see this advocacy in a political sense, in ways that move beyond the recognition of the potential benefits for teachers and the educational research community, to efforts that challenge and seek to unveil what Foucault has called "regimes of truth" (Gore, 1994). As long as we look at (or fail to look at) the challenges that teacher research poses to educational research more generally, seeing them as merely methodological or as merely adding teachers' voices to the research community, we ignore the reality that this is also about power and the authority of the voices heard.

I now think about my silence in the thesis committee meeting in terms of Allison's anger and disappointment. I saw what was happening, yet I did not intervene. I justified my silence at the time in terms of my being a member of both the research group and the thesis committee. I truly was in conflict about how to respond. I wanted to support my thesis committee colleagues in their questions and suggestions, yet I also wanted to support my co-researchers in challenging my colleagues' understanding of what counts as research. Should I have found a way to speak from my privileged position as a university-based researcher in support of these teachers' (my co-researchers') claims to be heard? YES, I should have. I now recognize this as a political act. While I am unsure of the forms that future advocacy will take, and while I recognize that it is problematic, I also recognize the necessity of those occupying the center speaking for those at the margins. This is not to suggest that those on the margins cannot speak for themselves, only that their voices need to be supported.

Teacher research as a way of knowing

Rethinking this myth has meant a fundamental realization that this issue is not merely or only methodological (that is, who and in what way research is conducted), it is also epistemological. Because epistemology is about what knowledge is worth knowing, and because this is always about power and position, I have come to see and experience that the challenge of teacher research (and therefore teachers) is intimately, ultimately, and fundamentally political in character. As indicated by Anderson and Herr (1999), many of the issues associated with teacher research have begun to be examined by the center (that is, the university research community). In discussing what they refer to as the "new paradigm wars", they explore the tensions, challenges, and ideological debates that have been engendered as teacher research has emerged as a viable, if marginalized, form of educational inquiry. While explicitly acknowledging the marginalization of teachers and teacher research within the educational research community, Anderson and Herr conclude:

> While we need not view categories like "academic" and "school practi-
> tioner" as monolithic, we clearly need to continue to struggle with the
> epistemological (e.g., inside vs outside), political (e.g., power and status
> relations), and material (e.g., work place conditions) differences. It is ulti-
> mately out of this struggle that new definitions of "rigor" will emerge for
> this new scholarship.
>
> (ibid., 1999, p. 20)

In light of my own experiences and work with teachers in seeking to understand what I mean by research, this statement captures my own struggle as an outsider speaking with insiders. My work with teachers makes me keenly aware of the political and ideological character embedded in our discourse surrounding research. It has forced me to consider the ways in which my own assumptions influence my understanding of research and how, through my work with teachers, I can both reinforce and challenge their marginalization and our collective understanding of research. Anderson and Herr's paper captures the complexity of this ideological and political terrain. What I find problematic about their conclusion, again represented in my own struggles, is how these ideological and political struggles become supplanted as a means to an end, new definitions of rigor. Privileging the methodological over the political, ideolog-ical, and epistemological serves only to leave unquestioned the dominant position of university researchers in the discourse about educational research.

Rethinking research, change, and thoughts on self-study

Much of this chapter focuses on how the teachers with whom I work have chal-lenged me to rethink the ways in which I understand research as a form of inquiry. By way of conclusion, I look beyond the self and raise a number of issues that have also emerged as a result of these interactions. In particular, I take up how we as teacher educators might see self-study as part of a larger project that seeks to extend our collective knowledge of teaching, learning, and schools in the context of wider societal relationships.

Beyond the self in self-study

I have come to recognize a danger in the study of self. Even though my own self-study has afforded me the opportunity to resituate my understanding of myself along a range of professional, ethical, and epistemological issues, I am wary of the ways in which this has allowed me to existentially isolate myself in relation to Anderson and Herr's (1999) notion of teacher researchers as the Other.

My research is certainly connected to the teachers with whom I work, but I did not initiate or conduct this project for them. And yet, in the ways I have come to see myself differently, it is through them that I own these understandings. The danger here for myself (and for self-study perhaps) is in perpetuating and failing to challenge the very boundaries, marginalization, and relations of power and privilege I have come to better understand through my self-study. I also wonder how much this is situated within the historical and methodological development of this area of inquiry. Through this project I have come to see that others, particularly the Others of teacher education – pre-service and in-service teachers – need to be more centrally situated in the study of the self. Self-study cannot be only about me and my work as a teacher educator, decontextualized from those for whom and with whom I undertake that work. Self-study has to be done in a way that honors their voices and integrates them more fully into both the process and the product of self-study, in a way that both recognizes and challenges our privileged and their marginalized voices.

A central tenet for scholars in feminist methodology is the notion of self in relation to others, particularly around issues of power, positionality, and identity. Like our own efforts at self-study, feminist research embarks on projects to answer women's questions about their own histories and work, while also seeking to answer questions respondents have about their lives (Harding, 1987; Bloom, 1998). As teacher educators, self-study cannot simply be about our lives, our practices, our histories. It must also understand these in relation to and through the lived realities, experiences, and perspectives of those with whom we are involved: students in teacher education and teachers, among others.

It is not simply the study of self, but the study of self-in-relation-to-others that both recognizes and seeks to get beyond the binary oppositions such as teacher educators/teachers; self-study/practitioner research; teacher education/ education; theory/practice and university/schools. We cannot simply objectify the teachers and students who contextualize our lives as teacher educators. Their lives, their concerns, their perspectives and their struggles must find a place in our study of the self. Thus thinking about self-study as the study of self-in-relation-to-others involves moving beyond recognition of my own complicity in the Othering of teachers in our discourses about teaching, teacher education, and research to a consideration of avenues for change.

Advocacy, power, and change

Self-study seems akin to practitioner research in that it seeks to examine one's practice as a foundation for change. While distinctions might be made about the systematic character and intentionality of practitioner research (Cochran-Smith and Lytle, 1993) and the reflective analysis of practice embedded in self-study, the two share a fundamental concern with change, at both individual and institutional levels. The irony of this, emerging only as I write, is perhaps something that should not be lost or overlooked. Much of the preceding analysis reflects my own efforts to engage in thinking about change at multiple levels (personally, professionally, and institutionally) and to apply this thinking to my practice. If it is true that there is an epistemological and methodological affinity between self-study in teacher education and teacher research, then perhaps the insider/outsider role of teacher educators engaged in self-study affords a collective voice from which to critique the regimes of truth of the center in a way that supports, though not necessarily validates, the epistemological and methodological challenges of teachers and teacher research.

Certainly our self-study efforts and our dialogues and scholarship about these challenges are important in and of themselves. My own efforts in this self-study have convinced me that this is not enough. While recognizing the potential dangers of speaking for those who have been marginalized (Alcoff, 1991), feminist research as well as feminist scholarship on research methodology has sought to find ways to view research as a foundation for coalition-building (Harstock, 1996), challenging existing power structures (Cancian, 1996), and advocating for those who have been marginalized (Bloom, 2001). Theoretically, methodologically, and politically, building upon efforts such as these, we too should consider how we might situate our efforts within a larger project that challenges existing inequalities and relationships of power. While recognizing that teachers themselves can, and must, speak about their own marginalization within the research of the scholarship on teaching, teacher educators, through our position within this intellectual class system, can and must envision our work in self-study in ways that support these efforts. In the struggle to understand and improve our work as teacher educators, we must struggle with our students, teachers, and marginalized others.

References

Alcoff, L. (1991) "The problem of speaking for others", *Cultural Critique* 20 (Winter): 5–32.

Altrichter, H., Posch, P. and Somekh, B. (1993) *Teachers Investigating Their Work: An introduction to the methods of action research*, New York: Routledge.

Anderson, G.L. and Herr, K. (1999) "The new paradigm wars: Is there room for rigorous practitioner knowledge in schools and universities?", *Educational Researcher*, 28 (5): 12–21, 40.

Anderson, G., Herr, K. and Nihlen, A. (1994) *Studying Your Own School: An educator's guide to qualitative practitioner research*, Thousand Oaks, CA: Corwin Press.

Arhar, J.M., Holly, M.L. and Kasten, W.C. (2001) *Action Research for Teachers: Traveling the Yellow Brick Road*, Columbus, OH: Merrill Prentice Hall.

Atweh, B., Kemmis, S. and Weeks, P. (eds) (1998) *Action Research in Practice: Partnerships for social justice in education*, New York: Routledge.

Bloom, L.R. (1998) *Under the Sign of Hope: Feminist methodology and narrative interpretation*, Albany, NY: State University of New York Press.

—— (2001) "'I'm poor, I'm single, I'm a mom, and I deserve respect': Advocating in schools as and with mothers in poverty", *Educational Studies*, 32 (3): 300–16.

Burnaford, G., Fischer, J. and Hobson, D. (eds) (1996) *Teachers Doing Research: Practical possibilities*, Mahwah, NJ: Lawrence Erlbaum.

Cancian, F. (1996) "Participatory research and alternative strategies for activist sociology", in H. Gottfried (ed.) *Feminism and Social Change: Bridging theory and practice*, Urbana, IL: University of Illinois Press, pp. 187–205.

Cochran-Smith, M. and Lytle, S.L. (1993) *Inside/outside: Teacher research and knowledge*, New York: Teachers College Press.

Fine, M. (1994) "Working the hyphens: Reinventing self and other in qualitative research", in N.K. Denzin and Y.S. Lincoln (eds) *Handbook of Qualitative Research*, Thousand Oaks, CA: Sage, pp. 83–98.

Freedman, S.W., Simons, E.R., Kalnin, J.S., Casareno, A. and the M-Class teams (1999) *Inside City Schools: Investigating Literacy in Multicultural Classrooms*, New York: Teachers College Press.

Gordon, A. (1997) *Ghostly Matters: Haunting and the Sociological Imagination*, Minneapolis, MN: University of Minnesota Press.

Gore, J.M. (1994) "Enticing challenges: An introduction to Foucault and educational discourses", in R.A. Martusewicz and W.M. Reynolds (eds) *Inside/out: Contemporary critical perspectives in education*, New York: St Martin's Press, pp. 109–20.

Goswami, D. and Stillman, P. (eds) (1986) *Reclaiming the Classroom: Teacher research as an agency for change*, Portsmouth, NH: Heinemann.

Harding, S. (1987) "Introduction: Is there a feminist method?", in *Feminism and Methodology: Social science issues*, Bloomington, IN: Indiana University Press, pp. 1–14.

Harstock, N. (1996) "Theoretical bases for coalition building: An assessment of postmodernism", in H. Gottfried (ed.) *Feminism and Social Change: Bridging theory and practice*, Urbana, IL: University of Illinois Press, pp. 256–74.

Hollingsworth, S. (1994) *Teacher Research and Urban Literacy Education: Lessons and conversations in a feminist key*, New York: Teachers College Press.

hooks, bell (1994) *Teaching to Transgress: education as the practice of freedom*, New York: Routledge.

Hopkins, D. (1985) *A Teacher's Guide to Classroom Research*, Philadelphia, PA: Open University Press.

Kincheloe, J.L. (1991) *Teachers as Researchers: qualitative inquiry as a path to empowerment*, New York: Falmer Press.

Kuhn, T. (1962) *The Structure of Scientific Revolutions*, Chicago, IL: University of Chicago Press.

Lincoln, Y. and Guba, E. (1985) *Naturalistic Inquiry*, Newbury Park, CA: Sage.

Noffke, S. and Stevenson, R. (1994) *Educational Action Research. Becoming practically critical*, New York: Sage.

Shulman, L. (1986) "Those who understand: Knowledge growth in teaching", *Educational Researcher*, 15 (2): 4–14.

Thomas, J. (1993) *Doing Critical Ethnography*, Newbury Park, CA: Sage.

Conclusion

16 Understanding self-study of teacher education practices

John Loughran

Introduction

The chapters in this book illustrate a range of approaches to self-study that have been initiated and conducted as a result of the importance of the question at the heart of each author's study. However, to place this work in perspective, it is helpful to outline how self-study has developed over time, while maintaining important features that are common even in the diversity of studies documented in this text.

In a 1992 AERA Division K symposium titled *Holding up the Mirror: Teacher Educators Reflect on their own Teaching*, the papers presented (Guilfoyle, 1992; Hamilton, 1992; Pinnegar, 1992; Placier, 1992 – collectively known as the Arizona Group – and Russell, 1992) were critiqued by Fred Korthagen from the University of Utrecht in the Netherlands. This was an interesting symposium in which the presenters publicly illustrated their personal struggles, as they endeavored to help their students learn about teaching while also questioning the very nature of the way they themselves conducted their own teaching.

The presentation highlighted the ongoing difficulty the Arizona Group was experiencing in coming to understand the unspoken rules about gaining tenure, and the apparent difficulties that this strand of their research created for themselves and others in similar positions. They lamented the fact that such research was not necessarily acceptable to the academy (a view reinforced by Zeichner, 1999). At the same time, Russell was questioning many of the taken-for-granted assumptions of teacher education that he considered negated the very essence of what teacher education purports to do – teach about teaching. He later described this by juxtaposing the tensions of teaching about teaching through the authority of position (as is commonly used in teacher education) and the valuing and responding to the authority of experience (Munby and Russell, 1994; Russell, 1995). This differentiation of pedagogies underpinning approaches to teacher education (Russell's views), combined with the personal struggles associated with attempting to teach in meaningful ways (the Arizona Group), seemed to embrace a growing groundswell of interest at that time. From this symposium, the gathering of like-minded teacher educators was encouraged as others rallied around, driven by similar tensions in their own practice.

A member of the audience at this 1992 symposium commented on the need to form a group, and at the 1993 AERA meeting the Self-Study of Teacher Education Practices (S-STEP) Special Interest Group was launched.

In retrospect, this situation may be viewed as a public response to earlier calls for studies of teaching about teaching and of teacher educators themselves (Lanier and Little, 1986), and it may seem that this symposium of ideas and concerns of teacher educators was a moment of particular good fortune – the right issues, at the right time, and in the right place.

In conjunction with similar work, also reported at that time, which high-lighted issues of concern to new faculty members (Diamond, 1988; Ducharme and Agne, 1989; Boice, 1991; Whitt, 1991) as well as studies associated with reconsidering the nature of learning to teach about teaching (Trumbull, 1990; Knowles and Cole, 1991), the initial work of the individuals in this symposium (later published – see Guilfoyle *et al.*, 1995; Russell and Korthagen, 1995) could well be regarded as having pricked the consciousness of many teacher educators.

Although not yet labeled, Self-Study of Teacher Education Practices was, at that time, in part an extension of the notion of reflection (Dewey, 1933; Schön, 1983, 1987) that was being encouraged through the work of other teacher education scholars (for example, Zeichner, 1983; Tom, 1985; Zeichner and Liston, 1987; Grimmett and Erickson, 1988; Clift, Houston and Pugach, 1990; Russell and Munby, 1992; Calderhead and Gates, 1993; LaBoskey, 1994). A number of the studies of reflective practice in teacher education were being conducted by researchers who were similarly questioning the nature of teacher education. Many were calling for teacher educators to challenge the *status quo* and to look more carefully at their own teaching practices.

This questioning of practice was also developing through studies in other associated fields by individuals involved in, for example, action research (McNiff, 1988) and teacher as researcher (Cochran-Smith and Lytle, 1993). A confluence of questions, challenges, and actions that could barely be ignored by the teacher education community led to many pursuing studies that could be characterized as *teacher educators as researchers of their own practices*.

Clearly, then, the threads of these areas of research were finding personal meaning in the lives and practice of many teacher educators. Collectively, these teacher educators were beginning to respond with a common sense of purpose as they tackled some of the salient questions that they perceived as needing to be answered, such as "How can I better help my students to learn?" and "How do I live my values more fully in my practice?" Some teacher educators were also beginning to publicly examine and respond to instances in practice of being "a living contradiction" (Whitehead, 1993, p. 79).

The desire to help students learn about teaching better, and to do so in ways that involve much more than telling, became a recognizable characteristic of, and purpose in, self-study. Thus a renewed focus on the complex nature of teaching about teaching and learning about teaching served as a catalyst for careful attention to teacher education practices by the very people responsible for conducting that practice. In so doing, though, there was an inevitability that premises and assumptions implicit in practice needed to be made explicit. There was a crucial need to question and articulate practice in ways that could make clear the pedagogical reasoning (Shulman, 1986) that underpins practice. This need to be able to access and examine the thoughts and actions of practitioners reflected similar developments in the work of those involved in studies of teacher thinking (for example, Clark and Peterson, 1986). However, in this case, the examination and articulation of the thinking was being conducted by the practitioners themselves.

As Clark examined the nature of teacher thinking and decision-making, he questioned teacher educators in ways that reflected the very essence of the important challenge of the time:

> Do teachers of teachers have the courage to think aloud as they themselves wrestle with troubling dilemmas such as striking a balance between depth and breadth of content studied, distribution of time and attention among individual students ... teaching disasters, and the human mistakes that even experienced teacher educators make ...
>
> (Clark, 1988, p. 10)

Responding to questions such as Clark's was one way of casting light on the pedagogy of teacher education and, for those teacher educators being drawn to self-study, it spawned a number of responses. One important outcome involved simply gaining access to teacher educators' thinking about their own teaching as it was beginning to be made much more explicit, both for themselves and for their student teachers. The modeling and think-aloud approach to teaching about teaching that developed illustrated ways of helping students learn about teaching in new ways. Some of the resultant research (Loughran, 1994, 1996) simultaneously highlighted aspects of teacher educators' knowledge of teaching about teaching that was a direct result of making the tacit explicit, and a clear indication to some of the possibilities for knowledge claims resulting from the process of self-study.

Through the growing commitment among teacher educators to this work, and a desire to move it forward in a systematic fashion, the Self-Study of Teacher Education Practices became a fully functioning AERA SIG and so, in 1994, self-study as a descriptor appeared for the first time in the AERA conference index. With such work now being categorized, and therefore more easily recognizable, it also became more accessible to others.

What matters in self-study of teacher education practice

In teaching generally, and in teacher education particularly, there has been a long history of research that has had little influence on practice. One reason often cited by teachers themselves is that much of the research has little to say to them as the end users of such research. S-STEP is largely driven by teacher educators' questions. Thus it is inevitable that the focus of inquiry is most commonly of immediate value to the practitioner, for it is in the manner of those inquiries that the results matter. Researchers intend to learn through their inquiries in ways that will inform their practice.

For teacher education to become better equipped to respond to the expectations placed before it, there is a realization that there must be change by teacher educators themselves before there can be genuine educational change. In essence, it can be argued that by focusing on personal practice and experience, teacher educators inquiring into their own practice can lead to a better understanding of the complexities of teaching and learning – for themselves and their students.

Feiman-Nemser and Floden (1986) also highlighted the importance of the individual or the "self" in research on practice. They outlined the shift in the research focus over the previous two decades from studying teaching at a distance to trying to understand how teachers define their own work. This shift in focus, they argued, was important because the knowledge of teachers (which is largely untapped) is an important source of insights for the improvement of teaching. The same clearly applies to S-STEP, as the knowledge that might be made available through such research is of immediate importance in informing teacher educators in their efforts to teach about teaching. Therefore, it seems reasonable to assert that teacher educators themselves should continually be adapting, adjusting, and altering their practice in response to the needs and concerns of *their* students in *their* context. Teacher educators' self-studies should then be important in helping others interpret and utilize the knowledge gained from such studies in their own work, as they interpret, shape, and (most importantly) teach about that knowledge in ways that seek to make it meaningful and valuable in the experiences of their students.

The impetus for self-study

> As a student in my teacher education classes, I was a student character in what we call the sacred theory–practice story. I was there to be filled with theory that I could then apply to my teaching practice … . As I began work as a university teacher educator, the same plot outline continued to shape the way I lived that story. Without being able to step outside to try to imagine competing plot lines, I could vary the story only in small ways.
>
> (Clandinin, 1995, pp. 28–9)

A sense of dissatisfaction with existing practice can be critical in initiating a self-study (consider, for example, the chapters by Brown and Kuzmic). Through being dissatisfied, a teacher educator begins to frame that which creates this sense of unease or discomfort. Thus the examination of a dilemma or contradiction in practice may well be the driver of self-study. This sense of unease is not necessarily (as Griffiths demonstrates) a negative aspect of practice though, for it can also be an impetus for finding ways to be better informed. Hence pursuing a self-study can help shape approaches to teaching about teaching by better understanding the complexity of this relationship.

Recognizing or feeling a sense of unease is linked to what Schön (1983) defined as reframing, whereby the problem that is the focus of the investigation should not necessarily be viewed as a singular, unchanging aspect of the teacher educator's work. The problem is not something that can necessarily be held still and studied in a linear fashion and then reviewed and slotted back into practice, because a common aspect of researching teaching about teaching is that new findings and teaching become interwoven, as illustrated by Dalmau and Guðjónsdóttir. In teaching there is a sense of the need to act immediately on new possibilities and to adjust one's teaching in accord with these possibilities. The research focus therefore alters and, as adjustments are made, new insights and possibilities emerge. Hence the intertwining of teaching and researching is such that as one alters so does the other. The problem develops, shifts, and changes in response to the continual shifts in the teaching; the two are almost symbiotic.

This means that one outcome of teacher educators researching their practice is that they commonly design and implement new approaches – classroom interventions that are intended to achieve change. These are not always successful, and may be "failures",[1] especially when first tried. For example, it may become clear to the teacher educator that the students did not see the purpose of the session, or that they did not apprehend the links between a particular session and the activities that preceded it. These failures may lead to valuable insights and to ways of avoiding and/or capitalizing on such failures in the future. In so doing, teacher educators then have to deal with the consequences of their interventions as part of their daily routine with the class. Negative consequences can affect a class for the remainder of the program/course, and that is also a matter of concern for teachers concerned with the teaching and learning environment in which they and their students collaborate. This means that such research can be a high-risk activity for teacher educators, and can therefore significantly affect their role as a teacher (as Bass, Anderson-Patton and Allender demonstrate).

When one considers these ideas, it becomes clear how important reframing must be to the process of self-study. It is not sufficient to simply view a situation from one perspective. Reframing is seeing a situation through others' eyes. For the teacher educator, a given dilemma, contradiction, or sense of discomfort may actually be associated with being the student rather than being the teacher. Hence there is an ongoing need to be able to view the teaching and learning situation from different perspectives. If all of the problems to be investigated are solely from the teacher educator's perspective, then a myriad of teaching and learning perspectives would, sadly, be ignored.

Learning through collaboration

In self-study there is sometimes a distinction between individual and collaborative self-studies. At the heart of this issue is the argument that reframing is much more difficult from an individual and personal perspective than when acting in collaboration with others. This point has been highlighted by many of the authors in this collection when they show that collaboration has been important in framing and reframing their studies. This issue of collaboration often revolves around the need for interpretations of data to be checked against a valued or trusted other.

Clearly then, a self-study designed for oneself (for example, Tidwell or Russell) will carry different expectations of evidence than will a self-study intended for teacher educators considering their teaching approaches together (Schuck and Segal or Fitzgerald, Farstad and Deemer) or indeed a self-study that focuses on an educational institution and its practices (Myers or Hamilton). Yet it may not be so much that the need for the type of data changes with the expectations of the study, but that perhaps, although all forms of data are always available, the relative importance of some data is highlighted over others in particular settings and for particular audiences.

Audience is also an important shaping issue for self-study accounts (Barnes, 1998). One audience is always the teacher educators themselves. However, beyond this, understanding the audience is caught up in the paradox of the term "self-study". Self-studies should not be viewed as being confined to an individual. Self-studies involve collaboration in varying numbers and across a range of participants (for example, teacher educators in the same program, across different programs, in similar programs but in different places, with students, by students), programs (pre-service, in-service, post-graduate), and institutions (as illustrated by Louie, Stackman, Drevdahl and Purdy).

Self-studies attempt to speak to individuals, groups, programs, and institutions as they seek to illustrate tensions, dilemmas, and concerns about practice and programs. Naturally, then, they are shaped and fashioned in ways that illustrate the research outcomes of those concerns in ways that will be meaningfully grasped by the target audience. As a matter of course, the learning through self-study is intended to be used. The usefulness of a self-study begins with the individual and works its way on so that, through teacher change, the possibility for genuine educational change might be enhanced. The interplay of the inquiry and its value and form of representation inevitably influence whether or not a self-study speaks to those envisaged as its audience.

Audience, in terms of self-study, has another defining aspect. Through self-study there is a growing sense of community whereby participants commonly view themselves as working together to be a positive influence in their field of endeavor – teaching about teaching. Therefore their sense of community is important in offering ways of learning from and through self-studies of teacher education practices.

Conclusion

The growing interest in self-study appears to focus largely on the desire by teacher educators to do more than just deliver a course in teacher education.

There has been a growing dissatisfaction among many teacher educators about the value of traditional approaches to teacher education (see, for example, Korthagen and Kessels, 1999; Korthagen *et al.*, 2001). The allure of self-study appears to relate to the desire of teacher educators to better understand the nature of teaching about teaching and to develop a genuine sense of professional satisfaction in that work. Put another way, self-study offers some teacher educators a way of being liberated in their practice in a system that is often far too restrictive. Thus self-study creates opportunities to develop the relationships and understandings in teaching and learning that tend to characterize much of the work of teachers, but have largely been ignored in the past by academia.

In his 1998 Division K Vice-Presidential address, Zeichner traced the development of teacher education research in the US over a twenty-year period. The subsequent paper, "The New Scholarship in Teacher Education" (Zeichner, 1999), explored the major research strands that have emerged.

> Researchers in the self-study movement in teacher education have employed a wide variety of qualitative methodologies and have focused on many different kinds of substantive issues … . A whole group of self-studies focuses on the tensions and contradictions involved in being a teacher educator in institutions that do not value this work … . Much of this work has provided a deep and critical look at practices and structures in teacher education …
>
> (Zeichner, 1999, p. 11)

In the chapters that comprise this book, this diverse range of issues has also been highlighted. However, these chapters are also personally important as they offer others opportunities to see (and perhaps feel) some of the reasons that drive S-STEP research and illustrate not only why it is pursued, but also why it is valued by teacher educators. In so doing, it is hoped that these chapters will encourage others to look more closely into their own practices.

Self-study allows teacher educators to maintain a focus on their teaching and on their students' learning. Both are high priorities in teacher education, and thus self-study complements their work. As a result, a most valuable aspect of self-study is apparent in the development of ways of knowing, or the professional knowledge of teaching and learning about teaching. This is demonstrated by the ways that Senese and Berry and Loughran, for example, have come to frame and name their practices. Their learning through self-study has enhanced their sense of what it is they have come to know and, importantly, are now able to articulate for themselves and others.

This book has, on purpose, set out to illustrate a range of approaches to self-study of teacher education practices and to highlight the importance of teacher educators taking the leading role in reframing and responding to their practice, not just to illuminate the field of the teacher educator but also to foster genuine educational change. We believe that this aim has been achieved, and we hope that readers will also embrace leading roles in educational change.

Notes

1 Failure in this case does not equate with the common understanding of failure as lack of success. Here failure refers to the fact that what was being implemented did not work "as planned". In light of the development of understanding of teaching through risk taking and learning from experience, failure is in fact an aid to the learning and understanding of pedagogy so that, as Dewey describes it,

> failure is not mere failure. It is instructive. The person who really thinks learns quite as much from his failures as from his successes. For a failure indicates to the person whose thinking has been involved in it, and who has not come to it by mere blind chance, what further observations should be made … . It either brings to light a new problem or helps to define and clarify the problem on which he has been engaged.

(Dewey, 1933, p. 114)

Therefore, failure is an important learning event in teacher research.

References

Barnes, D. (1998) "Looking forward: The concluding remarks at the Castle Conference", in M.L. Hamilton *et al.* (eds) *Reconceptualizing Teaching Practice: Self-study in Teacher Education*, London: Falmer Press, pp. ix–xiv.

Boice, R. (1991) "New faculty as teachers", *The Journal of Higher Education*, 62 (2): 150–73.

Calderhead, J. and Gates, P. (eds) (1993) *Conceptualizing Reflection in Teacher Development*, London: Falmer Press.

Clandinin, D.J. (1995) "Still learning to teach", in T. Russell and F. Korthagen (eds) *Teachers Who Teach Teachers: Reflections on teacher education*, London: Falmer Press, pp. 25–31.

Clark, C.M. (1988) "Asking the right questions about teacher preparation: contributions of research on teacher thinking", *Educational Researcher*, 17 (2): 5–12.

Clark, C. and Peterson, P. (1986) "Teacher's thought processes", in M.C. Wittrock (ed.) *Handbook of Research on Teaching*, 3rd edn, New York: Macmillan, pp. 255–96.

Clift, R.T., Houston, R.W. and Pugach, M.C. (eds) (1990) *Encouraging Reflective Practice in Teacher Education: an analysis of issues and programs*, New York: Teachers College Press.

Cochran-Smith, M. and Lytle, S.L. (1993) *Inside/Outside: Teacher research and knowledge*, New York: Teachers College Press.

Dewey, J. (1933) *How we Think*, New York: Heath & Co.

Diamond, P. (1988) "Construing a career: a developmental view of teacher education and the teacher educator", *Journal of Curriculum Studies*, 10: 133–40.

Ducharme, E. and Agne, R. (1989) "Professors of education: uneasy residents of academe", in R. Wisnieski and E. Ducharme (eds) *The Professors of Teaching*, Albany, NY: State University of New York Press, pp. 67–86.

Feiman-Nemser, S. and Floden, R. (1986) "The cultures of teaching", in M.C. Wittrock (ed.) *Handbook of Research on Teaching*, 3rd edn, New York: Macmillan, pp. 505–26.

Grimmett, P.P. and Erickson, G.L. (eds) (1988) *Reflection in Teacher Education*, New York: Teachers College Press.

Guilfoyle, K. (1992) *Communicating with students: the impact of interactive dialogue journals on the thinking and teaching of a teacher educator*, paper presented at the annual meeting of AERA, San Francisco, April.

Guilfoyle, K., Hamilton, M.L., Pinnegar, S. and Placier, M. (1995) "Becoming teachers of teachers: The paths of four beginners", in T. Russell and F. Korthagen (eds) *Teachers Who Teach Teachers: Reflections on teacher education*, London: Falmer Press, pp. 35–55.

Hamilton, M.L. (1992) *Making public the private voice of a teacher educator*, paper presented at the annual meeting of AERA, San Francisco, April.

Knowles, J.G. and Cole, A. (1991) *We're just like those we study – They as beginning teachers, we as beginning professors of teacher education: Letters of the first year*, paper presented at the Bergamo Conference on Curriculum Theory and Classroom Practice in Dayton, Ohio.

Korthagen, F.A.J. and Kessels, J.P.A.M. (1999) "Linking theory and practice: Changing the pedagogy of teacher education", *Educational Researcher*, 28 (4): 4–17.

Korthagen, F.A.J. with Kessels, J., Koster, B., Lagerwerf, B. and Wubbels, T. (2001) *Linking Practice and Theory: The pedagogy of realistic teacher education*, Hillsdale, NJ: Lawrence Erlbaum.

LaBoskey, V.K. (1994) *Development of Reflective Practice*, New York: Teachers College Press.

Lanier, J. and Little, J.W. (1986) "Research in teacher education", in M.C. Wittrock (ed.) *Handbook of Research on Teaching*, 3rd edn, New York: Macmillan, pp. 527–60.

Loughran, J.J. (1994) *Learning how to teach: Unpacking a teacher educator's thinking about pedagogy in pre-service education*, paper presented at the annual meeting of AERA, New Orleans, April.

—— (1996) *Developing Reflective Practice: Learning about Teaching and Learning through Modelling*, London: Falmer Press.

McNiff, J. (1988) *Action Research: Principles and Practice*, London: Routledge.

Munby, H. and Russell, T. (1994) "The authority of experience in learning to teach: Messages from a physics method class", *Journal of Teacher Education*, 45 (2): 86–95.

Pinnegar, S. (1992) *Student teaching as a teacher educator*, paper presented at the annual meeting of AERA, San Francisco, April.

Placier, P. (1992) *Maintaining practice: A struggle of too little time*, paper presented at the annual meeting of AERA, San Francisco, April.

Russell, T. (1992) *A teacher educator and his students reflect on teaching high-school physics*, paper presented at the annual meeting of AERA, San Francisco, April.

—— (1995) "Returning to the physics classroom to re-think how one learns to teach physics", in T. Russell and F. Korthagen (eds) *Teachers Who Teach Teachers: Reflections on teacher education*, London: Falmer Press, pp. 95–109.

Russell, T. and Korthagen, F. (eds) (1995) *Teachers who Teach Teachers: Reflections on teacher education*, London: Falmer Press.

Russell, T. and Munby, H. (eds) (1992) *Teachers and Teaching: From classroom to reflection*, London: Falmer Press.

Schön, D.A. (1983) *The Reflective Practitioner: How professionals think in action*, New York: Basic Books.

—— (1987) *Educating the Reflective Practitioner: Toward a new design for teaching and learning in the professions*, San Francisco, CA: Jossey-Bass.

Shulman, L.S. (1986) "Those who understand: Knowledge growth in teaching", *Educational Researcher*, 15 (2): 4–14.

Tom, A.R. (1985) "Inquiry into inquiry-oriented teacher education", *Journal of Teacher Education*, 36 (5): 35–44.

Trumbull, D. (1990) "Evolving conceptions of teaching: reflections of one teacher", *Curriculum Inquiry*, 20 (2): 161–82.

Whitehead, J. (1993) *The Growth of Educational Knowledge: Creating your own living educational theories*, Bournemouth: Hyde Publications.

Whitt, E. (1991) "'Hit the ground running': experiences of new faculty in a school of education", *The Review of Higher Education*, 14 (2): 177–97.

Zeichner, K. (1983) "Alternative paradigms of teacher education", *Journal of Teacher Education*, 34 (3): 3–9.

—— (1999) "The new scholarship in teacher education", *Educational Researcher*, 28 (9): 4–15.

Zeichner, K.M. and Liston, D.P. (1987) "Teaching student teachers to reflect", *Harvard Educational Review*, 57 (1): 23–48.

Name index

Subject index